AMERICAN COUNSELING
ASSOCIATION
6101 Stevenson Avenue, Suite 600
Alexandria, VA 22304
www.counseling.org

American Counseling Association

6101 Stevenson Avenue, Suite 600 | Alexandria, VA 22304

Associate Publisher | Carolyn C. Baker

Digital and Print Development Editor | Nancy Driver

Senior Production Manager | Bonny E. Gaston

Production Coordinator | Karen Thompson

Copy Editor | Beth Ciha

Cover and text design by Bonny E. Gaston

Library of Congress Cataloging-in-Publication Data

Names: Balkin, Richard S., author. | Kleist, David M., author.
Title: Counseling research : a practitioner-scholar approach / Richard S. Balkin, David M. Kleist.
Description: Alexandria, VA : American Counseling Association, [2017] | Includes bibliographical references and index.
Identifiers: LCCN 2016035461 | ISBN 9781556203572 (pbk. : alk. paper)
Subjects: LCSH: Counseling psychology—Research—Methodology. | Counseling psychology—Practice.
Classification: LCC BF636.65 .B35 2017 | DDC 158.3072—dc23 LC record available at https://lccn.loc.gov/2016035461

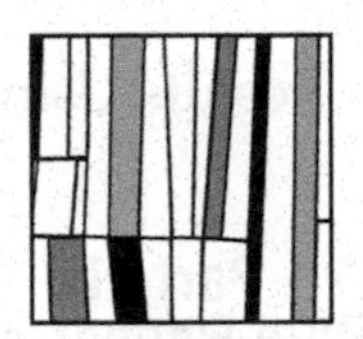

Table of Contents

Preface

Most of the counseling graduate students I (Rick) know do not wake up in the morning thinking, "Hot damn, I get to go to my research class today!" Rather, most of the students I have had in my research course come to class, at least in the beginning, with a lot of anxiety, much of which centers around discomfort with math. Honestly, I am not any different from the majority of counseling graduate students who have had this experience. When I was a graduate student, I walked into my research classes similar to most graduate students in counseling. I was anxious and felt unprepared. My experience with math was tumultuous at best. Much of counseling research is dependent on statistics, but I want to emphasize to you that research is not a computational nightmare but rather a process with logical steps to enhance our knowledge of the counseling profession. In fact, the math is not too difficult, as all we do is add, subtract, multiply, divide, and square root. So relax! The math is not really the main part. Focus on the process.

Of course, counseling research is not solely dependent on quantitative methods. I asked David M. Kleist to join me as a coauthor given his expertise in qualitative research as well as successful collaborations I have had with David in the past. You will find in this book a strong overview of qualitative research and common approaches used in counseling research that inform practice. Counselors make great qualitative researchers because of the natural fit of hearing our clients' narratives and to establishing meaning from them. These same skills can be used in developing meaningful counseling research.

The language used to describe research methods is technical, and both David and I attempt to reduce the confusion by using a conversational tone in this text. There will be times when the material may seem a little dry, but I think this book excels in providing research examples specific to counseling and bridging the technicalities of research and the realities of practice. Ultimately research is a useless exercise if it is not utilized to enhance the counseling practice.

In this book we strive to address two audiences: the counselor-in-training and the emerging researcher. If you are just being introduced to research in counseling, you will find this book helpful in providing an understanding of the primary methods of research used in the counseling profession. However, we also attempt to provide a bridge to individuals who have an understanding of research and wish to apply concepts to design studies. Hence, we feel this book will be useful to the master's student just beginning to understand research as well as to those considering topics for a thesis, dissertation, or the development of an initial study. To accommodate this broad audience, we include sections on research designs, respective to the content covered, near the end of each chapter. To assist with synthesizing and applying the content of each chapter, we provide a "Suggested Activities" section at the end of each chapter.

The text is divided into four parts. Part I, "The Essence of Research in the Counseling Profession," provides an overview of the practitioner-scholar model (Chapter 1), which informs the content of and approach to this text and emphasizes the connection between counseling practice and research. An introduction to the research process is presented in Chapter 2, addressing the choice of a research topic, review of the literature, and data collection and analysis. An emphasis on multicultural counseling and issues of diversity is essential to counseling, and the research process is no exception. We thus highlight research ethics and multicultural issues in Chapter 3. Chapter 4 includes an overview of the types of research that are delineated further in future chapters.

Part II, "Quantitative Research Designs," provides detailed descriptions of experimental (Chapters 5, 7, and 8) and correlational (Chapter 6) research. Meta-analysis is covered in Chapter 9 to provide an understanding of a genre of quantitative research that is especially important in identifying empirically supported treatments. Single-case research design is discussed in Chapter 8; this can be an important method for counseling researchers and practitioners who wish to evaluate the effectiveness of an intervention or treatment but do not have access to large numbers of potential participants.

Part III, "Qualitative Research Designs," provides an understanding of qualitative research. Chapter 10 posits key philosophies, concepts, and ideas about qualitative research and the development and design of qualitative studies. Chapter 11 provides an understanding of preeminent theories of qualitative inquiry and how they connect to the purpose, design, and analysis of qualitative research.

Part IV, "Practice-Based Research," is concerned with the development of measures that may be used for research and evaluation and for conducting program evaluations. Measurement is an essential component of research, and both practitioners and researchers often use measures to demonstrate efficacy and accountability. Program evaluation provides a connection between research and practice, and the process of program evaluation may incorporate elements of the various methods discussed throughout the text.

Throughout the text we emphasize practical research examples relevant to counseling practice and highlight opportunities to reflect on these examples in the "Suggested Activities" sections. Regardless of the extent of your training, we hope you will appreciate the importance of being a consumer of research—that when you join the American Counseling Association, you also benefit from the flagship journal *Journal of Counseling & Development*, division journals, and the multitude of resources this organization offers to advance the counseling profession. We hope that after reading this primer on research design, emerging researchers will be able to pursue further research studies and advanced coursework feeling well informed about the research process.

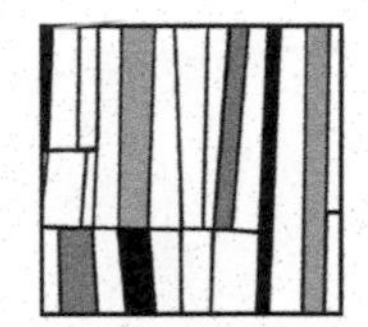

Acknowledgments

I (Rick) thank A. Stephen Lenz and Michael J. Walsh for their contributions to this book, Michelle Perepiczka for her reviews and insights on the quantitative chapters, and Quentin Hunter for his editorial assistance. David M. Kleist, thank you for joining me as a coauthor and contributing to the qualitative portion of this book. I needed someone to provide balance and expertise, and I am grateful for your friendship and collaboration. Most important, I thank my wife Melissa and my children Abigail, Gabriela, and Isabel, for their endless patience with me.

I (David) thank Rick for your patience with my process and belief in my ability to contribute to the book. I also thank my wife Jill and son Nathan, who seem to only see me sitting around the house with my laptop, and my daughter Mattie, whose own perseverance motivates me. Finally, I thank all of the doctoral students at Idaho State University who have expanded the envelope of qualitative research's relevance to the counseling profession.

We both wish to express our appreciation to Carolyn Baker, the staff at the American Counseling Association, and the individuals who reviewed this text.

About the Authors

Richard S. Balkin, PhD, is a professor and doctoral program coordinator at the University of Louisville. He is editor of the *Journal of Counseling & Development,* the flagship journal of the American Counseling Association (ACA), and past-president of the Association for Assessment and Research in Counseling. His primary research interests include counseling outcomes, research methods, counseling adolescents, and cultural differences in counseling. He is a past recipient of the ACA Best Practices Research Award and the Association for Counselor Education and Supervision (ACES) Counseling Vision and Innovation Award.

Rick has published more than 65 peer-reviewed manuscripts, books, and book chapters, the majority quantitative in nature. He is the author of *The Theory and Practice of Assessment in Counseling* (Pearson, 2014) and has authored book chapters on research methods as well as several journal articles related to research methods. Rick is a professor in the Department of Counseling and Human Development at the University of Louisville and a Fellow of ACA.

David M. Kleist, PhD, is a professor and chair of the Department of Counseling at Idaho State University. He is presently on the editorial board of *The Qualitative Report* and has held past editorial positions with *Counseling and Values* and *The Family Journal.* He has chaired more than 15 qualitative dissertations in his more than 20 years at Idaho State University. He is a past-president of ACES and has been honored with the International Association of Marriage and Family Counselors Mentoring Award. He has twice been selected as a Master Teacher at Idaho State University. His primary research interests include qualitative research methods, triadic supervision, and reflective processes in counselor education and supervision.

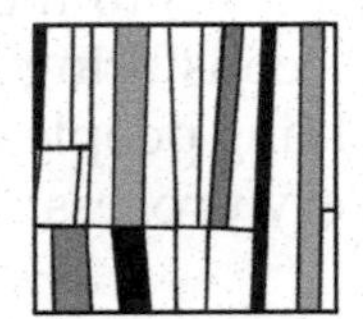

About the Contributors

A. Stephen Lenz, PhD, is an assistant professor of counselor education at Texas A&M University–Corpus Christi. Dr. Lenz has worked with children, adolescents, adults, and families as a licensed professional counselor in community-based, university, and private practice counseling settings. He is a specialist in the treatment of trauma and use of positive psychology interventions. His research interests include community-based program evaluation, counseling outcome research, the development and translation of psychological assessments, and meta-analysis.

Michael J. Walsh, PhD, is an assistant professor of neuropsychiatry and behavioral science in the University of South Carolina's Rehabilitation Counseling program (RCP). A graduate of the RCP, Mike began his career as a counselor with the South Carolina Department of Vocational Rehabilitation. He then transitioned to Mental Health America–Beaufort/Jasper as the executive director and clinical supervisor for the small nonprofit mental health agency. Mike has been with the RCP as a full-time faculty member since 2009. In addition to working as a professor, Mike has been active in the national counseling arena, having served two terms as president of the Association for Humanistic Counseling and one term as a member of the American Counseling Association's Governing Council. Mike also served on the American Counseling Association's Ethics Committee (2010–2013 and 2015 to the present) and as cochair of that committee in 2011. In addition to working as a counselor educator, Mike is active in the field, providing consulting and training to various mental health and vocational agencies. Since 2013, Mike has provided statewide counseling skills training to more than 450 vocational rehabilitation counselors used by the South Carolina Vocational Rehabilitation Department, and he continues to provide this training to newly hired vocational rehabilitation counselors. Mike also maintains active ties to the psychiatric rehabilitation community and provides consulting services to a mental health agency specializing in helping people with psychiatric disabilities move through the recovery process.

The Essence of Research in the Counseling Profession

If the emphasis on and role of research in the counseling profession was not a primary motivation for you to pursue a graduate degree in counseling, you are probably similar to most graduate students in the counseling profession. That being said, professional counseling—and as an extension counselor education—is not a static profession. Understanding how research is generated is important to maintaining competence and making contributions to an ever-changing field. Research traditions within the counseling profession emanate primarily from education and psychology. Hence, examining research traditions within these fields is important to understanding research within a counseling framework. In this text we emphasize the practitioner-scholar model, a model that places emphasis on the utility of research in the practice of counseling.

Along with introducing the practitioner-scholar model, in this section we introduce the research process, from the conceptualization of a study to the dissemination of the findings. Because the majority of counseling research is dependent on volunteer participants, we highlight the role of ethics as identified in federal law and the *ACA Code of Ethics* (American Counseling Association, 2014). Finally, we introduce the traditional families of research: quantitative and qualitative research. An overview of these methods is given in this section, with more detailed explanation in subsequent chapters.

References

American Counseling Association. (2014). *ACA code of ethics.* Alexandria, VA: Author.

The Counselor as a Practitioner-Scholar

Overview

This chapter introduces orientations toward research and provides conceptualizations to approaching research. The discussions regarding research orientation may seem academic and unimportant to the counseling professional. However, we believe that an understanding of orientation can set the stage for how a counselor appreciates research, becomes an intelligent consumer of research, and emerges as a producer of research. In this chapter you are exposed to two predominant ideologies of the role of research within the counseling profession (i.e., the scientist-practitioner model and the practitioner-scholar model) and two philosophies that govern one's approach to conducting research (i.e., positivist and constructivist).

Scientist-Practitioner Versus Practitioner-Scholar

The scientist-practitioner model and the practitioner-scholar model originated from psychology and impacted the philosophy of training. As these models have been adapted in higher education, the question of which model is appropriate for future practitioners, academics, and researchers has been widely debated. The essence of these debates, with respect to counseling, is focused on developing competent practitioners and scholars who can utilize new information and generate knowledge to move the counseling profession forward.

A committee representing various professionals in psychology, medicine, and education approved the scientist-practitioner model in 1949 in Boulder, Colorado; hence, the model is often referred to as the *Boulder model.* The emphasis in this model is that psychologists should adhere to the scientific method when engaging in applied practices. The scientist-practitioner model might therefore incorporate the following assumptions for counseling:

1. There is a solid link between research and practice.
2. The skills necessary to be a competent counselor are also necessary to be a competent researcher.
3. Institutions that endorse the scientist-practitioner model may have a stronger culture of research but emphasize competence in practice as well. (Stoltenberg et al., 2000)

An alternative model—the practitioner-scholar model—was approved in 1973 with the understanding that such a model might be more appropriate for future professionals (e.g., PsyD) who wish to focus primarily on clinical work. The emphasis on integrating research into practice was not lost; however, more focus was placed on clinical training as opposed to the generation and dissemination of research (Stoltenberg et al., 2000).

Counseling differs from psychology in many respects, particularly in regard to training and philosophical views of wellness, mental health, and well-being. "Counseling is a professional relationship that empowers diverse individuals, families, and groups to accomplish mental health, wellness, education, and career goals" (Kaplan, Tarvydas, & Gladding, 2014, p. 366). No other profession defines what it does primarily through a working relationship and encompassing the aforementioned global constructs.

Another distinguishing characteristic of counseling is that a license to practice independently is granted with the attainment of a master's degree in counseling; in psychology, one must attain a doctorate to practice independently in most states. Hence, a practitioner-scholar model may be more appropriate for professional counselors, as the emphasis in coursework and training is on applied practice. Not until one wishes to obtain a doctorate in counselor education, usually granted with a PhD, does the emphasis shift to research. The doctor of philosophy is a research degree, and therefore a strong balance between research and practice likely is obtained. As both models attempt to bridge research to practice, they serve as ideologies to which counseling students may align their interests consistent with how they are developing within the profession. Although counselors-in-training may initially align with the practitioner-scholar model early in their development, the pursuit of a doctorate may result in an inclination toward the scientist-practitioner model.

Integrating the Models: A Case Example

Prior to beginning work on my doctorate, I (Rick) was employed as a counselor at an acute care psychiatric hospital working with adolescents. To be admitted to the unit, adolescents had to meet criteria for being a danger to self or others. One of my clients was Ronny, a gay 14-year-old male with a history of substance use, suicidality, truancy, and oppositional behavior at school. He had been court ordered into the hospital after getting caught performing lewd acts with another boy in the bathroom at school. Unlike most adolescent clients who would begin earning privileges and working up the level system after 48 hours, Ronny remained under 15-minute observation by the nursing staff because of persistent threats to harm himself and his tendency to steal sugar packets from the cafeteria during meals and lick the packets when he thought no one was watching. Ronny did not make much progress during individual or group sessions. He consistently indicated that he would rather be in juvenile detention than in the hospital, as he thought he would be more likely to get together with other males in detention. He also indicated that if he left the hospital, he would continue to use drugs and may try to harm himself.

Ronny was resistant to establishing any type of working alliance with any of the staff at the hospital. The standard milieu of care consisting of individual and group counseling and 12-step support was not effective. Supportive therapeutic approaches and confrontation also did not appear to work. Frustrated with my lack of progress with this client, I sought consultation from my supervisor. After processing my conceptualization of Ronny my supervisor indicated, "Well, if nothing in the book is working, you might need to throw out the book and try something different."

So I brought Ronny into my office for his next individual session and indicated that given his lack of progress I was recommending him to long-term treatment, which would likely be court ordered by the judge. Ronny expressed his displeasure with this plan, indicating that he would rather the judge send him to juvenile detention. I told Ronny that if that was what he preferred, he could make that happen: "The judge is going to give you the opportunity to speak after he reads my recommendation. If you cuss him out, he will probably send you to detention." Ronny thought that was a great idea, so we role-played the scenario and rehearsed a number of highly inappropriate names he could call the judge in hopes that he would get sent to detention.

The next day Ronny went to court. On reviewing my letter the judge cleared the courtroom so that it was just Ronny, his parents, me, and the judge. The judge read out loud the letter that indicated Ronny's lack of progress, his behavior in the hospital, and my recommendation for long-term treatment. The judge then said, "Ronny, what do you have to say for yourself?" Ronny stood up, looked at the judge—and burst into tears. The judge responded, "Well, I guess I have no choice but to follow your counselor's recommendation and order you to long-term treatment."

Ronny's reaction—crying in the courtroom after the letter was read—was the first genuine affect he had shown since he had been hospitalized. It was the first instance of any emotional distress displayed by Ronny. So what does this mean with respect to research?

Research informed my work as a counselor. My primary theoretical orientation was Glasser's reality therapy, but when I saw how resistant Ronny was to not making any changes in his behaviors, I tried other approaches as well, such as focusing on being supportive and empathic as well as being confrontational. Whereas most clients appeared to make progress within 48 hours, Ronny required the highest level of care and documentation after 3 weeks. I do not believe that continued reliance on traditional, evidence-based treatment, as required by the scientist-practitioner model, would have been beneficial for Ronny.

The practitioner-scholar model, in contrast, allowed me to trust my instincts and experience with the client in order to get some type of therapeutic effect. I am not suggesting that evidence-based protocols be routinely dismissed. In fact, such protocols may be effective with clients. Stoltenberg and Pace (2007) emphasized that the scientist-practitioner model is an integrative, reciprocal model. If that is the case, the main difference between these models may in fact be the underlying philosophy rather than the implementation. Counselors should be aware of both models and understand that they need to balance research and applied skills rather than emphasize one model over the other.

Positivist Versus Constructivist Approaches

Exploring the philosophical underpinnings of counseling research may appear to be primarily an academic exercise. Nevertheless, similar to the orientation of practitioner-scholar versus scientist-practitioner, an understanding of positivism and constructivism is about not simply how a counselor conducts research but also who the counselor is as a person. Are you a little skeptical about that last statement—that research and counseling are so inherently related and part of a counselor's identity?

When academics discuss the philosophical underpinnings of research, they are talking about *epistemology*—the manner in which knowledge is generated. *Positivism,* also known as *empiricism,* is the belief that knowledge is generated from what can be observed and measured. Hence, research from a position of positivism relies on empirical data—data that were collected and assigned value. Positivism is tied to deductive reasoning (Trochim, 2006). If data can be observed and measured, then phenomena can be understood and generalized to the appropriate population. In other words, the goal of positivism is to gain a broad understanding of an experience that can be applied to many people after empirical data are analyzed. Many counseling theories, such as behaviorism, cognitive theory, and rational emotive behavior theory, use a positivist perspective. In each of these theories, measurement and evidence play a prominent role. For example, counselors who practice rational emotive behavior therapy may ask the client for evidence with respect to a specific belief in order to identify the belief as rational or irrational.

Constructivism, broadly speaking, asserts that knowledge is generated by individual perception, or construction, of reality and thus knowledge. Knowledge is generated through the construction of meaning with varying degrees of emphasis on the individual (personal construct theory, Kelly, 1955) to construction of meaning occurring primarily within cultural contexts (e.g., narrative therapy, White & Epston, 1990; relational-cultural theory, Comstock et al., 2008). Constructivism is more aligned with many popular counseling theories that endorse a phenomenological perspective (e.g., Adlerian, person-centered, existential, and personal construct theories). Constructivism purports that the ever-changing knowledge of human experiencing, essential to counseling research, is best described not through measurement but rather through an understanding of the meaning of the human experience. Meaning is always context bound and, depending on the qualitative method, can vary in its degree of emphasis on internal construction to relational interactions and conditions that influence meaning.

Ontologically speaking (i.e., What can be known?), constructivists believe that reality cannot be directly known; only humans' meaning making of the world around them can be known. Epistemologically speaking (i.e., What is the relationship between knower and known?), constructivists believe that knowledge is constructed by the knower (you and I) through our interaction with the world around us and our sense organs (Kelly, 1955; Schwandt, 2000), with inductive reasoning at its foundation and language, not numerical labels, as the means of capturing understanding. The focus for research is not on knowledge that is *found* through strict adherence to the scientific method but on how research participants and researchers interpret the phenomenon and the data. Knowledge products of research are viewed not as generalizable across all time and contexts but as context bound; thus, conclusions made are directed at the context from which the research was conducted.

But stepping into the wide world of constructivism is not so simple. You see, there is a wide range of philosophical positions, or stances, under this broad constructivist umbrella that a practitioner-scholar can take that have major impacts on the conceptualization and design of research and on data analysis (see Chapter 10 for more on constructivism, critical theory, and action research). From what has been called a weak constructivist stance (see Schwandt, 2000), a phenomenological study might commence seeking to understand the experience of sexual abuse survivors. But from a strong or radical constructivist stance, one might engage in participatory action research that seeks pragmatic change in treatment with such survivors. Here research might commence with sexual abuse survivors, but the focus is not merely on their experience but on pragmatic solutions to treatment dilemmas with abuse survivors wherein these survivors are viewed as coresearchers actively working with the practitioner-scholar. Curious about what this might look like? Oh wait, there's more—so much more in terms of constructivism's influence on research design and, most important, the relationship between the researcher and those researched. Even in counseling research, it's all about relationships.

Understanding Epistemology and Methodology

As alluded to before, discussing epistemology is mainly an academic exercise but does provide a perspective on how counselors approach research and eventually identify a methodological approach. Choosing positivism versus constructivism is not a requirement for engaging in research. More than likely, counselors will develop their philosophy over time and may even align their ideology in a manner that is consistent with their theoretical orientation. However, as counselors engage in research, a discussion of methodology is pertinent. *Methodology* is the systematic process used to gather information. Whereas *epistemology* refers to beliefs about how knowledge is generated, *methodology* is the process undertaken to acquire information (Trochim, 2006).

Conducting research and disseminating research findings is a formal process that requires expertise, transparency, and engagement. As intelligent consumers and potential producers of research, counselors need to know that the findings of a research study are credible. Hence, the methods used by the researcher need to stand up to critique through peer review and possibly public presentation. A good study is transparent, rigorous, and defendable.

The transparency of the research methods extends to what was done and the rationale for the procedure. Such details allow other researchers to replicate the study in case further verification is warranted or desired. The methodology of a research study should follow a prescribed system of data collection and analysis. Following a prescribed system entails using a research methodology that is appropriate for the study and grounded in the discipline. Research methodology is not an overly creative process (although the opportunity to explore a topic and generate new knowledge can be!). In addition, research studies are not perfect. Ultimately counseling research is highly dependent on evaluating human experiences, which are fraught with subjectivity. Even empirical studies grounded in measurement and supposed objectivity rely much on statistics, which contain error. In empirical studies researchers identify the amount of error that they are willing to tolerate and typically report error-related scores and measures. Researchers who choose to utilize narrative data (e.g., in qualitative studies) need to be concerned about subjectivity and bias, especially because they are the filter through which the narrative data derive meaning. Regardless of whether error is due to researcher bias (which can happen in quantitative research as well as qualitative research) or measurement and/or statistical error, no study is perfect, and researchers need to identify the type of error present in a study and either state how the error was addressed or minimized or identify the error as a limitation.

Another issue related to transparency is rigor. A rigorous study will have a detailed, accurate procedure. Researchers who use methods that allow for multiple types of error and bias produce results that are spurious (i.e., random and not easily replicable).

Especially when the effect of a treatment or intervention is being studied, counseling researchers need to be aware of treatment *fidelity*—that is, the consistency of a treatment or intervention. A research study should be replicable, and this may be considerably easier when scientists conduct studies in, for example, the physical sciences. However, the social sciences, and counseling research in particular, are dependent on consistency at a very human level. In human-subjects research there will be variability in the quality, interpretation, and replication of interactions, even for the most manualized or scripted treatments.

Take for example a study conducted by Lenz, Perepiczka, and Balkin (2013). In this study, Lenz et al. investigated changes in attitudes toward statistics among a small number ($N = 4$) of randomly assigned doctoral students who participated in a peer support group led by a facilitator. The authors hypothesized that students who participated in the small peer support group would demonstrate a more positive attitude toward statistics than those students in a control group. The following treatment was administered:

> Participants in the support group condition received four sessions of a peer-to-peer support group intervention. During support group meetings, the peer leader (first author), a doctoral candidate, established and maintained several controls related to group content and process to increase the internal validity related to evaluating the treatment. . . . Support group structure was as follows: a brief check-in among members, identification of present stressors related to statistics coursework, identification and sharing of coping skills by group members, and planning for engagement in coping practices. Group content did not include study tips from facilitator, content was reframed and redirected away from complaining about course requirements, and meetings were all between 30 and 40 min in length. (p. 30)

In reviewing treatment fidelity, Lenz et al. identified issues of structure, content, and time as essential to replicating the treatment method. However, the amount of time spent on the check-in, identification of stressors related to statistics coursework, or the processing of coping skills could vary from session to session, which would be natural depending on the orientation of the facilitator and the needs of the group members at each specific time. Hence, on the surface, the description of the treatment appears adequate, but in practice actual implementation could vary considerably, which could impact the results of future research should this study be replicated.

Rigor may also be affected when flaws occur in the methodology. Sometimes researchers inadvertently collect the wrong type of data. Take for example a variable such as age. Adolescents are typically defined as being between ages 12 and 17. So assume a researcher uses the following categories:

- Child = younger than 12 years of age
- Adolescent = 12–17 years of age
- Adult = 18 years of age or older

If the researcher has data from a 17-year-old participant, is the 17-year-old participant likely to be more similar to an 18-year-old (adult) or a 12-year-old (adolescent)? Of course the 17-year-old participant probably has more in common with the adult participants than the younger adolescent participants, but this information is lost when naturally occurring continuous data (e.g., age, income, weight) are artificially categorized. Although some variables are naturally categorized (e.g., sex, ethnicity, religion), variables such as age, income, or scores on a test are better studied in their naturally occurring continuous state. Otherwise information is lost.

Take for example a study by Ray, Armstrong, Warren, and Balkin (2005) in which the authors studied the relationships between the utilization of play therapy and the beliefs and training of elementary school counselors. The study participants, who were all elementary school counselors, were asked the number of hours per week they used play therapy. The participants responded by checking a box: 0–3 hours, 4–6 hours, 7–9 hours, 10–12 hours, or 13 or more hours. Notice that no rationale was provided for these categories. They are not equal intervals (0–3 has four values, 4–6 has three values, and 13 or more has a much larger range of values). In addition, participants who provided 3 hours of play therapy were placed in the same group as those who did not do any play therapy (0 hours) rather than those who used play therapy 4 hours per week. Finally, the types of analysis that can be conducted with categorical responses are quite different from and less powerful than (less likely to find a statistically significant effect if one exists) those that can be conducted with continuous data. Had the researchers simply asked, "How many hours per week do you utilize play therapy?" a more rigorous study could have been produced.

Ultimately published research is not necessarily perfect research. There are always limitations, and these should be identified within the study. Yet the significance of the findings should not be overshadowed by the limitations. In this regard, a study should be defendable—readers of a study should be able to understand the identified merits of the research and to replicate the methods.

Published research in the counseling profession goes through a blind peer-review process—that is, a process in which the manuscript is reviewed by experts in the field, the author of the manuscript remains unknown to the reviewers, and the reviewers remain unknown to the author. So there is merit to research that is published in counseling journals.

Chapter Summary

In this chapter we presented the underlying philosophies that govern the research traditions in the counseling profession with the ultimate goal of informing the counseling profession and bridging the technical aspects of research with the realities of counseling practice. Sometimes research may appear overly nuanced and technical. The methods and terminology used may seem foreign. We hope that by understanding how knowledge is generated in counseling research within the framework of transparency, rigor, and utility, counseling practitioners will continue to grow in their work with clients by improving their practice based on rigorous research methodologies.

Suggested Activities

I. Read the following article and discuss the questions below in small groups or as a class:

Lenz, A. S., Perepiczka, M., & Balkin, R. S. (2013). Evidence for the mitigating effects of a support group for attitudes toward statistics. *Counseling Outcome Research and Evaluation, 4*, 26–40. doi:10.1177/2150137812474000

1. What parts of the article were easy to understand? What parts were difficult?
2. Anxiety about research and research courses is normal. What is your experience so far?
3. Based on the article, to what extent do you believe that a support group would be beneficial to decreasing anxiety about statistics and research?
4. What do you think are prevalent attitudes regarding research in counseling?
5. How do you identify the importance of research in the counseling profession?

II. Discussion: Identify variables that are artificially categorized (e.g., we discussed age in Ray et al., 2005).
   1. What are the benefits and consequences of coding data in this way?
   2. Find a study that used artificially categorized variables.
      a. What type of information was collected?
      b. What information was lost?
      c. Was this addressed in the limitations?

References

American Counseling Association. (2014). *ACA code of ethics.* Alexandria, VA: Author.

Comstock, D. L., Hammer, T. R., Strentzsch, J., Cannon, K., Parsons, J., & Salazar, G., II. (2008). Relational-cultural theory: A framework for bridging relational, multicultural, and social justice competencies. *Journal of Counseling & Development, 86,* 279–287. doi:10.1002/j.1556-6678.2008.tb00510.x

Kaplan, D. M., Tarvydas, V. M., & Gladding, S. T. (2014). 20/20: A vision for the future of counseling: The new consensus definition of counseling. *Journal of Counseling & Development, 92,* 366–372. doi:10.1002/j.1556-6676.2014.00164.x

Kelly, G. A. (1955). *The psychology of personal constructs.* New York, NY: Norton.

Lenz, A. S., Perepiczka, M., & Balkin, R. S. (2013). Evidence for the mitigating effects of a support group for attitudes toward statistics. *Counseling Outcome Research and Evaluation, 4,* 26–40. doi:10.1177/2150137812474000

Ray, D., Armstrong, S. A., Warren, E. S., & Balkin, R. S. (2005). Play therapy practices among elementary school counselors. *Professional School Counseling, 8,* 360–365.

Schwandt, T. (2000). Three epistemological stances for qualitative inquiry: Interpretivism, hermeneutics, and social constructionism. In N. K. Denzin & Y. S. Lincoln (Eds.), *Handbook of qualitative research* (2nd ed., pp. 189–213). Newbury Park, CA: Sage.

Stoltenberg, C. D., & Pace, T. M. (2007). The scientist-practitioner model: Now more than ever. *Journal of Contemporary Psychotherapy, 37,* 195–203. doi:10.1007/s10879-007-9054-0

Stoltenberg, C. D., Pace, T. M., Kashubeck-West, S., Biever, J. L., Patterson, T., & Welch, I. D. (2000). Training models in counseling psychology: Scientist-practitioner versus practitioner-scholar. *The Counseling Psychologist, 28,* 622–640. doi:10.1177/0011000000285002

Trochim, W. M. K. (2006, October 20). *Research methods knowledge base* (2nd ed.). Retrieved from http://www.socialresearchmethods.net/kb/

White, M., & Epston, D. (1990). *Narrative means to therapeutic ends.* New York, NY: Norton.

The Research Process

Overview

In this chapter we walk you through the research process, from choosing a topic and reviewing previous research and literature to planning data collection and analysis. Although the choices available may appear overwhelming at times, we advocate that research is a systematic process in which each step in the process informs the next.

Choosing a Research Topic

In counseling research, the topics of study chosen by a researcher are often a result of who the researcher is as a person as much as the researcher having a sincere interest in the topic. More than likely the two are related, as research interests may be generated from personal experiences that influence the questions a researcher wishes to answer. This does not mean that research ideas are grounded in personal self-interest. Rather, research ideas often reflect a passion. Keep in mind that the research you initiate should sustain your attention for several months, and in the case of a dissertation perhaps a year or more. Choosing research topics that reflect your personal passion is important.

However, sometimes research interests are generated more from need as opposed to an identified passion. Regardless of your setting, you will likely encounter clients who attend counseling and present with problems that are unique or outside of your identified areas of training. In addition, you should keep in mind that although this text addresses the research process, from conceptualization, to data collection and analysis, to the reporting of findings, you may engage in all of these steps, or perhaps just some of them, especially as a practitioner and consumer of research. Consider the following as an example of some of the initial steps of the research process most counselors will engage.

Using Consultation and Resources

When I (Rick) started working in an outpatient counseling center, I quickly had three new clients, all of whom had identified compulsive behaviors related to cybersex. As I had completed my master's degree in 1992, this was not an area that had been addressed in my training, and despite numerous hours of continuing education in addiction, most of my training related to substance use as opposed to process addictions (see Smith, 2015). Consistent with the *ACA Code of Ethics* (American Counseling Association, 2014), I sought consultation to help address what I felt were deficits related to my understanding of Internet addiction (see Watson, 2015). My consultant was established in the area of treating addictions and recommended that I read work by Patrick Carnes, a noted scholar on addiction, and in particular sex addiction. Hence, working with clients who identified issues outside of my area of expertise necessitated acquiring consultation and resources that I might not have sought out otherwise. In this case, the need to develop competence in a particular area outweighed my passion for a particular topic. In addition, having an understanding of research helped in identifying appropriate resources that would be helpful to me in serving my clients.

A not-so-uncommon experience is having difficulty choosing a research topic. People often have difficulty selecting a single topic because they have varied or numerous interests or because they feel anxiety or uncertainty about where to begin the process. The former is usually the easier of the two to handle. A research study in counseling is not likely to metamorphose the profession, but each study has the potential to add to the knowledge base of the profession. No one can or should choose a research topic for you; this is something that emerging researchers must figure out for themselves. However, be aware that developing a researcher identity means establishing a research agenda that can be multifaceted. You do not need to choose *the* research topic but rather *a* research topic. Although it helps to choose a topic you are truly passionate about, having a topic that you are interested in and that can sustain your attention over a moderate to long period of time is most important.

Conceptualizing a research study as part of a longer term agenda may be helpful. This allows researchers to initiate a research agenda in manageable portions. For example, I (Rick) initiated research on therapeutic goal attainment for adolescents in crisis for a doctoral dissertation published in 2004. Two articles were developed from this dissertation exploring gender differences in therapeutic goal attainment for adolescents in crisis (Balkin & Roland, 2005) and a model for therapeutic goal attainment for adolescents in crisis (Balkin & Roland, 2007). Further research explored the relationship between therapeutic goal attainment and various psychosocial factors (e.g., Balkin, Leicht, Sartor, & Powell, 2011), culminating in the creation of an instrument to measure therapeutic goal attainment for adolescents in crisis (Balkin, 2013, 2014). Essentially, my experiences working as a counselor for adolescents admitted into crisis care in a psychiatric hospital setting were the catalyst for a dissertation and more than 10 years of published research. Hence, the research was influenced by professional experience, passion for the topic, and a line of research in which one study built on another.

However, not every study needs to be part of an extended research agenda, and often a person's first experiences with research are in assisting more established researchers with a particular study. As novice researchers engage in their first independent studies, some apprehension and anxiety are normal. Working with colleagues and engaging in supervised research help make this experience manageable and provide the necessary skills to be able to engage in more independent research. The process of becoming a competent researcher is not so different from that of becoming competent as a counselor.

1. *Develop research skills.* The ability to identify and review contemporary research is important to competent, ethical practice. A single research class in a master's program likely will be sufficient preparation to become an intelligent consumer of research, consistent with the practitioner-scholar model. A basic understanding of statistics and how to read and interpret them is helpful in evaluating what new models or techniques may be effective for clients. Research can be helpful when a counselor feels stumped by a particular client or encounters a new issue or problem. For example, Internet addiction is a

more recent phenomenon, and training regarding this type of addiction, even by today's standards, is quite limited. Although it is unlikely that many counselors have received training in this area, individuals are more often seeking treatment for this issue (Watson, 2015).

2. *Be a research participant.* Similar to counseling, participating in the research process can provide a more intimate understanding of the process. By participating in a research study, particularly a good research study, future researchers gain experience with the methods and procedures used, such as informed consent, methods and procedures used to identify and access potential participants, and means researchers use to communicate with their participants.
3. *Engage in research with an experienced researcher.* Students can gain valuable experience in research by working with faculty who conduct research, especially if they seek out faculty who conduct research in areas that reflect their own interests. Initially this involvement may focus on writing, such as putting together a literature review. This type of experience is important to learning how to be concise and write in the style set forth by the American Psychological Association. As students gain more advanced understanding of the research process, such as by taking additional courses in research methods, statistics, and qualitative research, they may have the opportunity to participate in conducting analyses and interpreting, writing, and disseminating the results of a study.
4. *Initiate a solo research study.* Students who work on their doctorate will eventually initiate a solo study to complete the dissertation. However, one does not have to be a doctoral student in order to conduct research. Research takes many forms, including program evaluation and single-case research designs. Such research is not necessarily complex and can be useful for demonstrating accountability, evaluating outcomes, and supporting current practice and procedures.

   Take for example a single-case research design by Cox, Lenz, and James (2015) in which the investigators examined the effect of a cognitive–behavioral counseling intervention for adult offenders who were diagnosed with co-occurring psychiatric and substance use disorders. Although eight participants began the study, only three participants completed it. Data were collected and evaluated prior to the onset of the intervention (A), during the intervention (B), and after the completion of the intervention (A), thereby constituting an A-B-A design. Data were graphed so that both researchers and consumers of research could evaluate the efficacy of the treatment based on visual analysis. In addition, basic metrics were used to further explain the effectiveness of the intervention (see Lenz, 2013). The study was not overly complex; used a small number of participants ($n = 3$); and lent itself to visual inspection of data, so consumers of the research did not need to be familiar with sophisticated statistics. This method can be replicated easily by practitioners as well as more seasoned researchers.

5. *Collaborate with or mentor other researchers and emerging researchers.* Collaborating on research can be beneficial for increasing productivity, decreasing researcher bias, and mentoring others in research. When researchers collaborate, they can discuss methods and procedures more thoroughly to address any weaknesses or limitations. Students and colleagues whose research interests align may also choose to further a particular line of research. For example, research on therapeutic goal attainment for adolescents in crisis (e.g., Balkin, 2014; Balkin & Roland, 2007) was furthered by dissertation research by students who worked with the lead author (e.g., Schmit, 2015; Smith, 2015).

Finding What's Out There: Reviewing the Literature

A Case Example

When working in the adolescent unit of a psychiatric hospital, I (Rick) was assigned a client diagnosed with anorexia. Similar to many of the adolescents in the hospital, she had been admitted against her will and did not believe her issues warranted any intervention. She regularly purged after meals and when prevented from doing so would exercise vigorously. Hence, some of the interventions with this client related to monitoring her very closely, especially after meals. An obvious goal for the client was to gain weight while in the hospital. During an initial team meeting (that included the nursing staff, psychiatrist, counselors, and support staff) to discuss the client and her care, the following question was asked: "When weighing the client, should we weigh her on the scale so that she can see the numbers and her weight gain, or should we have her stand on the scale with her back to the numbers so she does not notice her weight gain?"

The ramifications of this decision were deemed important. If, for example, the client were weighed so that she could see the numbers and note her weight gain, she might have been inclined to sabotage these efforts, which would have set her back in her treatment. Hence, the client identifying her weight gain might have been contraindicative. However, not allowing the client to see her weight gain ignored the issue. Eventually the client would be discharged from the hospital and would need to face the reality that she had gained weight. How could the treatment team prepare her for that reality and teach her coping skills if the issue were ignored?

Some readers of this case may feel that the answer is obvious, but this issue truly stumped the treatment team. At the core of the issue was nonmaleficence—Do no harm. Careful consideration of what constituted harm to the client needed to be considered. This dialogue among the treatment team transformed into a vigorous debate with various factions screaming at each other in the meeting about whether the client should see her weight gain. At no time did anyone suggest, "I wonder what is in the literature."

Rather than guessing at what outcome would be best, reviewing the literature can provide the knowledge needed to fully understand and address a particular topic. In a research study, reviewing the literature can provide the necessary background, highlight gaps in the literature, and provide the rationale for a study. Think about this client diagnosed with anorexia. Exploring the literature would provide the basis for understanding counseling and treatment as well as promote further ideas on what is still needed to understand, counsel, and treat clients with anorexia. Hence, in this section we talk about both reviewing the literature and writing a literature review.

Reviewing the Literature

Identifying pertinent literature is paramount when writing a literature review for counseling research. By *pertinent literature* we are referring to peer-reviewed articles, relevant texts, and essential documents necessary to cover the topic thoroughly within the field of counseling.

Peer-reviewed articles are articles published in academic journals that generally were accepted under a double-blind peer-review process. Although there are some exceptions to this rule, such as when an editor invites an author to submit a manuscript on a particular topic, articles published under a double-blind peer-review process are published under the following conditions:

1. An author or team of authors submits a de-identified manuscript. All potential identifiers of the author have been removed from the manuscript. Hence, no one who reviews the manuscript will be able to identify the author.
2. The manuscript is assigned to reviewers who remain anonymous to the author. Reviewers are scholars within the profession who agree to read and critique manuscripts submitted for publication. Reviewers represent the profession and are the gatekeepers of research: They identify research, whether theoretical/conceptual or data driven, that contributes to the profession and adds to the knowledge base. The reviewers provide an anonymous critique to the editor, who then makes a decision as to whether the manuscript merits publication. The reviewers are members of the editorial team who are anonymous to the author, and the author is anonymous to the reviewers—hence the term *double-blind peer review.*

Peer-reviewed manuscripts are published in scholarly journals that may be found in library databases or on the Internet (known as *open-access* journals). Database companies (e.g., EBSCO, ProQuest) purposefully select journals based on their meeting established criteria (e.g., being peer reviewed, publishing a certain number of issues). Although not all journals are equal in terms of rigor, content, and publication standards, journals in library databases generally can be trusted to have utilized the double-blind peer-review process and to conform to professional standards that represent scholarly work in a given field. In counseling research, popular library databases include EBSCO, PsycINFO, ProQuest, and the *Mental Measurements Yearbook*. EBSCO and ProQuest contain full-text articles for many counseling and counseling-related journals. ProQuest also has access to dissertation abstracts. However, exercise caution when citing dissertations, as there is a lot of variability among them and in standards for completing them across the country. EBSCO consists of several databases, including Academic Search Complete, PsycINFO, and *Mental Measurements Yearbook.* Academic Search Complete includes full-text articles. PsycINFO includes some full text but also abstracts of published manuscripts. PsycINFO is among the largest social science research databases, but not all counseling journals appear in PsycINFO. So researchers in the counseling profession would do well to search both Academic Search Complete and PsycINFO. *Mental Measure-*

ments Yearbook is a very specific database focused on reviews of published measures. It can be very helpful when one is trying to identify whether a measure is appropriate for a particular study.

Users of these databases use Boolean search strategies to identify manuscripts. Boolean search strategies include identifying topics and using *and, or,* or *not* to expand or limit potential manuscripts that fit a given set of identified topics. Parentheses can be used to group terms together. Users can also specify publication dates in order to isolate the most recent publications, for example. Typically researchers want to limit their searches to peer-reviewed articles in order to maintain scholarly standards, but such a limit prevents books and dissertations from being listed in the search results. Counseling researchers should be cautious about limiting their searches to full-text articles only. Although imposing such a limit is convenient, many journals do not allow the full texts of articles to be included in these databases or place a moratorium on access for a period of time to add value to the journal publication. Researchers should check university libraries to access such articles.

Open-access journals may or may not be of similar quality to traditional academic journals. Open-access journals are electronic journals published on the Internet. Everyone has access to these journals, which can increase citations of their articles and provide broader dissemination of the research due to easy accessibility. However, unlike journals in library databases, open-access journals charge authors a fee to publish, which sets up a highly disconcerting conflict of interest. Is the manuscript being published because the authors met a high standard, or is the manuscript being published because the authors paid a fee?

Textbooks and professional texts can be important sources of information for research, especially when their authors are recognized for a particular area of expertise. However, readers should be cautious when using books as a source of information. Not all books are created equal, and authors often insert their opinion based on their expertise (and this book is no exception). Some books may be considered seminal texts. For example, in a piece on cultural humanism, Lemberger (2012) cited seminal humanistic theorists Alfred Adler (1938) and Carl Rogers (1951), who indicated that individuals are part of a larger cultural and social environment. Lemberger would have been remiss if these texts had not been included in his review of the literature. Furthermore, some constructs studied in counseling require the citing of important works that are not necessarily traditional, scholarly texts. Balkin, Watts, and

Ali (2014) discussed issues of faith, sexual orientation, and gender within the counseling profession from Jewish, Christian, and Muslim perspectives. The authors made reference to various religious texts in the article, which given the context of the subject was appropriate and pertinent for sufficient coverage of the information.

Although not peer reviewed, some websites offer important information related to counseling topics. Researchers are encouraged to be judicious when deciding to use a website as a reference. For example, when addressing the topic of counseling adolescents in crisis, Balkin and Roland (2007) cited information from the American Academy of Child and Adolescent Psychiatry website. Reiner, Dobmeier, and Hernández (2013) discussed licensure portability in light of professional identity and cited the website of the American Association of State Counseling Boards. What determines whether a website should serve as a reference? Consider the source, who the source represents, and the reputation of the author or agency. Many websites represent professional organizations pertinent to the profession. The website should be developed to inform aligned professionals and the public. Often such websites include important position papers of a scholarly nature that did not go through the peer-review process. When websites are used as references, accuracy and transparency are important and may lend credibility to the content provided.

However, the same cannot be said for websites such as Wikipedia, blogs, or news websites that are biased (e.g., Fox News, MSNBC). Information garnered from such websites may not be accurate. The purpose of these websites may be considerably different from those of reputable professional organizations such as the American Counseling Association or American Academy of Child and Adolescent Psychiatry. Best practice is to support your assertions with peer-reviewed references; however, when such references appear to be unavailable, texts and information from reputable websites only may be used.

Writing the Literature Review

Writing a literature review for a research study, especially for a dissertation, may seem like a daunting process. A well-written literature review provides a foundation for the topic that is informative and places the current research study into perspective. A good literature review essentially indicates *what is known and what still needs to be learned.* Organizing the literature into a coherent narrative is key to creating a publishable study. The key to writing a coherent narrative is to understand the difference between a linear literature review and an integrated literature review.

A *linear literature review* is organized by study. Essentially, the author mentions a study, summarizes it, and then mentions another study to summarize. This process continues until all of the appropriate studies have been identified. The problem with this approach is twofold:

1. None of the study summaries are connected. Although a study may be connected to the topic, how the study fits into the overall picture of the research may be lost.
2. Such a literature review fails to connect ideas from one study to another.

Remember, a well-formulated literature review provides a picture of what has been covered with regard to the topic and what requires further investigation. Without a literature review that is grounded in recent and past research, the researcher is in danger of investigating a topic or question for which much information is already known or key components are missing, which will affect the design and outcome of the study.

An integrated literature review addresses these concerns. In an *integrated literature review,* research is organized by topic and the researcher provides summaries of each topic, noting confirming and disconfirming evidence from extant research. One advantage of this method is that the reader gains an understanding of various perspectives, as the researcher provides findings from various points of view. Such a review is easier to understand and provides a foundation for the topic of study.

Providing a comprehensive literature review is important to demonstrating a complete understanding of and expertise around the topic of study. Without a comprehensive approach to a topic, the researcher is in danger of developing, conducting, and disseminating a study grounded in bias. Consider the following example.

Balkin, Freeman, and Lyman (2009) reviewed the literature related to the role of reconciliation in the forgiveness process. Within the framework of the literature review, two contrasting perspectives on the role of reconciliation were discussed:

> *Reconciliation* has often been linked to forgiveness (Hargrave, 1994; Power, 1994); however, other clinicians and researchers (Aponte, 1998; Coyle & Enright, 1997; Freedman & Enright, 1996; Hart & Shapiro, 2002) have argued that reconciliation is distinct from the decision to forgive. (p. 154, italics in the original)

Now consider for a moment if only one of these perspectives were presented. As a reader you may not agree that reconciliation should be linked to forgiveness (and I [Rick] certainly disagree with linking reconciliation to forgiveness). However, to ignore this assertion would result in incomplete coverage of the topic and a rather biased review of the literature. Not only would a biased literature review misinform the public who reads the manuscript, it would also potentially bias the researcher with respect to the research question and what is ultimately reported.

However, some researchers (e.g., Esterberg, 2002; Mertens, 2010) have identified a trend among some qualitative researchers in which a comprehensive literature review is avoided because of researcher bias. The thinking here is that if a researcher were aware of various studies and results, this could bias the researcher during the analysis and interpretation of the findings. However, sound analysis and interpretation is based, to some degree, on expertise or developing expertise on the subject matter. In qualitative research, the researcher is the instrument through which all data are filtered. Hence, providing a comprehensive literature review is always advisable.

Defining the Gap . . . What Do I Still Need to Know?

After providing an overview of what has been covered on a given topic, a literature review often concludes by addressing the gaps in the literature, which in turn introduces the research questions or hypotheses that govern the study. If the goal of a research study is to produce knowledge that contributes to the counseling profession, then the researcher needs to have a strong understanding of the extant research in order to identify gaps in this research and formulate research questions or hypotheses. A cursory knowledge of the literature simply does not allow for this.

Students and other emerging researchers often have a sincere interest in a topic but have not explored the gaps. For example, a student who says, "I want to study the effects of abuse on children," probably has not reviewed the literature. The fact is that there is already considerable information about the effects of abuse on children. Although the topic may be of interest, the student has yet to define a gap, especially given what is already known about the topic. What new research can be generated from this topic? Without a comprehensive review of the literature, and in particular a review of the extant research, a person's ability to contribute to this area of interest is limited. In other words, researchers should avoid reinventing the wheel.

With this in mind, there is nothing wrong with conducting research in order to see whether results can be replicated. Confirmation of past research is necessary in order to build a knowledge base. In addition, sometimes studies may be replicated with the intent of improving on the research. For example, perhaps limitations in the design, measure, or participants in the study led to results that were circumspect. Replicating or improving on such a study could be a valuable contribution. Hence, not all research is entirely original. Rather, simply making minor adjustments that may confirm or disconfirm past research findings may fill gaps. A common phenomenon in counseling research is to identify a research topic for which findings are mixed. Research may then be undertaken to provide further evidence in support of one set of findings over another. For example, Balkin, Perepiczka, Whitely, and Kimbrough (2009) found that emotional awareness was not linked to the decision to engage in sexual activity and was not related to the sexual values of college freshmen participants. This finding was contrary to other findings in the extant research (e.g., Davidson & Gottlieb, 1955; Harrod & Scheer, 2005; Livingstone & Day, 2005; Moriarty, Stough, Tidmarsh, Eger, & Dennison, 2001; Salovey, Mayer, Goldman, Turvey, & Palfai, 1995; Shaughnessy & Shakesby, 1992) that linked emotional awareness and emotional intelligence to the decision to engage in sexual activity. Hence, Balkin, Perepiczka, et al.'s (2009) research study provided evidence disconfirming prior research. Further study on the topic is warranted.

Operationalizing the Study: Research Questions or Hypotheses

Once the gap in the literature is identified, the researcher can introduce the purpose of the study. The purpose of the study is a narrative of expression about the nature of the investigation or inquiry. Research questions or hypotheses operationalize the purpose of the study. The decision to state research questions or hypotheses is up to the researcher, but both are not necessary. Rather, use either questions or hypotheses, as the inclusion of both tends to be superfluous. However, with respect to the dissertation process, some dissertation chairs will use the antiquated method of including both.

Research questions and hypotheses may provide direction for the design of the study and the analytic strategy. For example, research questions that address between-groups differences will likely signal the use of some type of experimental; quasi-experimental; or explanatory, nonexperimental design. In contrast, research questions that attempt to establish relationships between or among variables may dictate the use of a correlational design. Qualitative researchers use research questions, hypotheses, or purpose statements that are indicative of a more naturalistic inquiry. Consider the following examples.

Example 1: The Use of Research Questions

Gnilka, Chang, and Dew (2012) designed a study around the supervisory working alliance for students in counseling. They identified the purpose of the study followed by research questions:

> The purpose of this study was to explore the relationships between perceived stress levels, coping resources, the working alliance, and the supervisory working alliance among a sample of counselor supervisees currently enrolled in a master's-level program. The research questions were (a) What are the relationships between current perceived stress levels, specific types of coping resources, and the working alliance among supervisees? (b) Are perceived stress and specific coping resources predictive of the working alliance from a supervisee's perspective? (c) What are the relationships between current perceived stress levels, coping resources, and supervisory working alliance among supervisees? (d) Are perceived stress levels and coping resources predictive of the supervisory working alliance from a supervisee's perspective? (p. 64)

In this example, the research questions inform the reader about how the purpose of the study will ultimately be addressed. The researchers used key phrases, such as asking "What are the relationships . . ." or "Are perceived stress and specific coping resources predictive . . .," to denote a correlational design.

Example 2: The Use of Research Questions and Hypotheses

Research questions and research hypotheses can both be incorporated into a study. Lenz, Perepiczka, and Balkin (2013) investigated whether a peer support group would have an influence on doctoral students' attitudes toward statistics. Notice the use of both research questions and hypotheses to guide the study:

> This study evaluated the following research question: Does a peer-to-peer supportive group intervention have an influence on first semester doctoral students' attitudes about their statistics? We hypothesized [that] participants attending a regular statistics support group would demonstrate more positive attitudes toward statistics when compared to a control group. (p. 28)

In this example, the research questions are followed by a research hypothesis—what the researchers expect to find in the study based on a comprehensive review of the literature. An advantage of research hypotheses is that the researchers provide a clear statement about expectations; however, the depiction of expectations could be viewed as evidence of researcher bias in the study. Hypotheses should be based on what currently exists in the literature, not what the researcher prefers to find. When the extant research findings are ambiguous or mixed, research questions may be preferred over research hypotheses.

Example 3: The Use of Purpose Statements

As mentioned previously, qualitative researchers may use purpose statements that guide their inquiry. Gibson, Dollarhide, and Moss (2010) sought to identify a theory related to developing professional identity in counselor training:

> This study was designed to provide a theory of professional identity development from entry into the program through the completion of internship, as described by the trainees. Professional identity development is highlighted at nodal points in counselor training (before course work, before practicum, before internship, and at graduation) to articulate a grounded theory of the construction of professional identity. (p. 23)

Here the authors clearly indicate using a qualitative paradigm, grounded theory, to develop a theory related to professional identity in counselor training.

The transition from the literature review, to the gap in the literature, to the research questions or hypotheses should be seamless. Without a thorough grounding in the literature, researchers may be at risk for conducting research that makes only a limited contribution or even identifying the wrong research questions or hypotheses. This may have been the issue with Project DARE (Drug Abuse Resistance Education), in which researchers indicated that the program did not reduce or prevent drug use (e.g., Ennett, Tobler, Ringwalt, & Flewelling, 1994; Lynam et al., 1999). DARE was a funded program in which police officers went into schools to deliver drug education and prevention programs. However, one benefit of the program that was not presented was the presence of police officers in the schools delivering programs to the youth in the community. Although DARE may not have impacted drug use among youth, the program may have had an impact on youths' perception of police officers (this was not investigated). Hence, the results of a study may be impacted by the type of question asked.

Researcher and Participant Bias in Counseling Research

Perhaps no issue clouds the results of human-subjects research more than the presence of bias. Individuals may be extremely skeptical of research findings, especially when research is tainted by strong social and political contexts. For example, consider research on addictions. Despite overwhelming evidence for a genetic predisposition to addiction, many individuals continue to view addiction as a chosen behavior. The tendency to ignore research findings that may be overwhelmingly persuasive is not exclusive to social science research, as this debate exists with respect to many other areas, such as genetics and climate change.

So what does the denial of research findings have to do with bias? Such skepticism ties directly into research design and the belief about what researchers do. A common myth is that researchers can essentially make the data say whatever they want. Aside from falsifying the data, this is simply not true. Data should not be anthropomorphized. Data cannot *say* anything. Rather, researchers put in place a design and strategy for interpretation that is transparent. A well-executed design, in either quantitative or qualitative research, can help guard against many types of research bias.

Researcher Expectations

Perhaps the most obvious type of bias researchers must guard against is their own biases or desire for a particular finding. Both quantitative and qualitative domains use rigorous methodologies to protect the integrity of the research. Nevertheless, researcher bias persists. The nature of a research question, the variables selected for study, the amount of error allowed in a study, the type of sampling processes used, and the mechanisms put in place to demonstrate research integrity are all subjective decisions that both protect and inform bias. For example, a research question chosen by the researcher is likely driven by personal interest, and the researcher likely has an informed opinion about or even expertise in the selected topic. Hopefully, however, the procedures the researcher has put in place will protect the integrity of the research and reduce potential researcher bias.

Publication Bias

A question often asked by doctoral students and novice researchers is, "What happens if I do not find anything?" Such a statement is generated from the fear that if nothing is found, then the research cannot be published. This is somewhat true, in that the vast majority of research indicates some type of finding that hopefully moves the field forward. Moving the field forward can be accomplished when research provides information and/or evidence on where to look for answers. However, knowing where not to look for answers is also helpful. Thus, nonfindings may not be published as frequently as findings, but it is not impossible to publish such studies, and doing so may even be helpful to the field.

Administration of Treatment

The investigation of interventions, also known as *treatments*, can be complicated because of the issue of *treatment fidelity*—the consistency with which a treatment is delivered. Consider for example the previously mentioned study by Lenz et al. (2013) investigating whether a peer support group would have an influence on doctoral students' attitudes toward statistics. Consider the description of the implementation of the treatment:

> . . . a brief check-in among members, identification of present stressors related to statistics coursework, identification and sharing of coping skills by group members, and planning for engagement in coping practices. Group content did not include study tips from facilitator, content was reframed and redirected away from complaining about course requirements, and meetings were all between 30 and 40 min in length. (p. 30)

Based on this description, consider the extent to which the intervention could be replicated. Are the details sufficient to replicate the study? To what extent can a researcher adhere to the described treatment? How would the integration of supportive comments, confrontational comments, and educational comments to group members produce variability (i.e., lack of consistency) within the design? Also consider the skill of the facilitator—who is to say that a replication of this study would include a facilitator with skills in implementing a support group? Clearly these issues can affect the results of the study, thereby contributing to researcher bias.

Scoring of Measures

In many instances of counseling research the scoring of instruments is straightforward. For example, many measures utilize a Likert or

Likert-type scale (e.g., 1 = *strongly disagree*, 2 = *disagree*, 3 = *neither disagree nor agree*, 4 = *agree*, 5 = *strongly agree*). Such measures are often self-reports, meaning that the research participant completes the measure. Other measures, though, may be completed by a rater, including the researcher. In this case, the prejudicial judgments of the rater can influence the results of the study. Even with the best of intentions, researchers who are motivated or biased toward a particular finding may administer, score, or interpret instruments erroneously. Procedures to address fidelity in scoring measures, such as through evidence of interrater reliability, are important when such measures are used in a research study. In addition, the moods or motivations of participants can also influence a study. Masling (1966) described what is often referred to as the *screw you effect*, in which participants respond in a dishonest manner with the intent of providing inaccurate results or negatively influencing the integrity of a study.

Interaction With Participants

Additional factors contributing to bias include collecting data using observations or interviews or even the researcher providing directions to the participants. The clarity and consistency (or lack thereof) of communications can impact a study and the subsequent results. Researchers need to be careful that directions and interactions remain consistent and objective. Such a task can be particularly difficult in qualitative research, in which the quality of interactions can be pertinent to the research. Often qualitative researchers will engage in interviews using guided or semistructured approaches in order to provide consistency to the inquiry. Even the extent to which participants are responsive to the researcher due to appearance, verbal requests, and nonverbal communications can impact participants' responsiveness to a study. Obviously, some of these qualities are out of the control of the researcher, but one should consider the extent to which interactions can impact a study when designing and implementing research and when discussing the limitations of a given study.

Collecting and Analyzing Data

Novice researchers may view the collection and analysis of data as the culminating step in executing a research study. A statistical test in quantitative research or the process of generating themes in qualitative research can be rather meaningless without a transparent and coherent design. The type of data collected is determined by the research questions and/or hypotheses. Once data are collected, researchers discern a plan for analysis.

Research can be an intimidating process if after the collection of the data the researcher has not identified a plan for analyzing those data. For example, survey designs are popular in counseling research. Those individuals who create surveys often do not consider how the data will be analyzed. Common problems occur when survey questions are analyzed individually. In other words, survey research can be problematic when single items are used to compare groups or evaluate a construct.

For example, the Beck Depression Inventory–II (Beck, Steer, & Brown, 1996) contains 21 items that evaluate the presence and severity of depressive symptoms. The thought behind this is that assessing depression is complicated and requires more than a single item. Why not simply ask, "On a scale of 1 to 5, with 1 being *no problem* and 5 being *severe,* how would you rate your depression?" If one item were sufficient to assess a construct consistently and accurately, then there would not be a need for multidimensional measures.

Hence, having a plan for how data will be managed and analyzed prior to collecting the data is very important. Such planning informs the researcher about the nature of the data to be collected. Putting a plan in place *before* collecting data is more transparent and ethical than what is often referred to as *data mining*—running analyses without preordained research questions or hypotheses to see what can be found. Such processes increase the likelihood of error in a study and are not replicable because of the haphazard nature of conducting analyses without considering the overarching purpose of the study.

Let's look at a rather entertaining study by Park and Henley (2007) in which they investigated the relationship between personality factors and character references from virtual role-playing games. They hypothesized that people were likely to create fantasy role-playing characters that were reflections of their own personalities. The authors collected data on personality and fantasy role-playing attributes, such as species (e.g., elf, human, orc), occupations (e.g., fighter, thief, magician), and attributes (e.g., intelligence, strength, charisma). Overall, 31 role-playing attributes were correlated with five personality factors, resulting in 155 correlation coefficients. Although the study was somewhat creative and enjoyable, the nature of the analysis (i.e., running 155 correlation coefficients) produced a likely error rate of 68%. In other words, running so many statistical tests, with each test allowing for a 5% chance of indicating statistical significance when there actually was not significance, likely produced erroneous results. Although this type of exploratory research may be fun and interesting, and in this case was even publishable, given its high error rate the study is not likely to make a valuable contribution to the field. Rather, researchers should be more purposeful about what they want to analyze so as to avoid accruing so much error.

Similar issues could occur in qualitative research. Though some researchers resist the use of semistructured and guided interview approaches, relying on spontaneity and informal interview approaches may hinder one's ability to compare respondents and develop themes. Qualitative researchers should consider the benefits of standardizing some aspects of the inquiry process.

Chapter Summary

The research process is both developmental and systematic. Conducting research is a skill and like any skill must be learned and practiced repeatedly to be honed. Moreover, the process is almost always sequential. A topic must be chosen in order for the literature review to be conducted and research questions or hypotheses generated. The generation of research questions or hypotheses without a thorough grounding in the literature can lead to research that is unnecessary or ill informed. Researchers need to be aware of contributing factors of bias and be thoughtful in their planning and execution of a study. Careful thought about the type of data needed for a study will lead to a thoughtful plan for analysis that is both concise and efficient. Some research can be exploratory, but when exploratory research is conducted, the results may be spurious and the conclusions more unsound.

Suggested Activities

I. There are many tutorials on using library databases. Complete a tutorial that introduces you to using library databases if you are not already familiar with them.

II. Using your library databases (e.g., EBSCO Academic Search Complete, PsycINFO), search on a topic of your choosing related to the counseling profession. When conducting the search, make the following alterations:

1. Use more than one library database. Do you find more resources with one than another?

2. Notice what happens when you limit your search to only peer-reviewed resources.
3. Notice what happens when you use Boolean search strategies (e.g., *and, or*). Using *and* will limit your search (by requiring all terms), whereas using *or* will increase your search results (by picking up articles that use any term).

III. Select a topic related to counseling and search the *Mental Measurements Yearbook* database. Identify measures related to your research topic. Select a review of a measure that might be interesting to use for a study.

References

Adler, A. (1938). *Social interest: A challenge to mankind* (J. Linton & R. Vaughan, Trans.). London, England: Faber & Faber.

American Counseling Association. (2014). *ACA code of ethics.* Alexandria, VA: Author.

Balkin, R. S. (2013). Validation of the Goal Attainment Scale of Stabilization. *Measurement and Evaluation in Counseling and Development, 46,* 261–269. doi:10.1177/0748175613497040

Balkin, R. S. (2014). *The Crisis Stabilization Scale manual and sampler set.* Menlo Park, CA: Mind Garden.

Balkin, R. S., Freeman, S. J., & Lyman, S. R. (2009). Forgiveness, reconciliation, and mechila: Integrating the Jewish concept of forgiveness into clinical practice. *Counseling and Values, 53,* 153–160. doi:10.1002/j.2161-007X.2009.tb00121.x

Balkin, R. S., Leicht, D. J., Sartor, T., & Powell, J. (2011). Assessing the relationship between therapeutic goal attainment and psychosocial characteristics for adolescents in crisis residence. *Journal of Mental Health, 20,* 32–42. doi:10.3109/09638237.2010.537402

Balkin, R. S., Perepiczka, M., Whitely, R., & Kimbrough, S. (2009). The relationship of values and emotional awareness to sexual activity in young adulthood. *Adultspan Journal, 8,* 17–28.

Balkin, R. S., & Roland, C. B. (2005). Identification of differences in gender for adolescents in crisis residence. *Journal of Mental Health, 14,* 637–646.

Balkin, R. S., & Roland, C. B. (2007). Re-conceptualizing stabilization for counseling adolescents in brief psychiatric hospitalization: A new model. *Journal of Counseling & Development, 85,* 64–72. doi:10.1002/j.1556-6678.2007.tb00445.x

Balkin, R. S., Watts, R. E., & Ali, S. R. (2014). A conversation about the intersection of faith, sexual orientation, and gender: Jewish, Christian, and Muslim perspectives. *Journal of Counseling & Development, 92,* 187–193. doi:10.1002/j.1556-6676.2014.00147.x

Beck, A. T., Steer, R. A., & Brown, G. K. (1996). *BDI-II manual.* San Antonio, TX: Psychological Corporation.

Cox, R. M., Lenz, A. S., & James, R. K. (2015). A pilot evaluation of the ARRAY program with offenders with mental illness. *Journal of Counseling & Development, 93,* 471–480. doi:10.1002/jcad.12045

Davidson, H. H., & Gottlieb, L. S. (1955). The emotional maturity of pre- and post-menarcheal girls. *Journal of Genetic Psychology, 86,* 261–266.

Ennett, S. T., Tobler, N. S., Ringwalt, C. L., & Flewelling, R. L. (1994). How effective is drug abuse resistance education? A meta-analysis of Project DARE outcome evaluations. *American Journal of Public Health, 84,* 1394–1401. doi:10.2105/AJPH.84.9.1394

Esterberg, K. G. (2002). *Qualitative methods in social research.* New York, NY: McGraw-Hill.

Gibson, D. M., Dollarhide, C. T., & Moss, J. M. (2010). Professional identity development: A grounded theory of transformational tasks of new counselors. *Counselor Education and Supervision, 50,* 21–38.

Gnilka, P. B., Chang, C. V., & Dew, B. J. (2012). The relationship between supervisee stress, coping resources, the working alliance, and the supervisory working alliance. *Journal of Counseling & Development, 90,* 63–70.

Harrod, N. R., & Scheer, S. D. (2005). An explanation of adolescent emotional intelligence in relation to demographic characteristics. *Adolescence, 40,* 503–512.

Lemberger, M. E. (2012). A reply to Hansen's cultural humanism. *Journal of Humanistic Counseling, 51,* 180–183.

Lenz, A. S. (2013). Calculating effect size in single-case research: A comparison of nonoverlap methods. *Measurement and Evaluation in Counseling and Development, 46,* 64–73. doi:10.1177/0748175612456401

Lenz, A. S., Perepiczka, M., & Balkin, R. S. (2013). Evidence for the mitigating effects of a support group for attitudes toward statistics. *Counseling Outcome Research and Evaluation, 4,* 26–40. doi:10.1177/2150137812474000

Livingstone, H. A., & Day, A. L. (2005). Comparing the construct and criterion-related validity of ability-based and mixed-model measures of emotional intelligence. *Educational & Psychological Measurement, 65,* 851–873.

Lynam, D. R., Milich, R., Zimmerman, R., Novak, S. P., Logan, T. K., Martin, C., . . . Clayton, R. (1999). Project DARE: No effects at 10-year follow-up. *Journal of Consulting and Clinical Psychology, 67,* 590–593. doi:10.1037/0022-006X.67.4.590

Masling, J. (1966). Role-related behavior of the subject and psychologist and its effect upon psychological data. In D. Levine (Ed.), *The Nebraska symposium on motivation* (pp. 67–103). Lincoln, NE: University of Nebraska Press.

Mertens, D. (2010). *Research and evaluation in education and psychology* (3rd ed.). Thousand Oaks, CA: Sage.

Moriarty, N., Stough, C., Tidmarsh, P., Eger, D., & Dennison, S. (2001). Deficits in emotional intelligence underlying adolescent sex offending. *Journal of Adolescence, 24,* 743–752.

Park, A. E., & Henley, T. B. (2007). Personality and fantasy game character preferences. *Imagination, Cognition, and Personality, 27,* 37–46.

Reiner, S. M., Dobmeier, R. A., & Hernández, T. J. (2013). Perceived impact of professional counselor identity: An exploratory study. *Journal of Counseling & Development, 91,* 174–183. doi:10.1002/j.1556-6676.2013.00084.x

Rogers, C. R. (1951). *Client-centered therapy: Its current practice, implications and theory.* Boston, MA: Houghton Mifflin.

Salovey, P., Mayer, J. D., Goldman, S. L., Turvey, C., & Palfai, T. (1995). Emotional attention, clarity, and repair: Exploring emotional intelligence using the Trait Meta-Mood Scale. In J. W. Pennebaker (Ed.), *Emotion, disclosure, and health* (pp. 125–154). Washington, DC: American Psychological Association.

Schmit, E. L. (2015). *The relationship between working alliance and therapeutic goal attainment in an adolescent inpatient, acute care behavioral hospital* (Doctoral dissertation). Available from ProQuest Dissertations and Theses database. (UMI No. 3700674)

Shaughnessy, M. E., & Shakesby, P. (1992). Adolescent sexual and emotional intimacy. *Adolescence, 27,* 475–480.

Smith, P. L. (2015). *The relationship between spirituality and spiritual/religious coping, goal attainment, and change in symptoms of adolescents in crisis residence* (Doctoral dissertation). Available from ProQuest Dissertations and Theses database. (UMI No. 3642855)

Watson, J. C. (2015). Internet addiction. In R. L. Smith (Ed.), *Treatment strategies for substance and process addictions* (pp. 293–311). Alexandria, VA: American Counseling Association.

Ethical and Multicultural Issues in Counseling Research

Overview

The historical antecedents leading to the formation and implementation of institutional review boards (IRBs) are rooted in human tragedies from a multicultural context. An understanding and practice of ethical behavior in research is a federal mandate as well as a professional obligation. The requirements of meeting this charge, from both a legal and moral standpoint, are explored in this chapter.

How Did We Get Here?

Research ethics may seem a bit mundane, but the importance of conducting ethical research cannot be overstated. In the United States the development of research ethics is tied directly to flagrant corruption, inequity, and exploitation resulting in racial discrimination and social injustices. Nowhere is this more apparent than in the Tuskegee Study of Untreated Syphilis in the Negro Male (1932–1972), which originated with the U.S. Public Health Service (PHS; DuBois, 2008). There are varying accounts as to whether the Tuskegee study began innocently enough—to observe how untreated syphilis progressed among Black men—or was grounded in racist philosophies from the onset. In 1932 theories that promulgated the idea that the course of syphilis could vary among ethnic groups were still under debate (DuBois, 2008).

Black men in rural Alabama (399 with syphilis and 200 in a control group) were enrolled in the study. The actual purpose of the study was not disclosed to the enrollees. Rather, they were deceived to believe that they had "bad blood" and were promised free medical care, which consisted of a documented history and physical, a spinal tap without anesthesia, subsequent visits, and an eventual autopsy (DuBois, 2008, pp. 15–16).

In addition to being deceived during the 30-year course of this study, participants were denied important medical care when such advances were available. As penicillin became available in the 1940s, efforts were undertaken to deny participants use of the medication to treat syphilis and knowledge about available treatments. From 1952 to 1972, state and local health departments assisted the PHS in retaining men in the experimental group and denying or preventing health care services for the treatment of syphilis. The study persisted until 1972 when public health official Peter Buxton went to the press (DuBois, 2008).

As reported by Thomas and Quinn (1991), Buxton had attempted to address the ethical concerns of the Tuskegee syphilis study internally through the PHS. Buxton was a social worker and interviewer working for PHS and had initially communicated ethical concerns to the director of the Division of Venereal Diseases. Another letter was sent in 1968 in which Buxton noted the ongoing racial discord in the United States and the racial composition of the study (100% African American). This was enough to get the attention of the National Communicable Disease Center 3 months later in 1969. The Center realized that the study could be a public relations fiasco but decided that it should continue to its logical conclusion and that no treatment should be offered to participants. Buxton finally put an end to the study in July 1972 by making a report to the Associated Press. The Center faced litigation for what its leaders identified as "genocide" (p. 1502), and the government settled out of court for $10 million in 1974.

Although the modern-day Office for Human Research Protections (OHRP) did not come into existence until 1979 as a response to the Tuskegee syphilis study, as well as other egregious human-subjects violations (e.g., the 1972 Stanford prison study, Willowbrook hepatitis study), the decision to continue the Tuskegee syphilis study and deny treatment and resources to the participants occurred in the post-Nuremberg era (DuBois, 2008). The Nuremberg Code was a 1947 verdict from an American military tribunal focused on the prosecution of German doctors who performed medical experiments on Holocaust victims. The German doctors attempted to defend themselves by indicating that the experiments performed were consistent with human experiments in the United States. Two American doctors, Andrew Ivy and Leo Alexander, worked with military prosecutors to develop six points addressing principles of legitimate research. On rendering their verdict, the military tribunal expanded the initial six points to 10 (see Exhibit 3.1).

Although the Tuskegee syphilis study began prior to World War II, written documentation related to medical ethics and human-subjects research was firmly in place during the study. Yet this widely recognized ethical code developed by American doctors appears to have been ignored prior to Buxton informing the press. In 1979, primarily in response to the Tuskegee syphilis study, the National Commission for the Protection of Human Subjects of Biomedical and Behavioral Research issued *The Belmont Report: Ethical Principles and Guidelines for the Protections of Human Subjects of Research*. The *Belmont Report* represented the first time the federal government mandated ethical conduct as part of legal behavior and proceedings (DuBois, 2008). Three ethical principles—respect for persons, beneficence, and justice—became the cornerstone of human-subjects research with three essential applications: informed consent, assessment of risk and benefit, and selection of subjects. From this framework, the modern process for reviewing and approving human-subjects research was initiated. The *Belmont Report* can be found online at http://www.hhs.gov/ohrp/regulations-and-policy/belmont-report.

The IRB

The federal mandate for research ethics and the protection of human subjects spawned regulations from the U.S. Department of Health and Human Services: 45 *Code of Federal Regulations* (CFR) part 46 (OHRP, 2009), which established the Common Rule (subpart A) and three additional subparts: subpart B—additional protections for pregnant women, human fetuses, and neonates involved in research; subpart C—additional protections pertaining to biomedical and behavioral research involving prisoners as subjects; subpart D—additional protections for children involved as subjects in research. The Common Rule and subsequent sections were originally published in 1991 and most recently revised in 2009. The Common Rule, also known as subpart A of 45 CFR part 46, outlined the following: compliance through the establishment of IRBs, rules and

PERMISSIBLE MEDICAL EXPERIMENTS

The great weight of the evidence before us is to the effect that certain types of medical experiments on human beings, when kept within reasonably well-defined bounds, conform to the ethics of the medical profession generally. The protagonists of the practice of human experimentation justify their views on the basis that such experiments yield results for the good of society that are unprocurable by other methods or means of study. All agree, however, that certain basic principles must be observed in order to satisfy moral, ethical and legal concepts:

1. **The voluntary consent of the human subject is absolutely essential.**
   This means that the person involved should have legal capacity to give consent; should be so situated as to be able to exercise free power of choice, without the intervention of any element of force, fraud, deceit, duress, over-reaching, or other ulterior form of constraint or coercion; and should have sufficient knowledge and comprehension of the elements of the subject matter involved as to enable him to make an understanding and enlightened decision. This latter element requires that before the acceptance of an affirmative decision by the experimental subject there should be made known to him the nature, duration, and purpose of the experiment; the method and means by which it is to be conducted; all inconveniences and hazards reasonably to be expected; and the effects upon his health or person which may possibly come from his participation in the experiment.
   The duty and responsibility for ascertaining the quality of the consent rests upon each individual who initiates, directs or engages in the experiment. It is a personal duty and responsibility which may not be delegated to another with impunity.
2. **The experiment should be such as to yield fruitful results for the good of society, unprocurable by other methods or means of study, and not random and unnecessary in nature.**
3. **The experiment should be so designed and based on the results of animal experimentation and a knowledge of the natural history of the disease or other problem under study that the anticipated results will justify the performance of the experiment.**
4. **The experiment should be so conducted as to avoid all unnecessary physical and mental suffering and injury.**
5. **No experiment should be conducted where there is an a priori reason to believe that death or disabling injury will occur; except, perhaps, in those experiments where the experimental physicians also serve as subjects.**
6. **The degree of risk to be taken should never exceed that determined by the humanitarian importance of the problem to be solved by the experiment.**
7. **Proper preparations should be made and adequate facilities provided to protect the experimental subject against even remote possibilities of injury, disability, or death.**
8. **The experiment should be conducted only by scientifically qualified persons. The highest degree of skill and care should be required through all stages of the experiment of those who conduct or engage in the experiment.**
9. **During the course of the experiment the human subject should be at liberty to bring the experiment to an end if he has reached the physical or mental state where continuation of the experiment seems to him to be impossible.**
10. **During the course of the experiment the scientist in charge must be prepared to terminate the experiment at any stage, if he has probable cause to believe, in the exercise of the good faith, superior skill and careful judgment required of him that a continuation of the experiment is likely to result in injury, disability, or death to the experimental subject.**

EXHIBIT 3.1

Note. From Nuremberg Military Tribunals. (1949). *Trials of war criminals before the Nuremberg military tribunals under Control Council Law No. 10 Nuremberg, October 1946–April 1949.* Washington, DC: U.S. Government Printing Office.

procedures for IRBs, and requirements for informed consent. Fifteen federal agencies and departments adopted the Common Rule; as these 15 agencies and departments share subpart A, but not necessarily subparts B, C, and D, subpart A was deemed the "Common Rule." These regulations can be found online at http://www.hhs.gov/ohrp/regulations-and-policy/regulations/index.html.

The function of an IRB is to protect human subjects in compliance with federal regulations (i.e., 45 CFR part 46). Thus, IRBs function in a role of legal compliance. Failure of agencies, organizations, and institutions to properly address and protect participants of human-subjects research is a violation of federal law. As a result of failing to protect these research participants, agencies, organizations, and institutions put themselves at risk for litigation and federal sanctions, which could affect their ability to obtain external funding through government grants and contracts as well as conduct research. However, although IRBs exist in organizations that receive federal funding and conduct research, agencies and organizations that do not receive federal funding are not technically required to submit to an IRB. When agencies or organizations that do not receive federal funding wish to conduct research, they can typically partner with an organization (e.g., a hospital or university) that has an established IRB or submit a research protocol that addresses the required guidelines directly to the National Institutes of Health or another federal organization.

Members of an IRB often draw the ire of those individuals wishing to conduct human-subjects research. Individuals who submit protocols to an IRB should keep in mind that members of the IRB are volunteers with the function of overseeing compliance with federal regulations as it pertains to the safety of participants in research. The initial concern of any IRB, therefore, is whether the initiative put forth by a researcher is by definition *research.*

According to OHRP (2009),

> *Research* means a systematic investigation, including research development, testing and evaluation, designed to develop or contribute to generalizable knowledge. Activities which meet this definition constitute research for purposes of this policy, whether or not they are conducted or supported under a program which is considered research for other purposes. For example, some demonstration and service programs may include research activities. (p. 4, italics in the original)

Similar to most ethical constructs, what constitutes research is left to interpretation and thus may be interpreted differently by different

IRBs. Each IRB is tasked with interpreting 45 CFR part 46, implementing the code, and ensuring compliance.

For example, research "means a systematic investigation, including research development, testing and evaluation, designed to develop or contribute to generalizable knowledge" (OHRP, 2009, p. 4). Some agencies, institutions, and organizations (e.g., hospitals) exclude qualitative research from IRB review under the guiding principle that qualitative research is not generalizable. Academic institutions, in contrast, likely review qualitative research under the belief that qualitative research may contribute to generalizable knowledge. The idea that qualitative inquiry does not constitute research as defined by the Common Rule may seem offensive, particularly to qualitative researchers, but some professionals may separate how research is defined according to OHRP (2009) and how research is defined in academe (as discussed in Chapter 1). Nonetheless, the collection of qualitative data can be quite sensitive, and reviewing how qualitative data are collected and maintained is important to the protection of participants.

Another key issue is whether the collection and recording of data constitute research. Again, the focus is on whether the collection of data is "designed to develop or contribute to generalizable knowledge" (OHRP, 2009, p. 4). The collection of sensitive data, which occurs in agencies, organizations, and institutions quite often, does not necessarily constitute research. Understanding how the data are likely to be used is key to understanding whether the collection of data is regarded as research.

Counselors document sensitive data on their clients. The data from an initial intake are quite sensitive. However, the data collected are not "designed to develop or contribute to generalizable knowledge" (OHRP, 2009, p. 4). The same could be said if a counselor were to try a new intervention strategy. An approved research protocol from an IRB would not be necessary because the counselor does not intend to develop or contribute to generalizable knowledge. However, if a counselor were to establish a new intervention and wished to publicize his or her findings, such proceedings would fall under OHRP guidelines. In addition, other ethical guidelines could play a role, and the client may still need to be informed if a strategy or intervention is based on recognized practice. The introduction to Section C of the *ACA Code of Ethics* states that "counselors have a responsibility to the public to engage in counseling practices that are based on rigorous research methodologies" (American Counseling Association [ACA], 2014, p. 8).

Does this mean that a counselor cannot use creative strategies or that a school counselor cannot be innovative with a guidance curriculum? The answer is both no and yes. Understand that two sets of ethical guidelines need to be taken into account: federal guidelines (i.e., OHRP, 2009) and the *ACA Code of Ethics* (ACA, 2014).

Federal Guidelines and Exceptions

From the perspective of OHRP, data that are not shared or presented—in other words, data that are not being presented as generalizable—are not research and therefore not under the auspices of an IRB. However, once data are compiled and either presented or published, federal guidelines may apply. Businesses, agencies, and organizations collect data from their stakeholders, consumers, and employees all of the time, but unless these data are presented or published, they are likely considered internal and not research. Even if the process of collecting and disseminating data transpired, thereby falling under the definition of *research,* there are conditions under which such studies are exempt or follow an expedited process through the IRB. Studies that are *exempt* do not require regulatory oversight through the IRB and meet one or more of the following criteria:

1. Research conducted in established or commonly accepted educational settings, involving normal educational practices, such as (i) research on regular and special education instructional strategies, or (ii) research on the effectiveness of or the comparison among instructional techniques, curricula, or classroom management methods.
2. Research involving the use of educational tests (cognitive, diagnostic, aptitude, achievement), survey procedures, interview procedures or observation of public behavior, unless: (i) information obtained is recorded in such manner that human subjects can be identified, directly or through identifiers linked to the subjects; and (ii) any disclosure of the human subjects' responses outside the research could reasonably place the subjects at risk of criminal or civil liability or be damaging to the subjects' financial standing, employability, or reputation.
3. Research involving the use of educational tests (cognitive, diagnostic, aptitude, achievement), survey procedures, interview procedures, or observation of public behavior that is not exempt under paragraph (b)(2) of this section, if: (i) the human subjects are elected or appointed public officials or candidates for public office; or (ii) federal statute(s) require(s)

without exception that the confidentiality of the personally identifiable information will be maintained throughout the research and thereafter.

4. Research involving the collection or study of existing data, documents, records, pathological specimens, or diagnostic specimens, if these sources are publicly available or if the information is recorded by the investigator in such a manner that subjects cannot be identified, directly or through identifiers linked to the subjects.
5. Research and demonstration projects which are conducted by or subject to the approval of department or agency heads, and which are designed to study, evaluate, or otherwise examine: (i) Public benefit or service programs; (ii) procedures for obtaining benefits or services under those programs; (iii) possible changes in or alternatives to those programs or procedures; or (iv) possible changes in methods or levels of payment for benefits or services under those programs. (OHRP, 2009, p. 3)

Hence, when research involves "normal educational practices" (p. 3), the research may be exempt from IRB oversight. In addition, analyses of publicly available data that are de-identified are also exempt, as are program evaluations. With all of this being said, consultation should be the normal practice. It is always a good idea to consult with an IRB coordinator or fellow professional and not make this decision on your own.

Simply because OHRP (2009) regulations indicate that a study may be exempt does not necessarily mean that it will be. The exemption of research activities is at the discretion of the institution or organization. The listing of criteria for exemptions is precluded by the introduction "Unless otherwise required by department or agency heads" (p. 3), indicating that the institution has the final decision on whether a study is exempt. IRBs may have a particular culture. Whereas an IRB at one institution may declare a study exempt, another may indicate that the study requires full review. Many IRBs are cautious when a study includes minors, even if the study is in a school setting and could otherwise be considered exempt.

When studies involve procedures that are "no more than minimal risk" or require "minor changes in approved research" (OHRP, 2009, p. 6) an expedited procedure may be used. In an *expedited* review the IRB chair or designated member (and sometimes more than one) will review a protocol and either approve or request revision. Only a full board review can disapprove a study.

When a research protocol is neither exempt nor expedited, it is reviewed by the IRB. This is a formal committee meeting in which the merits and concerns of the research are discussed by the IRB. Discussion is led by the chair and culminates in a vote on whether the research is approved, tabled in order to be revised, or disapproved.

Ultimately the IRB is tasked with determining whether the researchers have satisfied the OHRP (2009) requirements. A research protocol is approved when all of the following conditions have been met:

1. The study poses minimal risk, as evidenced by the use of an established and valid research design.
2. The risks are reasonable, particularly in light of the benefits of the study.
3. The selection of participants is equitable. In other words, a rationale for inclusion and exclusion must be provided. Individuals should not be excluded from the research simply because of inconvenience. Equal opportunity to participate must be provided.
4. Each potential participant will provide informed consent in accordance with OHRP guidelines.
5. Informed consent will be documented.
6. The researchers provide a plan for how data will be collected that ensures the safety and welfare of the participants.
7. Adequate processes are in place to protect confidentiality.
8. Additional safeguards are in place for vulnerable populations.

Within these guidelines are five concepts that require further discussion: minimal risk, equitable selection, informed consent, conflicts of interest, and vulnerable populations.

Minimal Risk

The issue of minimal risk is an important one for IRBs and one that is certainly subject to interpretation. OHRP (2009) defines *minimal risk* as "the probability and magnitude of harm or discomfort anticipated in the research [being] not greater in and of themselves than those ordinarily encountered in daily life or during the performance of routine physical or psychological examinations or tests" (p. 4). Hence, the IRB is tasked with determining the probability of harm and what activities constitute daily life or routine physical and psychological examinations. Although most members of an IRB may have experienced a routine physical examination, the same cannot be said for psychological evaluations. Depending on the experiences and expertise of IRB members, quite a bit of discussion can emanate from the task of interpreting these issues. For example, many counselors routinely ask their clients whether there has been any history of physical or sexual abuse. A doctor may inquire in a routine physical exam whether a patient is sexually active. If such questions are indeed routine, then including questions about sexual abuse or sexual activity in a questionnaire or survey may be considered to pose minimal risk. However, the IRB is tasked with making this decision and assuming responsibility for the research.

Consider a study by Balkin, Perepiczka, Whitely, and Kimbrough (2009) in which the researchers studied emotional awareness, sexual values, and sexual activity among college freshmen. The participants were all consenting adults 18 years old or older. In this study,

> sexual activity was identified by marking one of the following categories: (a) I have not had intercourse; (b) I have had intercourse, but I am not engaging in intercourse currently; (c) I engage in intercourse but limit my activity to monogamous relationships; and (d) I engage in intercourse and do not limit my activity to monogamous relationships. (p. 24)

In addition, participants completed a questionnaire related to identifying their own values related to sexual activity and abstinence. When this research study was proposed, the issues in front of the IRB related to whether the research protocol exceeded minimal risk.

Despite the fact that this study did not involve a protected population, it should not have been exempt. The study did not occur in an educational setting (e.g., a classroom) or involve educational practices or tests; the data collected were not publicly available or used for program evaluation purposes. Therefore, some review and oversight by an IRB was necessary. But should the study have gone for full review or been expedited? Recall that for a study to be expedited "no more than minimal risk" (OHRP, 2009, p. 6) should be involved. Were the questions related to sexual activity and values outside the scope of what might be asked in a routine physical or psychological evaluation? The chair of the IRB to which this particular study was submitted believed so and sent the study for full review as opposed to expediting it. However, another IRB chair may have chosen differently. Ultimately subjective decisions must be made by IRBs, as the federal guidelines, similar to other written documents, are subject to interpretation.

Equitable Selection

When selecting participants for a study, researchers need to be aware of the potential for bias when individuals are excluded (inadvertently or not) or unable to participate. Consider work by Porter and Wright (2011). Porter and Wright indicated a disparity between Whites and African Americans who were imprisoned for using crack cocaine. According to a national survey by the Substance Abuse and Mental Health Services Administration, between 2008 and 2009 users of crack cocaine had the following ethnic classifications: 50% White, 37% African American, and 13% Latino. "Despite this, African Americans constitute about 80% of persons incarcerated in federal prisons for crack offenses" (p. 10). Because the majority of incarcerations were of African American users, and because of the violence associated with the drug trade, different sentencing guidelines were adopted by many states, leading to harsher sentences for crack cocaine users (who were disproportionately African American) than for cocaine users (who were disproportionately White). The issue here is that sentencing guidelines related to crack cocaine were determined based on racial bias.

Researchers will inevitably produce more useful and meaningful results when multicultural considerations are considered, and this can be addressed through the use of equitable sampling procedures. When researchers make sure that all eligible participants have the opportunity to participate, the implementation of ethically responsible research protocols becomes more likely. When some participants are excluded, the generalizability of the research is compromised. This can have serious consequences, particularly when research findings are used to guide decisions and policy.

Informed Consent

With few exceptions, informed consent is a requirement for human-subjects research, and the process of obtaining and documenting informed consent is a necessary part of the research protocol reviewed by the IRB. Although informed consent documents inform the research participant about the research study, consenting to participate does not release the institution, the IRB, or the researcher from liability or charges of negligence. Informed consent must be provided in a timely manner in order for the potential participant to be able to consider the study and not be coerced or pressured into making a decision. The information must be understandable, so technical language and jargon should be avoided (OHRP, 2009). Requirements of informed consent include the following:

- An explanation and description of the research, including the duration and procedures
- A description of risks
- A description of benefits
- A description of the manner in which confidentiality or anonymity will be maintained
- A description of any processes that involve more than minimal risk and procedures in the event that discomfort or injury occur
- Contact information for the researcher and IRB
- A statement that participation is voluntary, that the participant can withdraw at any time, and that there will be no loss of benefits or penalty for refusing to participate or withdrawing from the study

Can Informed Consent Be Waived?

OHRP (2009) provides guidelines for approving research with altered informed consent or waiving informed consent, such as studies in which there is deception or the documentation of informed consent is unreasonable. For example, a research study involving adolescents completing a survey over social media may have parental informed consent waived, as it would be unreasonable to obtain informed consent for such dissemination of a survey. Adolescents would be more likely to complete the survey if they did not have to obtain a parent's permission; obtaining parental consent in this case would likely deter participation. When informed consent processes are altered or waived, participants cannot be exposed to anything beyond minimal risk, the rights and welfare of the participants remain protected, and a debriefing is provided in the case of deception. In the event that informed consent is altered or waived, it is still required that information be provided to the research participant.

Assent

Assent refers to "a child's affirmative agreement to participate in research" (OHRP, 2009, p. 12). OHRP specifically states that assent cannot be inferred. Simply because a minor fails to object to participating in a study does not imply assent. For research studies involving minors, the researcher is tasked with identifying how assent is solicited and documented. Assent procedures need to be understandable to the minor. Especially with young children, signing a document may not be reasonable, and documentation of verbal agreement is necessary. A common practice in research has been to have a young child provide assent by circling a smiling face to participate or an unsmiling face to decline. However, some IRBs discourage this type of document, as it communicates a value judgment (i.e., happy vs. sad) for participating in the study, which could be viewed as coercion.

Data Management

Pertinent to counseling research and the issues of risk and informed consent is the management of data. Much of the risk assumed in counseling research may be in terms of how data are protected. Researchers need to be aware of confidentiality versus anonymity. When data are *confidential*, the researcher can connect the data to the participant but makes assurances that such connections will remain unknown to the public. When data are *anonymous*, the researcher is not able to connect the data to the participant. For example, research studies in which data are collected from participants multiple times would require the researcher to connect the data to a participant. In such cases, the researcher has to document how confidentiality will be maintained, such as by keeping data in a locked, secure location. When researchers do not require identifying data, the data may be anonymous. In this case, signed consents are kept separate from other data to limit the ability of the researcher or public to connect data to a particular individual.

Conflicts of Interest

Conflicts of interest can undermine research integrity. The National Institutes of Health (2010) identified two key areas of conflicts of interest: objectivity and benefit. Conflicts of interest related to objectivity occur when a researcher's feelings, beliefs, or attitudes are incompatible with the responsibility of conducting research in a pragmatic and unbiased manner (DuBois, 2008). As mentioned in Chapter 2, research often evolves from an interest or passion on the part of the researcher. In other words, we investigate phenomena in order to learn something or confirm our ideas. So what happens when the focus is more about confirmation of what we believe than the methods used? Clearly researchers need to be aware of how biases may play a role in identifying methods and analyzing results. Researchers need to be open to the idea that their ideas or attitudes may be disconfirmed. Ultimately learning where not to look for answers can be as informative as finding answers.

Beneficial conflicts of interest may occur when researchers receive some type of welfare, service, or profit for engaging in the research.

Simply because a researcher received financial benefits does not mean that the research was compromised. However, conflicts of interest need to be addressed and often will appear in publications, especially when research is funded. Conflicts of interest are often identified a priori—before the research is conducted. IRB protocols are required to include statements that address conflicts of interest, and these are evaluated by IRB members. Furthermore, publications in scholarly journals often include statements related to funding and conflicts of interest. Being up front and allowing consumers of the research to be aware and evaluate the role of the researcher is essential to the research process.

Vulnerable Populations

Vulnerable populations may include "children, prisoners, pregnant women, mentally disabled persons, or economically or educationally disadvantaged persons" (OHRP, 2009, p. 7). Sections outside the Common Rule (subpart A) include subpart B—additional protections for pregnant women, human fetuses, and neonates involved in research; subpart C—additional protections pertaining to biomedical and behavioral research involving prisoners as subjects; and subpart D—additional protections for children involved as subjects in research. Generally speaking, counseling research does not involve issues related to subpart B, so attention is focused here on research related to prisoners and minors.

IRBs are concerned with three essential areas when addressing research with vulnerable populations: coercion and assent (in the case of children) and representation (in the case of prisoners or individuals in institutional settings). Researchers are obligated to include additional provisions to protect against undue influence or coercion. Some provisions are documented by OHRP (2009) in subsections c and d; however, other populations are left for interpretation by the IRB, such as individuals who could be identified as elderly, economically or educationally disadvantaged, or emotionally or mentally disadvantaged. In these instances, obtaining informed consent or assent could be challenging because of impaired ability to understand the nature of the research or study. Documenting in the protocol how such situations will be managed by the researcher is important, as is noting the risks and benefits to the participants and populations. Of particular note is that equal opportunity to participate in the research must be provided, and the research must not harm the participants. For example, if a counselor wanted to study the emotional characteristics of individuals in a prison population, the data collected could not be used by a parole board, incentives to participate could not be so overwhelming that the decision to participate would be influenced, and all eligible members of the population would need to have an equal opportunity to participate.

In addition, children and other vulnerable populations should not feel unduly coerced to participate in research. This could occur in the assent process for children. Counselors who wish to conduct research with children are required to obtain both consent and assent, but care must be taken to make sure that the child is not coerced into participating. If requests to participate are made to the parent or guardian and child together, so that consent and assent are documented simultaneously, the child could feel coerced into participating. The simple fact that the parent is providing permission in the presence of the child could cause the child to agree to participate without truly wanting to participate. For this reason, the consent and assent processes should be separate, in order for the child to avoid feeling unduly influenced.

When researchers focus on participants in institutional settings (e.g., prison, psychiatric hospitals, nursing homes), adequate representation on the IRB is necessary. In such cases a representative from the institution will represent the interests of the potential participant(s) in the full IRB review process. Such representation is necessary when working with children or adults who are incarcerated; wards of the state; or in special settings, such as a foster placement. The representatives serve as advocates for the potential participants to make sure that their best interests are represented. Representatives need to have the appropriate authority, background, and experience to represent potential participants in such settings.

Unanticipated Problems and Adverse Events

Occasionally unanticipated problems arise when conducting research, such as a laptop with confidential data is stolen, a physical injury to a participant occurs, or a participant experiences emotional distress. The Common Rule mentions "unanticipated problems" once, indicating that assurances are needed that federally supported research includes "written procedures for ensuring prompt reporting to the IRB" (OHRP, 2009, p. 5) in the event of risk or injury to participants, noncompliance with the protocol, or any other reason the research is suspended or terminated. OHRP does not provide any other regulatory requirements, but in 2007 it published a guiding statement of recommendations. In this statement, OHRP (2007) differentiated between *unanticipated problems,* which refers to unexpected events that likely occur as a result of participation in the research that place participants at greater risk than previously recognized, and *adverse events,* which refers to the occurrence of physical or psychological harm to participants in a study. Adverse events need to be reported if they are unexpected—an unanticipated problem. If a participant in a study is in an unrelated automobile accident, this does not qualify as an unanticipated problem because the accident did not occur as a result of participation in the study. The occurrence of unanticipated problems or adverse events can result in revised protocols, suspension or termination of the study, and reports to monitoring agencies.

ACA Code of Ethics

In addition to following federal guidelines, counselors who conduct research subscribe to principles outlined in the *ACA Code of Ethics* (ACA, 2014). Section G of the *ACA Code of Ethics,* "Research and Publication," is divided into five subsections: "Research Responsibilities," "Rights of Research Participants," "Managing and Maintaining Boundaries," "Reporting Results," and "Publications and Presentations."

Counselors who conduct research are obliged to follow federal, state, and institutional regulations, even if they practice independently. Hence, if counselors decide to try an innovative intervention with clients, they should do so under the auspices of consultation and be certain that (a) appropriate safeguards are in place, especially if they are deviating from standard practice; and (b) clients are informed of the exploratory or untried nature of the intervention and have the right of refusal. Moreover, the processes identified by the Common Rule and applicable subsections should be implemented specific to the issues of informed consent and assent.

An area in which ACA (2014) has expanded on the Common Rule is protecting students and supervisees as well as colleagues. Students and colleagues are provided with provisions to protect them from exploitation and to ensure that they receive credit for what they contribute; in particular, if a student serves as the primary contributor, he or she should get credit as the primary author. This is an important provision because of the power structure in academic institutions. Counseling research is primarily conducted in academic institutions. Within academe a power structure exists in which students may perform work under the supervision of professors, and professional colleagues who work together may be of different ranks and tenure (e.g., assistant, associate, or full professor). Hence, ACA (2014) addresses how contentious issues such as credit and the order of authorship are handled. Essentially agreement needs to be made in advance with respect to the delineation of tasks and publication credit.

With respect to reporting and distributing research, counselors have an ethical responsibility to report findings accurately, even if the results are unfavorable to stakeholders and entities with an interest in the research. Authors should submit to only one publication outlet at a time. Dual submissions are unethical. Journals and publication outlets dedicate considerable resources, often from volunteers in the academic community, to review manuscripts for publication. In connection with this, counselors who review research should do so in a manner that remains unbiased and is based on "valid and defensible standards" (ACA, 2014, Standard G.5.h.).

The *ACA Code of Ethics* (ACA, 2014) expands on the Common Rule by emphasizing protections and treatments for all individuals involved in the research process, not just the participants. Furthermore, ACA (2014) expands on responsibilities throughout the research process, including behaviors for reviewing research, publishing, and presenting. Counselors should take care to consider how to integrate the *ACA Code of Ethics* with IRB processes explicated by the Common Rule and appropriate subsections.

Completing the IRB Protocol

The IRB assumes the responsibility for reviewing research and instructing the university to assume liability. Keep in mind that the vast majority of research conducted in academic settings is not funded, and the IRB is a group of volunteers who are assuming risk and assigning risk to an institution at the request of a researcher or set of researchers for which there may be few or minimal benefits or incentives. In addition, members of an IRB may have varying degrees of experience with human-subjects research. For this reason, some IRBs take particular caution.

A research project should be worthwhile. Some IRBs may relegate themselves to simply reviewing protection of human subjects. However, if in the explanation of a study a research design is so flawed that the study is unlikely to make a contribution, should the IRB approve the study? This may be a matter of debate among IRB members. If a researcher is asking participants to dedicate time to a flawed study, protecting human subjects could be interpreted as establishing that participation in the study is not a waste of time and effort. As research may ultimately be a reflection on an institution, decisions of IRBs impact protection of human subjects, the researcher, and the institution. A university becomes vested in the research because of the affiliation of faculty. Students who conduct research at a university must work with a faculty member who is affiliated with the university, serves as a point of contact, and is willing to assume risk.

IRB protocols vary among institutions and organizations, but the type of information requested is fairly standard in order to comply with federal guidelines. In general, researchers need to be prepared to provide information related to the following:

- A description of the research
- Participants
- Risks and benefits
- Informed consent
- Confidentiality or anonymity and data security
- Methods and measures

The IRB will not need a full literature review; however, a working title of the study and an overview of the research questions or hypotheses will be requested. Providing brief, general background information can be helpful to the IRB if your topic is more specialized.

Information regarding participants is mandatory, so you will need to consider whose participation you are soliciting. How many participants will you need? Are certain characteristics required (e.g., the ability to read and/or speak English, a certain age)? Who will be included and/or excluded from the study? Keep in mind that there must be a rationale for exclusion, as equitable opportunity to participate in research should be provided otherwise. Protocols typically go to full review when research is being conducted with a protected population. Exceptions to this occur when research is being conducted with minors in an educational setting using established educational strategies. When research is being conducted with minors or other vulnerable populations (e.g., the elderly, prisoners) in a clinical setting (e.g., a counseling clinic, a psychiatric hospital), researchers need to acknowledge that the population of interest is a *double-protected population*—that is to say, the minors constitute a protected population, as do individuals receiving mental health care. Hence, researchers need to consider their protocols carefully and make sure that external organizations or agencies (e.g., schools, counseling centers, hospitals) are supportive of the research. Common practice can include having a representative from the agency or organization with the IRB during the full review proceedings.

Risk needs to be carefully considered. Risk can be due to physical damage, emotional damage, or the disclosure of damaging information. These risks need to be identified in consent and, if necessary, assent procedures and documentation. Ultimately a rationale for assuming the risk should be addressed and hopefully outweighed by the potential benefits of conducting the research. Risks and benefits of the study must be communicated to the participants. In the case of damaging information, procedures need to be scrutinized with respect to maintaining confidentiality or anonymity.

Researchers must be careful to distinguish between confidentiality and anonymity in the protocol. When data are anonymous, it will be inherently easier to protect participants' identities. When data are confidential, as opposed to anonymous, data security is an even more important consideration that must be detailed, along with a rationale for why the data need to be confidential. Participants should be informed about how data security will be maintained and whether information will be confidential or anonymous.

IRBs will request a description of the methods and measures to be used in the study. When possible, measures are often submitted as part of the IRB protocol. Methods often include how participants will be solicited, how informed consent or assent will be collected, what tasks participants will need to complete (and the time expected to complete them), how confidentiality or anonymity will be maintained, how data will be kept secure, and how data will be analyzed. Some of this information may seem repetitive, as it appears in both the protocol form and the informed consent.

The aforementioned considerations are common areas of deliberation among IRBs. Researchers need to be aware of the Common Rule and appropriate subsections in order to understand categories of consideration (e.g., exempt, expedited, full review) and properly advocate for their research. IRBs may be governed by OHRP guidelines as well as the experience of the members and the research culture of the institution. Researchers should focus on required training for research and ethics (e.g., Collaborative Institutional Training Initiative, Public Responsibility in Medicine and Research) in order to have a comprehensive understanding of the Common Rule and the information required by institutional protocols.

Chapter Summary

Given the appalling exploitation of and injustice to African Americans by the Tuskegee Study of Untreated Syphilis in the Negro Male from 1932 to 1972, the U.S. government created oversight processes for human-subjects research that have resulted in the most current federal regulations from OHRP (2009). Any institution, agency, or organization that receives federal funding must abide by OHRP regulations and utilize an IRB for all research. Agencies and organizations that do not receive federal funding may still need to comply with OHRP regulations and can access IRBs by collaborating with local organizations, such as hospitals or universities, or utilizing IRB services through the National Institutes of Health.

In addition, the *ACA Code of Ethics* (ACA, 2014) devotes Section G to research and publication, including issues outside the scope of OHRP regulations, such as authorship considerations, treatment of supervisees and students, and publishing and presenting research. Hence, counselors are required to follow both the *ACA Code of Ethics* and OHRP regulations. With respect to conducting research, both documents appear to support each other, and the *ACA Code of Ethics* provides further information with respect to publishing; presenting; and providing opportunities and recognition to students, supervisees, and coauthors. Should conflicts arise, members of ACA can take advantage of a free ethics consultation from ACA as a benefit of membership.

Suggested Activities

I. Review criteria for exempt, expedited, and full IRB reviews. Then read the following article:

Balkin, R. S., Perepiczka, M., Whitely, R., & Kimbrough, S. (2009). The relationship of values and emotional awareness to sexual activity in young adulthood. *Adultspan Journal, 8,* 17–28.

As mentioned in the chapter, this study required a full IRB review. Consider the following:

1. Do you agree with the decision of full review?
2. Did the items go beyond the type of questions asked in a physical or psychological evaluation?
3. What was the risk? If data had been compromised (e.g., individuals' responses identified), what would have been some possible ramifications?

II. Review the *ACA Code of Ethics* (ACA, 2014) "Research and Publication" section and your institution's IRB protocol.

1. What information in the *ACA Code of Ethics* is not included in the IRB protocol?
2. In what ways does the *ACA Code of Ethics* complement federal guidelines?

III. Talk with faculty at your institution about their experiences with the IRB. What is the impression you get from listening to their experiences related to the IRB process?

References

American Counseling Association. (2014). *ACA code of ethics.* Alexandria, VA: Author.

Balkin, R. S., Perepiczka, M., Whitely, R., & Kimbrough, S. (2009). The relationship of values and emotional awareness to sexual activity in young adulthood. *Adultspan Journal, 8,* 17–28.

DuBois, J. M. (2008). *Ethics in mental health research: Principles, guidance, and cases.* New York, NY: Oxford University Press.

National Commission for the Protection of Human Subjects of Biomedical and Behavioral Research. (1979). *The Belmont report: Ethical principles and guidelines for the protections of human subjects of research.* Washington, DC: U.S. Department of Health and Human Services, Office for Human Research Protections.

National Institutes of Health. (2010). *Conflict of interest information resources available on the Web.* Retrieved from http://grants.nih.gov/grants/policy/coi/resources.htm

Nuremberg Military Tribunals. (1949). *Trials of war criminals before the Nuremberg military tribunals under Control Council Law No. 10 Nuremberg, October 1946-April 1949.* Washington, DC: U.S. Government Printing Office, 1949–1953.

Office for Human Research Protections. (2007). *1. What are unanticipated problems?* Retrieved from http://www.hhs.gov/ohrp/policy/advevntguid.html#Q1

Office for Human Research Protections. (2009). *U.S. Department of Health and Human Services, Code of Federal Regulations, Title 45 Public Welfare, Part 46, Protection of Human Subjects.* Washington, DC: Author.

Porter, N. D., & Wright, V. (2011). *Cracked justice.* Retrieved from http://www.sentencingproject.org/wp-content/uploads/2016/01/Cracked-Justice.pdf

Thomas, S. B., & Quinn, S. C. (1991). The Tuskegee Syphilis Study, 1932 to 1972: Implications for HIV education and AIDS risk education programs in the Black community. *American Journal of Public Health, 81*, 1498–1504.

Types of Research

Overview

In this chapter we provide an overview of unifying concepts in quantitative and qualitative research. In both quantitative and qualitative research, there will be differences based on the purpose of the study and the framework in which the study is conceptualized. We present concepts in each type of research that tend to be common throughout various analytic tools or theoretical perspectives. Finally, we discuss trends in research and choosing a type of research for a study.

Research in the counseling profession generally falls into one of four categories: quantitative, qualitative, mixed methods, and single-case research design (SCRD). Each of these methods makes valuable contributions to the counseling profession by informing practitioners of procedures, practices, and theories that contribute to the overall well-being of clients.

Although counseling researchers tend to prefer particular methods and types of research, such preferences should not be used to indicate the superiority of one method over another. Both qualitative and quantitative methods are important. For example, qualitative research may be used to develop theory, whereas quantitative research may be helpful in testing such a theory. Counseling researchers should use methods based on their research questions. In other words, the nature of the research question—not the investigator's preference for one research method over another—drives the study.

As each type of research is discussed, it is tempting to try to identify the purpose and role of each type of research. However, this is a foolhardy task, as most research can be easily modified to fit one method or another. As noted earlier, the research question is the primary determinant of the proposed method to be utilized in a study. In addition, rather than focusing on the strengths and weaknesses of a given type of research, consider the types of data and various purposes of the given research method with a focus on how each type of research may be used to promote the growing knowledge base of the counseling profession.

Unifying Concepts in Quantitative Research

Quantitative research is useful when the research question examines relationships between variables, examines differences between groups, or identifies specific trends in a given population. Quantitative research is concerned with *generalizability*—the extent to which findings from a study for a particular set of participants can be attributed to a larger population. Gall, Gall, and Borg (2007) provided a nice synopsis of the relationship between sampling and generalizability. If results are to be considered generalizable, one must consider, "Generalizable to whom?" Ideally, results of a study are generalizable to a population of interest, known as a *target population.* The problem is that counseling researchers rarely evaluate data based on a target population because of the nature of human-subjects research requiring informed consent (see Chapter 3) and simply not having access to a target population. From the target population, researchers collect data from an *accessible population*—those whom the researcher can realistically access. From the accessible population, the researcher collects data from participants, who may also be referred to as a *sample.* So an important characteristic of generalizability is *representativeness*—the participants in your study may be identified with the accessible population, who are identified with the target population.

In quantitative research the typical process includes gathering participants, obtaining measures, evaluating data, and communicating results. In quantitative research, the nature of collecting data involves providing numeric values for phenomena. These values are then analyzed to make inferences. In most cases, such inferences are centered around understanding the relationships between various phenomena, known as *correlational research;* understanding the effectiveness of treatments or interventions, known as *experimental research;* or understanding how various groups differ across a particular phenomenon, known as *explanatory, nonexperimental research.*

Before we discuss these various types of research, it may be helpful to identify the unifying concepts of quantitative research. Quantitative researchers are concerned with generalizability and the application of numerical data, and therefore the choice of sampling methods (e.g., collecting data from participants), the use of numeric values, and reliance on statistics to answer research questions.

Assigning Value to Data

The application of numerical data to measure phenomena of interest can occur through two primary means: direct observation or evaluation of a construct. Some quantitative data in counseling research, that is, an exact value for a particular phenomenon, can be collected through direct observation. For example, the number of days prior to experiencing a panic attack, the number of suicidal ideations in a week, or the amount of alcohol consumed could be measured through direct observation.

However, most counseling research does not evaluate data gathered through direct observation. Rather, researchers gather data by measuring *constructs*—phenomena that cannot be directly observed. Often counseling research is concerned with measuring abstract concepts such as multicultural competence, symptom severity, levels of distress, and so forth. Concepts such as these are not easily quantifiable and require an operational definition to define and measure. An *operational definition* provides a clear description of what is to be measured, and researchers go to great lengths to develop valid measures that can accurately and consistently measure constructs across an accessible population. For example, Balkin, Miller, Ricard, Garcia, and Lancaster (2011) examined the relationship of antisocial behavior, anger control, emotional distress, and positive self as measured by the Reynolds Adolescent Adjustment Screening Inventory (RAASI; Reynolds, 2001) to the likelihood of reoffending among adjudicated adolescents. Adolescent adjustment was a construct and was operationally defined by the subscales of the RAASI; reoffenses, however, were tracked through direct observation. In this example, a score can be used to represent each variable (i.e., reoffenses and adolescent adjustment). The amount of time that passes until a reoffense occurs can serve as one type of quantitative data (direct observation), and the RAASI can be used to quantify adolescent adjustment. In the case of the RAASI, items are presented to the participant and scored from 0 (*never or almost never*) to 2 (*nearly all the time*); these items can then be added and used as a score in the research. Not every research study will use direct observation or constructs, but most research in counseling tends to rely on the measurement of constructs. The quality of the operational definition and validity of the measure play an important role in the measurement of the construct and ultimately the generalizability of the results.

Essential Concepts in Quantitative Sampling

The means by which a researcher solicits and collects data from participants is known as *sampling*, and traditionally in counseling research the notion of random sampling is emphasized. Here we talk about the theory behind random sampling, briefly cover the four types of sampling, and then discuss the notion of random sampling and its practicality in counseling research.

Random sampling draws from the idea that a generalizable sample will likely result when individuals for a study are selected at random. Truly random sampling would in theory provide participants that are most like the target population. Hence, a random sample that is representative of the target population would likely have some homogenous characteristics but would also include individuals who are quite different in terms of cultural variables (e.g., ethnicity, religion), sex, gender identity, socioeconomic status, and so forth. For example, Balkin, Schlosser, and Levitt (2009) randomly selected 500 counselors who were members of the American Counseling Association (ACA) to participate in a study about counselor religious identity, homophobia, sexism, and multicultural competence. One could argue that this was a random sample, as the 500 participants were randomly selected from the ACA database, and each member in the database had an equal chance of being selected.

Simple random sampling refers to the idea that all individuals from an accessible sample have an equal chance of being selected for participation in a study. The Balkin et al. (2009) study mentioned previously is an example of simple random sampling. How can simple random sampling be done? If a researcher is using a database, random sampling can be done by identifying the total number in the database and randomly selecting individuals through such methods as random computer generation or the use of software like that found at https://www.random.org. This website can be used to identify random numbers that could be tied to a list of potential participants. For example, if a researcher has a list of

2,100 potential participants and would like a sample of 500, the researcher could use the website to generate numbers at random. Then the researcher could simply count down the list and mark the intended participants to solicit for the study.

Stratified random sampling also ensures an equal chance of participation but places a stipulation on desired characteristics. For example, assume that Balkin et al. (2009) wanted to account for religious affiliation in their study by perhaps identifying that 50% of the participants self-identify as Christian and 50% self-identify as non-Christian. This type of information would be known from the database, and the same simple random sampling would be used. Stratified random sampling may also be proportional by stipulating specific percentages reflected from a particular group. For example, researchers can stipulate that participants in the study reflect identified proportions in the target population. Balkin et al. (2009) reported that 72% of their participants self-identified as Christian. If this study were reflective of a stratified proportional sample (it was not), then one would expect a similar percentage of counselors who are members of ACA to self-identify as Christian.

Cluster random sampling refers to soliciting and obtaining participants based on randomly selected groups as opposed to randomly selected individuals. Cluster random sampling may be more common in educational research, in which schools or classrooms, as opposed to individual students, are randomly selected. *Systematic random sampling* uses a combination of cluster sampling and simple random sampling. In systematic sampling, potential participants from the accessible population are placed into groups. For example, 30 individuals are listed in each of 40 groups. The researcher randomly selects a number from 1 to 30 (e.g., 13), and the 13th member of each of the 40 groups is selected to participate.

Nonprobability sampling, also referred to as *convenience sampling,* is a process of recruiting and selecting participants for research who are accessible to the researcher. Nonprobability sampling represents the most common type of sampling in counseling research. However, a consequence of using nonprobability sampling is that the generalizability of the research findings is extremely limited. Social science research, as a general rule, is overrepresented by college student participants. Do findings based on college students really generalize to an adult population? Arguments for how college students are developmentally different from the overall population are quite salient. Furthermore, researchers who use college students as participants might be limited by type of college or geographic region. A final thought is that research conducted with actual clients in a variety of settings is not random, but such research on client outcomes and the efficacy of counseling is essential to moving the counseling profession forward. Most research in counseling depends on the use of convenience sampling, and counseling researchers need to be able to identify the appropriateness of a sample, particularly when nonprobability sampling is utilized. Let's take a look at how this is done.

The Representative Sample Versus the Random Sample

You have had a brief review of random sampling, so let's talk about why random sampling may be impractical in counseling research and perhaps in most social science research.

Although we would hesitate to say that *all* counseling research is devoid of random sampling, most counseling research is devoid of random sampling and highly reliant on convenience sampling. Ethical human-subjects research requires informed consent, and when minors are involved assent is typically required as well. When working with protected populations (e.g., individuals in medical, clinical, or correctional institutions; individuals classified as elders or minors), consent, assent, and permission from both the institution sponsoring the research and the research site is required. Given these various stipulations, participants in research are volunteers, and so there is limited randomness to their selection. Rather than considering whether a sample is truly random, view random sampling on a continuum. Consider the study by Balkin et al. (2009), in which 500 counselors who were members of ACA were randomly selected to participate in a study about counselor religious identity, homophobia, sexism, and multicultural competence. Of the 500 randomly selected potential participants, only 111 completed the instruments to participate in the research. So was this a random sample? Not really. Sure, there was a degree of random selection, but only 22% of the identified individuals participated in the study. These 111 individuals completed the instruments and gave permission to use their results in the study. So these individuals likely had some interest in the study that led them to participate. When voluntary participation and potential interest in the study are accounted for, the randomness of the selection process appears compromised.

The key therefore is not the randomness of the sample but rather the representativeness of the sample. Researchers show representativeness by reporting demographic information about their participants. Typically researchers include at a minimum frequencies and percentages for sex and ethnicity and the mean and standard deviation for age. Of course, other pertinent demographic information may also be reported depending on the nature of the research. Balkin et al. (2009) reported religious affiliation along with typical demographics, including sex, ethnicity, and age.

The importance of reporting demographic information cannot be overstated, as these data provide pertinent information so readers can determine the extent to which the participants in a study represent the target population. Information on sex and ethnicity in particular provide an opportunity to generalize to diverse populations, and failure to report this information often will result in an article being rejected for publication because of the inability to ascertain generalizability to the target population.

Random Assignment

A concept often confused with random sampling is random assignment. Random assignment is a specific feature of experimental research. Whereas random sampling is a rare phenomenon in social science research, random assignment is quite important in studies that utilize treatments or interventions and therefore contribute to evidence-based research. Essentially, random assignment is a process by which all extraneous variables that could confound a study are theoretically dispersed equally between or among the various groups in a study.

Random Assignment Is a Process

Once a researcher obtains a representative sample of participants for a study, he or she may randomly assign the participants to a group, such as a treatment group, comparison group, or control group. Of course, not all studies can include random assignment. In a study that makes comparisons between males and females or by ethnicity, random assignment is not possible (e.g., if you are male, you cannot be randomly assigned to either the male or female group). Random assignment is only possible when (a) a sample of participants exist, (b) two or more groups exist, and (c) the groups being compared can be assigned.

Extraneous Variables Can Confound a Study

When participants agree to be in a study, they not only agree to provide the researcher with an understanding of a phenomenon of interest but also bring in their subjective experiences—what we refer to as their *stuff.* Sometimes, just like a teenager with a messy room, people's stuff can get in the way of what a researcher is looking for. For example, Lenz, Perepiczka, and Balkin (2013) conducted an SCRD in which doctoral students enrolled in their first statistics course were randomly assigned to a peer-to-peer support group or a control group (no support group). Each participant in the study was administered the Attitudes Towards Statistics Scale. Participants also brought their own stuff: Perhaps some participants in the study experienced torment by a middle school math teacher who made them feel inadequate at math, and therefore they worked hard to avoid math in high school, only to relent and take college algebra in college and have no idea how they actually passed this class, culminating in a career choice in which math could be completely avoided, only to find utter despair that this fear would have to be confronted once again in pursuing a doctorate. Clearly this stuff would affect the study. A mechanism like random assignment needs to be implemented, as seen in Lenz et al., to control this stuff.

Extraneous Variables Are Theoretically Dispersed Equally Between or Among Groups in a Study

The purpose of random assignment, then, is to create equal groups. How does this work? Well, if each participant brings his or her stuff to the study, and the researcher has no idea what that stuff is, then by randomly assigning participants the researcher randomizes and disperses all of the participants' stuff equally between or among the groups. When something is chosen by chance, the odds are even, and the placement of individuals in groups is no exception.

Experimental Designs

Experimental design involves conducting studies in which comparisons between groups are made, sometimes over time. We present an overview here but provide more detail in Chapter 7. Essentially, group comparisons are made when one group receives a treatment or intervention and another group either does not receive one or receives an alternative one. When comparing groups, the common conceptualization includes preexperimental, quasi-experimental, and true experimental design. Table 4.1 provides a summary of this information.

Preexperimental designs do not include random assignment or the use of a comparison group. Essentially, preexperimental designs are not generalizable, and so the publication of such research is rare or conducted under the auspices of another design or mixed method. A preexperimental design would involve a researcher using

TABLE 4.1
A Simple Comparison of Preexperimental, Quasi-Experimental, and True Experimental Designs

Design	Random Assignment	Control/Comparison Group
Preexperimental	No	No
Quasi-experimental	No	Yes
True experimental	Yes	Yes

a single group, administering a pretest, conducting an intervention, and then administering a posttest.

For example, for a given research class, students purchase a textbook. Before they read the text, the course instructor assigns a pretest, and the students learn from the pretest that they do not know much about research. At the end of the course, many students earn an A. Can one conclude that the grade earned was reflective of using this text? Of course not, as too many confounding variables could have influenced the grading, and there was not a comparison group against which to compare efforts and interventions. For example, student performance could have been influenced by teaching style, the ease of the assignments, supplementary material, and so forth. Because no conclusion can be drawn about the outcome, the value of preexperimental research is quite limited.

Quasi-experimental designs also do not include random assignment but do include a comparison group. This means that one group receives an intervention and another group does not. So are the results generalizable? They can be. For example, the researcher can include a pretest and run a statistical test (e.g., an independent-samples *t* test) to see whether the groups are statistically significantly different. If no statistical significance is evident, then the groups can be considered equivalent. However, other issues arise with this type of design, such as a testing effect—when an instrument is used on more than one occasion, which can confound the results. (Additional information on problems that occur in experimental research is given in Chapter 7.)

In this example, the quasi-experimental design includes a group that receives treatment and a group that does not, thereby providing the *experimental* nature of the design—a manipulated independent variable. An individual could just as easily be in one group or the other and receive or not receive the intervention. However, what happens when such a variable cannot be manipulated? Davis, Balkin, and Juhnke (2014) compared scores on the Juhnke-Balkin Life Balance Inventory between individuals who were currently seeking counseling services (clinical) and individuals not seeking counseling services (nonclinical). Whether or not a participant was currently in counseling could not be randomly assigned. When such a treatment or intervention cannot be manipulated or randomly assigned, then the study cannot be considered quasi-experimental. However, when comparisons can be made based on nonrandomized, nonmanipulated groups, the design can be identified as *exploratory, nonexperimental* (Johnson, 2001). The purpose of exploratory, nonexperimental research is often to describe differences between preexisting groups when an independent variable cannot be manipulated. However, controlling for extraneous or confounding variables can be more difficult.

True experimental research includes both random assignment and comparison groups. Extraneous variables are controlled, and results tend to be generalizable without the added burden of trying to demonstrate group equivalence through statistical tools. These studies are less common in social science research, as true experimental research is difficult to conduct. Finding participants who will consent to randomized control is time consuming and challenging. As a result, most published social science research is not experimental but rather correlational.

Correlational Research

Correlational research is likely the dominant form of quantitative research published in the counseling literature. Correlational research provides opportunities for researchers to examine how various phenomena relate to one another. According to Erford et al. (2011), correlational research was the dominant form of counseling research published in the *Journal of Counseling & Development*, ACA's flagship journal, from 1994 to 2009, and this trend likely continues.

Correlational research involves investigating the relationship between or among variables. Typical correlational designs include various regression procedures (simple regression, multiple regression, logistic regression, hierarchical linear regression, etc.), canonical correlation, structural equation modeling, and other advanced methods. The advantage of correlational designs is that comparison groups are not needed, so relationships between or among variables can be investigated with a single set of participants without concern for controlling for extraneous variables, which needs to be addressed when conducting group comparisons. This is not to say that extraneous variables do not affect correlational research (they do), but other procedures exist for identifying outliers so that these effects can be minimized.

Another reason correlational research is popular is because examining how psychosocial variables relate to one another is both interesting and important to counseling research. For example, Balkin et al. (2009) provided insight into characteristics of religious counselors that contribute to or protect against bias toward clients. Counselors completed four instruments to measure (a) religious identity, (b) multicultural competence, (c) sexism, and (d) homophobia. Correlational research was used to evaluate how attitudes were related across these constructs. For example, counselors who professed more rigid and authoritarian views were more likely to exhibit homophobic and sexist attitudes. In another example, Balkin and Roland (2007) examined the relationship between therapeutic goal attainment for adolescents in crisis and psychiatric symptoms among adolescents in acute care psychiatric hospitalization. In other words, a correlational design evaluated the relationship between two measures (one evaluating therapeutic goal attainment for adolescents in crisis, and the other evaluating symptom severity); each participant completed both measures. The more adolescents in crisis met their goals in counseling, the less severe their symptomatology. Thus, correlational research can be helpful in examining aspects that influence counselor practice and client-centered outcomes.

Unifying Concepts in Qualitative Research

So far our discussion of research has been focused on quantitative methods—methods that explore phenomena and assign values to the constructs or direct observations. Whereas the goal of quantitative research is generalizability, qualitative research is focused on *transferability*, or the extent to which a study is coherent, insightful, and useful to other individuals or settings (Lincoln & Guba, 1985). Whereas quantitative research relies heavily on statistics (along with proper methods) to determine generalizability, the extent to which a qualitative study is transferable is determined by the reader and likely will be enhanced when the study is well written, informative, practical, and beneficial.

Narrative Data

Data in qualitative research are narrative in nature rather than numerical as in quantitative research. Qualitative data, therefore, come in the form of transcribed interviews, observations, or documents. These data are evaluated and compared to derive themes to inform the reader. This process of evaluating and comparing various data sources is rigorous and methodical in order to provide findings that are both driven by the data and less influenced by researcher bias. Indeed, many of the unifying concepts discussed here are in place to address and reduce bias.

Theoretical Sensitivity

Theoretical sensitivity refers to the personal, professional, and research experiences that facilitate the researcher providing meaning and understanding to the data (Corbin & Strauss, 2015). Unlike in quantitative research, in which measures are used to evaluate a construct, in qualitative research the researcher is the instrument (Patton, 2015). The narrative data collected are analyzed, interpreted, and disseminated through the researcher. Theoretical sensitivity, therefore, addresses both the expertise and biases of the researcher. Essentially, readers need to know why the researcher is a good instrument for the study. Discussion of the personal, professional, and research expertise of the researcher lends credibility to the qualitative inquiry. Theoretical sensitivity may also be described in *the role of the researcher* portion of a qualitative study. This section provides an understanding of not only researcher expertise but also transparency (Hunt, 2011). For example, a counselor conducting a qualitative study on addiction may also have personal experience with addiction as opposed to merely a professional interest. The researcher could have intimate knowledge of addiction from either struggling with addiction or having family members who have struggled with addiction. Hence, in the study the researcher should note both professional and personal experiences.

That the disclosure of personal and professional experiences, in the writing of qualitative methods, occurs in the first person is worth noting and is a somewhat more distinguishing characteristic of qualitative inquiry. As the researcher is the instrument, the personal perspective of the researcher plays a more prominent role in the methods.

Trustworthiness

Trustworthiness may best be described as the rigor and credibility of a qualitative study (Hunt, 2011). Trustworthiness is often described as *validity* in a qualitative study in order to liken the process to quantitative research; however, this is a misnomer, as the concept of validity in quantitative research has continually evolved and does not accurately depict the unique aspects of ensuring credibility in qualitative inquiry. "The rigor of qualitative research can stand on its own, without being compared to quantitative research, and researchers are responsible for showing readers the steps they took to ensure quality and trustworthiness" (Hunt, 2011, p. 298). Patton (2015) identified procedures for ensuring trustworthiness, which include *prolonged engagement* (ensuring adequate time in the field), *persistent engagement* (an evaluation of confirming and disconfirming evidence), *triangulation* (comparisons across a variety of sources and theoretical frameworks), *peer debriefing* (a process in which the data evaluation is checked by other experts), *member checks* (an evaluation of the data by the actual participants), and the *audit trail* (a presentation of the raw data). In a qualitative study, not all of these procedures may be mentioned, but several of these processes should be depicted.

Purposeful Sampling

Recall that in our discussion of quantitative research an emphasis on probability and nonprobability (i.e., convenience) sampling was presented. Qualitative research uses *purposeful sampling*, in which the researcher intentionally selects participants. In qualitative inquiry, data are collected from information-rich sources, so thoughtful consideration by the researcher is necessary in order to consider who is an information-rich resource. Researchers provide a description of the participants and the rationale for their selection in the study. Unlike probability sampling, which can be delineated into just a few categories, there are numerous categories of purposeful sampling, which are discussed later (see Chapter 10).

Data Analysis

Data analysis in qualitative research is an extension of the methods that leads to themes that emerge from the narrative data. The process of analyzing, evaluating, and comparing the various data sources should be depicted clearly (Hunt, 2011). The process used to analyze the data will depend on the type of qualitative theory (e.g., phenomenology, grounded theory, consensual qualitative research) used for the study and often involves *coding*—a systematic method of identifying themes in narrative data using a word or short phrase that captures the essence of the phenomenon being studied (Saldaña, 2013).

Findings

A key component of describing the findings or results in qualitative research is support from the data. In communicating themes, qualitative researchers identify and cite examples from the narrative data to support the findings. Such support is often presented in the form of quotes from various participants, documents, and observations, which enhance credibility and lend the participants' "voice" to the research (Hunt, 2011, p. 299). In this way, examples of the actual data may be presented as well as used to confirm the themes or patterns identified by the researcher.

Emerging Trends in Counseling Research

Mixed-methods research and SCRD are not new but are becoming more popular in counseling research. Leech and Onwuegbuzie (2010) provided a description of the benefits and uses of mixed-methods research. Such designs should be accompanied by a clear rationale. In the case of mixed-methods research, researchers often seek to provide more information about the participants in the study than can be provided by a single method. A quantitative study may focus on comparisons between groups; a qualitative study may seek to explore individual responses in depth. Through mixed-methods research, both of these areas can be addressed. In particular, when participants receive a particular intervention, an in-depth interview can provide additional information about the effects of the intervention that may be missed when looking at scores for a group. Furthermore, combining quantitative and qualitative findings may produce a more meaningful study.

SCRD is a growing method in counseling research but has been used quite extensively in behavioral research and research in special education. Within counseling research, SCRD has been utilized extensively in studying the effects of play therapy. Lenz (2015) indicated that SCRD was "a practical strategy for making inferences about the efficacy of an intervention, establishing evidentiary support for counseling practices, and giving voice to counseling activities with small or understudied populations" (p. 387). SCRD combines the benefits of experimental design with the study of individual cases in order to identify a functional relationship between an intervention and an effect (O'Neill, McDonnell, Billingsley, & Jenson, 2010). In addition, qualitative data can be easily incorporated into SCRD to add richness to quantitative findings. SCRD is covered in more detail in Chapter 8.

Choosing a Type of Research

The types of research discussed in this chapter are typical of counseling research but by no means exhaustive. Researchers commonly pick a methodology that they are comfortable with and tailor their research to that particular methodology. A fundamental tenet of strong research, however, is that *the research question drives the method* and not vice versa. New researchers need to be cautious about (a) limiting their skill set to only one particular methodology and (b) choosing a methodology because it is convenient instead of the best method for the study.

The ability to review and conduct a variety of studies using a diverse set of methods is an integral skill in developing a researcher identity in the counseling profession. A complete set of skills requires study and practice with the aforementioned research typologies. By only focusing on a particular skill set (e.g., quantitative or qualitative), researchers limit the types of research questions they can investigate. Research questions become specifically adjusted to fit a particular method, which may result in the researcher eliminating data collection methods that truly would enhance the phenomenon of interest.

Despite needing a comprehensive set of skills, counselors often specialize in a particular type of research, not out of avoidance of a particular method but more as a result of their theoretical orientation to research. For example, Hansen (2012) advocated for qualitative research to be a standard method of inquiry in counseling research because of (a) the ability of qualitative research to better address human issues holistically and from multiple perspectives; (b) an understanding that human nature is complex, and qualitative research better addresses this complexity; and (c) the limitations of quantitative research, which can oversimplify human complexity and reduce this complexity to a mere number or label. Lemberger (2012b), in a response to Hansen, indicated the value of quantitative research:

> Consider Hansen's (2012) preferred brand—qualitative methodologies—as an exemplar. The researcher enters research inquiry with a certain position in relationship to the phenomena that are to be studied. The researcher then uses select mechanisms, typically words (e.g., codes, themes), to symbolically capture the experience of the phenomena (Moustakas, 1994). These mechanisms, although imprecise, provide the researcher and the consumer of the research a way to catalogue and interpret the meanings of the phenomena considered. The limitations of this mode of inquiry pertain to the usefulness and veracity of the words as symbols to describe the phenomena and also the interpretative capacity of the researcher and consumer. Now juxtapose the qualitative method with the quantitative method. In the case of quantitative research, the researcher approaches [a phenomenon] and assigns it a numeric symbol to encapsulate its

> assumed essence (Smith, 1983). This symbol is limited by each of the aforementioned considerations and yet is valuable because it is compared with prior findings in related literatures and from within the interpretative relevance of the researcher and consumer alike. In other words, quantitative research, like qualitative research, is only usable by virtue of how it is interpreted by the individuals to whom the findings are made accessible. (p. 170)

In this regard, some researchers gravitate toward a particular methodology out of their sincerely held beliefs about the nature of counseling research. Carl Rogers (1963), a pioneer in humanistic counseling, argued that research should focus on objective knowing (knowledge based on measurements of constructs), subjective knowing (knowledge based on internalized beliefs), and interpersonal knowing (knowledge based on empathic understanding of one another). Hence, both paradigms hold value, and what the researcher is left with is to determine a type of research that will best answer the question of interest.

Chapter Summary

In this chapter we explored unifying concepts in quantitative and qualitative research and identified some trends that may bridge these two distinct families of research. The goals, sampling strategies, and methods of data collection and analysis are part of what makes quantitative and qualitative inquiry distinct from each other. Although you will likely develop your own preferences toward research, the selection of a research strategy is determined primarily by research questions or hypotheses rather than personal preference. At the heart of this debate lies the issue of depth versus breadth. When a researcher wants to dive deeply into a topic and understand the details and nuances, qualitative inquiry presents a compelling model. When the researcher's goal is to generalize findings across a large population, quantitative research presents the best opportunity. Although it is a bit of an overgeneralization, qualitative research is a wonderful tool for developing theory, and quantitative research provides an opportunity to test theory. Both are necessary to move a field forward.

Suggested Activities

I. A special issue of the *Journal of Humanistic Counseling* (Dollarhide, 2012) presents a compelling discussion of the nature of counseling and counseling research that speaks directly to choosing a type of research. Review this issue and consider the following:

1. Consider Hansen's (2012) assertion that using scientific methods to investigate complex human issues is dehumanizing and the response by Lemberger (2012a). Is the scientific method dehumanizing? How should the counseling profession respond to issues of research, diagnosis, and assessment?
2. In Liebert's (2012) response to Hansen, economic pressures appear to be a driving force behind trends, practice, and knowledge in counseling. What is your perspective on addressing these external influences on the counseling profession?

II. Each division of ACA publishes a journal. Select three counseling journals associated with ACA and its divisions and review the author guidelines and research published in the past few issues.

1. What type of research is being conducted?
2. What trends in published research, if any, can you identify?

References

Balkin, R. S., Miller, J., Ricard, R. J., Garcia, R., & Lancaster, C. (2011). Assessing factors in adolescent adjustment as precursors to recidivism in court-referred youth. *Measurement and Evaluation in Counseling and Development, 44,* 52–59. doi:10.1177/0748175610391611

Balkin, R. S., & Roland, C. B. (2007). Re-conceptualizing stabilization for counseling adolescents in brief psychiatric hospitalization: A new model. *Journal of Counseling & Development, 85,* 64–72. doi:10.1002/j.1556-6678.2007.tb00445.x

Balkin, R. S., Schlosser, L. Z., & Levitt, D. H. (2009). Religious identity and cultural diversity: Exploring the relationships between religious identity, homophobia, sexism, and multicultural competence. *Journal of Counseling & Development, 87,* 420–427. doi:10.1002/j.1556-6678.2009.tb00126.x

Corbin, J., & Strauss, A. (2015). *Basics of qualitative research: Techniques and procedures for developing grounded theory* (4th ed.). Thousand Oaks, CA: Sage.

Davis, R. J., Balkin, R. S., & Juhnke, G. A. (2014). Validation of the Juhnke-Balkin Life Balance Inventory. *Measurement and Evaluation in Counseling & Development, 47,* 181–198. doi:10.1177/0748175614531796

Dollarhide, C. T. (Ed.). (2012). Humanism redefined [Special issue]. *Journal of Humanistic Counseling, 51*(2).

Erford, B. T., Miller, E. M., Schein, H., McDonald, A., Ludwig, L., & Leishear, K. (2011). *Journal of Counseling & Development* publication patterns: Author and article characteristics from 1994 to 2009. *Journal of Counseling & Development, 89,* 73–80. doi:10.1002/j.1556-6678.2011.tb00062.x

Gall, M. D., Gall, J. P., & Borg, W. R. (2007). *Educational research: An introduction* (8th ed.). Boston, MA: Pearson.

Hansen, J. T. (2012). Extending the humanistic vision: Toward a humanities foundation for the counseling profession. *Journal of Humanistic Counseling, 51,* 133–144. doi:10.1002/j.2161-1939.2012.00011.x

Hunt, B. (2011). Publishing qualitative research in counseling journals. *Journal of Counseling & Development, 89,* 296–300. doi:10.1002/j.1556-6678.2011.tb00092.x

Johnson, B. (2001). Toward a new classification of nonexperimental quantitative research. *Educational Researcher, 30,* 3–13. doi:10.3102/0013189X030002003

Leech, N. L., & Onwuegbuzie, A. J. (2010). Guidelines for conducting and reporting mixed research in the field of counseling and beyond. *Journal of Counseling & Development, 88,* 61–69. doi:10.1002/j.1556-6678.2010.tb00151.x

Lemberger, M. E. (2012a). A reply to Hansen's cultural humanism. *Journal of Humanistic Counseling, 51,* 180–183. doi:10.1002/j.2161-1939.2012.00017.x

Lemberger, M. E. (2012b). A return to the human in humanism: A response to Hansen's humanistic vision. *Journal of Humanistic Counseling, 51,* 164–175. doi:10.1002/j.2161-1939.2012.00015.x

Lenz, A. S. (2015). Using single-case research designs to demonstrate evidence for counseling practices. *Journal of Counseling & Development, 93,* 387–393. doi:10.1002jcad.12036

Lenz, A. S., Perepiczka, M., & Balkin, R. S. (2013). Evidence for the mitigating effects of a support group for attitudes toward statistics. *Counseling Outcome Research and Evaluation, 4,* 26–40. doi:10.1177/2150137812474000

Liebert, T. W. (2012). Response to Hansen: Economic pressures, not science, undermine humanistic counseling. *Journal of Humanistic Counseling, 51,* 206–216. doi:10.1002/j.2161-1939.2012.00021.x

Lincoln, Y. S., & Guba, E. G. (1985). *Naturalistic inquiry.* Newbury Park, CA: Sage.

O'Neill, R. E., McDonnell, J. J., Billingsley, F. E., & Jenson, W. R. (2010). *Single case research designs in educational and community settings.* Upper Saddle River, NJ: Pearson.

Patton, M. Q. (2015). *Qualitative research and valuation methods: Integrating theory and practice.* Thousand Oaks, CA: Sage.
Reynolds, W. M. (2001). *Reynolds Adolescent Adjustment Screening Inventory. RAASI: Professional manual.* Lutz, FL: Psychological Assessment Resources.
Rogers, C. R. (1963). Toward a science of the person. *Journal of Humanistic Psychology, 3,* 72–92. doi:10.1177/002216786300300208
Saldaña, J. (2013). *The coding manual for qualitative researchers* (2nd ed.). Thousand Oaks, CA: Sage.

Quantitative Research Designs

All statistics are correlational and stem from the general linear model (Thompson, 2006), which means that quantitative research is about the examination of relationships. These relationships may be manifested in different ways. Chapter 5 provides an overview of fundamental concepts in understanding, evaluating, and designing quantitative research. Chapter 6 covers how to evaluate relationships between or among variables. For example, how do coping skills, as measured by the Crisis Stabilization Scale, influence a decrease in symptoms, as measured by the Target Symptom Rating scale

(Balkin, 2013, 2014; Balkin, Leicht, Sartor, & Powell, 2011). Chapter 7 focuses on how relationships with a variable may differ depending on group assignment. For example, adolescent females who experience a crisis may have a stronger commitment to follow-up counseling services than males (Balkin & Roland, 2005). Chapter 8 identifies methods and procedures for understanding how scores may change over time, such as the evaluation of pretest and posttest data. Finally, Chapter 9 concludes this section by examining how the overall effectiveness of counseling interventions and practices may be evaluated through meta-analyses.

References

Balkin, R. S. (2013). Validation of the Goal Attainment Scale of Stabilization. *Measurement and Evaluation in Counseling and Development, 46,* 261–269. doi:10.1177/0748175613497040

Balkin, R. S. (2014). *The Crisis Stabilization Scale manual and sampler set.* Menlo Park, CA: Mind Garden.

Balkin, R. S., Leicht, D. J., Sartor, T., & Powell, J. (2011). Assessing the relationship between therapeutic goal attainment and psychosocial characteristics for adolescents in crisis residence. *Journal of Mental Health, 20,* 32–42.

Balkin, R. S., & Roland, C. B. (2005). Identification of differences in gender for adolescence in crisis residence. *Journal of Mental Health, 14,* 637–646.

Thompson, B. (2006). *Foundations of behavioral statistics: An insight based approach.* New York, NY: Guilford Press.

Fundamental Concepts in Quantitative Research

Overview

This chapter provides an overview on defining constructs and variables, measuring constructs and variables, understanding statistics and error, and understanding hypothesis testing that is essential to evaluating quantitative research and designing studies. Understanding statistics at a conceptual level is essential to evaluating and formulating research. Moreover, an argument can be made that understanding statistics at a procedural level (i.e., being able to compute and generate statistics) strengthens a person's ability to synthesize and generate research. The focus of this chapter is to explain and evaluate statistical concepts at a conceptual level. Moreover, the criticism of relying too much on statistical inference to make determinations related to the practice of counseling is highlighted.

Defining Constructs and Variables

Counseling research is inextricably linked to the evaluation and measurement of constructs. A *construct* is a phenomenon of interest that cannot be measured directly. Phenomena like height and weight can be measured directly. Rulers and scales were developed so that regardless of who is doing the measuring, a consistent and accurate result is obtained. However, a construct, such as coping skills, self-esteem, depression, or intelligence, cannot be measured directly. Hence, counseling researchers rely on measures (e.g., assessments, surveys) to evaluate constructs. Keep in mind that such measures may vary based on how a construct is operationally defined and the type of assessment being administered. For example, the Stanford–Binet Intelligence Scale, Fifth Edition (Roid, 2003), and the Wechsler Adult Intelligence Scale, Fourth Edition (Wechsler, 2008), both measure intelligence, but each uses a different method for doing so. Such differences highlight the variety of ways in which a construct can be measured and interpreted. For this reason, an operational definition of the construct of interest is important. An *operational definition* is a guiding description of a phenomenon. It provides a framework for which measures may be developed in order to evaluate a construct. For example, Balkin, Harris, Freeman, and Huntington (2014) developed the Forgiveness Reconciliation Inventory (FRI) from a theoretically derived model from Balkin, Freeman, and Lyman (2009) that outlined a therapeutic process for addressing issues of forgiveness and conflict in counseling. The stages identified in the Balkin et al. (2009) model were incorporated into an empirically validated measure (see Balkin et al., 2014) to evaluate a client's perception of the forgiveness process with respect to a specific issue of the client. In this sense, the content (i.e., the items) of a measurement instrument is theoretically tied to the operational definition of the intended construct to be measured.

Variables are types of measures that may be discrete or continuous and may measure a construct or directly observable phenomenon. A *discrete* variable is categorical in nature. Examples of discrete variables include sex, ethnicity, religious affiliation, and so forth. Discrete variables use *levels* within each variable. For example, sex is a variable that often includes two levels: male and female. In contrast, a variable like ethnicity can have multiple levels, such as African American, Caucasian, Native American, Latino, Asian, and so forth. A *continuous* variable is a score or measure. Scores on the Crisis Stabilization Scale (CriSS; Balkin, 2014) or FRI are examples of continuous variables.

Variables generally function on one of four scales: nominal, ordinal, interval, or ratio.

Nominal

Variables measured on a nominal scale are discrete, categorical variables, such as those mentioned previously (e.g., sex, ethnicity, religious affiliation). Numbers may be assigned to nominal variables (sex: male = 1, female = 2), but these numbers have no direct value.

In other words, no mathematical operations may be used with nominal variables; nominal variables are used strictly to classify.

Ordinal

Variables measured on an ordinal scale are most often discrete, as they represent an ordered sequence, but the magnitude between each value is unspecified. For example, a client completes the Occupational Information Network Interest Profiler and obtains a Holland code of S-A-E, indicating that his or her highest scores were on the Social, Artistic, and Enterprising scales. From this report, the counselor can infer that the client's highest score was on the Social scale, and scores on the Artistic and Enterprising scales were the next highest, respectively. What is not known is the extent or magnitude to which the client prefers Social to Artistic or Enterprising or another category (i.e., Realistic, Conventional, or Investigative). Classifications such as high, middle, or low socioeconomic status may be considered ordinal. Likert-type scales (e.g., 1 = *strongly disagree*, 2 = *disagree*, 3 = *neither disagree nor agree*, 4 = *agree*, 5 = *strongly agree*) also may be considered ordinal because they lack a true, objective metric. Participants who complete a survey in this format may have varying opinions of what constitutes *agree* versus *strongly agree.* For instance, responses to an item that measures pain ("I experience a lot of pain every day") might vary across participants. Two people could experience the same level of pain but endorse it differently based on their pain tolerance.

Interval

Variables measured on an interval scale maintain an ordered sequence, as with an ordinal scale, but also main values that are equidistant. Interval scales do not use a true zero, meaning that no absence of a phenomenon exists. Because of this, interval scales rarely exist in counseling research. More typically counseling researchers use quasi-interval variables. For *quasi-interval* variables, the subjective variability between values is treated as if the values were objective and definite. For example, although two people could experience the same level of pain but endorse it differently based on their pain tolerance, their subjective assessment is treated as definitive. In this way, scores on such a scale can be subjected to mathematical operations and therefore considered continuous data. The vast majority of quantitative research in the counseling field uses this type of quasi-interval measure. Myriad scales have been developed to measure various constructs that technically use an ordinal measure but are treated as interval. Hence, when evaluating research from a practitioner-scholar approach, keep in mind that the integrity of the findings is limited by the fact that the differences among participants completing a scale most often are perceived, not actual.

Ratio

Variables measured on a ratio scale have the aforementioned qualities of the interval scale but also include a true zero, indicating the absence of a phenomenon. Ratio scales often are not constructs and represent a phenomenon that may be observed directly. Demographic variables such as age and number of years in school are common examples of ratio variables. A counseling researcher may be interested in the number of days of sobriety until relapse or the number of times clients engage in cutting, which could be objectively measured. A true zero (i.e., the absence of a phenomenon) is possible.

When designing studies, counseling researchers should keep in mind that naturally occurring continuous variables can always be reduced to interval, ordinal, or nominal scales; however, a scale at the lower level cannot be converted to a higher level scale. A counseling student can record the actual number of credit hours taken in a semester. Because values range from 0 to an unspecified amount, the variable is considered continuous or ratio. The number of credit hours enrolled could easily be converted to an ordinal scale: 0–3, 6–9, 12 or more. Furthermore, the variable could be converted to a nominal scale: part time or full time. However, if only the category was collected (part time or full time), those values could not be converted to an ordinal, interval, or ratio scale.

Measuring Constructs and Variables

Measuring constructs is a complex process. The development of measures for counseling research must follow a rigorous process. A researcher who wants to measure the impact of counseling when working with adolescents in crisis should be certain that any measures utilized in such a study operationally define how adolescents who are in crisis will be identified and what will be measured to indicate impact or improvement. Constructs in counseling are quite complex. The extent to which adolescents address relevant goals related to stabilizing a crisis situation can be measured using the CriSS. The CriSS, similar to other measures, includes numerous items to measure clients' progress toward stabilization. Why not just have a single item that the counselor completes, such as "Is the client stable?" A single item is not adequate to encompass a complex construct such as crisis stabilization. For this reason, items on the CriSS were developed to align theoretically with research related to crisis stabilization. The result was a 25-item instrument. Another instrument that is used quite often in counseling and counseling research is the Beck Depression Inventory–II (BDI-II; Beck, Steer, & Brown, 1996). The BDI-II is a 21-item instrument developed in 1996 to assess the presence and severity of depressive symptoms. Because of the complexity and implications of diagnosing and evaluating the severity of symptoms, the importance of using an instrument that is comprehensive, consistent, and accurate cannot be overstated.

A key to quantitative research, therefore, is to make sure that instruments used in a research study align with the intended construct being measured and measure the said construct accurately and consistently. The American Educational Research Association, American Psychological Association, and National Council on Measurement in Education (AERA, APA, & NCME; 2014) jointly published *Standards for Educational and Psychological Testing*. The standards outline issues related to instrument development, fairness and bias, and the application of results to various settings (e.g., educational, vocational, psychological settings). With respect to evaluating research, issues of test construction, specifically evaluating validity and reliability, need to be addressed.

Validity

"Validity refers to the degree to which evidence and theory support the interpretations of test scores entailed by proposed uses of test" (AERA, APA, & NCME, 2014, p. 11). Validity, therefore, concerns not simply the alignment of an instrument with theory and research but also how the scores are used. AERA, APA, and NCME identified five types of evidence for evaluating the validity of a measure: evidence based on test content, evidence based on response processes, evidence based on internal structure, evidence based on relationships to other variables, and evidence based on consequences of testing.

Evidence based on test content is specifically related to the extent to which the items are aligned with existing theory and the operational definition of the construct. Evidence of test content often is established through documentation of a review of the extant literature and expert review. *Evidence based on response processes* includes an analysis of how respondents answer or perform on given items. In counseling research, some documentation about how respondents interpret the items may be noted. *Evidence based on internal structure* refers to the psychometric properties of the instrument. For example, items on a scale should be correlated, as they measure the same construct, but they should not be overly correlated, as that could indicate that the items are not measuring anything unique. Generally speaking, factor analysis and reliability estimates are used to indicate adequate factor structure and accurate and consistent responses for scores. As a rule of thumb, items should have factor loadings, which are essentially correlation coefficients, of around .40 or higher to indicate that they are sufficiently measuring the intended construct. In terms of reliability (i.e., the accuracy and consistency of scores), estimates of .70 indicate adequate consistency of scores, .80 indicate good consistency of scores, and .90 or higher indicate very good consistency of scores. *Evidence based on relationships to other variables* is usually demonstrated through some type of correlational research in which the scores on instrument are correlated with scores on another instrument. When an instrument is correlated with another instrument, this provides evidence that the same construct is being measured by both instruments. *Evidence based on consequences of testing* refers to the need to document the effects and ramifications, either intended or unintended, of the administration, scoring, and interpretation of the test (AERA, APA, & NCME, 2014). When evaluating or conceptualizing a research study, consider whether the instrument(s) used in the study meet the intended guidelines. The choice to use scores on an instrument for a research study should be aligned with theory and practice.

Researchers often utilize multiple constructs and variables in a research study. How these variables are utilized within the study is discussed later in this chapter and in subsequent chapters. Now that you understand how constructs are operationalized and variables are measured, we can turn our attention to examining what counseling researchers do with such variables.

Understanding Statistics and Error

At the most basic level, data are often reported as frequencies and percentages, measures of central tendency, measures of variability, and measures of relationship. Data such as these are often referred to as *descriptive statistics* and may be presented in a narrative or table. These data are important for three reasons. First, data specify information about the participants in a study, which provides an indication of the generalizability of the results. Second, data provide descriptive information about measures used in the study in order to establish relationships among other variables or between or among groups, which may be important to hypothesis testing and the research question(s). Third, descriptive statistics may be pertinent to replicating a study.

Frequencies and Percentages

Frequencies and percentages are often helpful in describing the participants of a study or nominal variables. For example, Balkin et al. (2014) validated the FRI for use in assessing clients who are struggling with issues of forgiveness and conflict. The following information was provided about the participants in the study:

> Two hundred participants from the United States were solicited from nonclinical and clinical settings; the nonclinical setting included undergraduate and graduate students on a university campus in the South and consenting professionals from a community-based education program (N = 131, 65.5%), and the clinical settings included a correctional setting, outpatient women's recovery center, and domestic abuse shelter in the Northeast, and a domestic abuse shelter in the South (N = 69, 34.5%). Participants were 35 (17.5%) males and 165 (82.5%) females with the following ethnic breakdown: white (N = 115, 57.5%), Latino/a (N = 47, 23.5%), African American (N = 18, 9.5%), Asian (N = 8, 4%), other (N = 8, 4%), and missing (N = 4, 2%). Mean age was 33.33 (SD = 14.21). (p. 5)

When evaluating this study given the information presented, one can ascertain that the participants were primarily female. Compared to many studies, this study had a more balanced ratio between White and minority clients. These issues should be taken into consideration when evaluating the generalizability of the study. For example, would this study necessarily be generalizable to male clients? Clearly this could be a limitation!

Common Descriptive Statistics

The most common descriptive statistics can be classified as measures of central tendency, measures of variability, and measures of relationship. Typically these values come in the form of means, standard deviations, and correlation coefficients.

The *mean* is the most common measure of central tendency and represents the average score for a set of observations. Other measures of central tendency include the *median,* which is the middle score in a set of observations, and the *mode,* which is the most frequent score in a set of observations. Most statistical tests used in counseling research use the mean, but there are some exceptions when the median is used. The mean is useful, as a single score is used to represent an entire group. The mean represents the best estimate of how an individual or group will perform when nothing else is really known. For example, if we know that the average individual attending outpatient counseling typically scores around 22 on the BDI-II, we can gauge how much more or less severe a client's symptoms are based on the mean.

However, if the mean is used as an approximation to evaluate the scores of other individuals or groups, we need to keep in mind that the mean is simply an estimate. Some people score above the mean; others score below the mean. Because the mean is an estimate, researchers need to account for inaccuracies, known as *error.* The most common estimate of error is the *standard deviation,* which indicates the average amount of error from the mean. The *variance* is another measure of error and represents the squared value of the standard deviation. This value has many important statistical properties in the reporting of quantitative research. The *range* is also a measure of variability and simply indicates the distance between the highest and lowest scores. The standard deviation, or average distance from the mean, is difficult to conceptualize, so we will follow this idea through an example.

In developing the BDI-II, researchers administered the measure to 500 individuals in outpatient counseling. The mean score for these 500 participants was 22.45. Keep in mind that for each individual, the BDI-II was scored in increments of 1 point, but when the average was computed (i.e., all of the participants' scores are summed and divided by 500), the mean was 22.45. Clearly not all 500 participants scored at the mean. It would be helpful to know how accurate the mean is in providing an estimate for an individual or group. The extent to which individuals score above or below the mean is an indication of error. The standard deviation provides an indication of the average amount of error from the mean, or rather, the average amount by which individuals score above or below the mean. For the 500 outpatient participants who were administered the BDI-II, the standard deviation was 12.75, meaning that on average a score varied from the mean by 12.75 points.

The standard deviation is often converted to units or standard scores, and there are many ways to do this. In using standard scores, the goal is to convert scores to a value that is more easily interpreted and understood. Standard scores can easily be converted to percentiles so that a score can be compared to that of a normative sample or group. To further understand this point, it helps to be familiar with the *normal curve* or bell-shaped distribution.

Properties of the Normal Curve

The normal curve is the basis for parametric statistics, which encompass the majority of statistical tests used in counseling research. In parametric statistics, scores are assumed to be normally distributed—that is, in the shape of a normal curve. But are most groups normally distributed? Actually in most cases this assumption is met, and scores tend to represent a normal distribution. Not all variables are normally distributed, such as income, but many of the constructs measured in counseling research meet this criterion.

In a normal distribution, the mean, median, and mode (all measures of central tendency) are equal, and the area under the normal curve can be approximated using the 68–95–99 rule. For a normally distributed set of scores, 68% of the participants will have scores that are between –1 and +1 *SD* units. In the previous example of the BDI-II with a mean of 22.45 and a standard deviation of 12.75, the average individual entering outpatient counseling will score between 9.7 (22.45 – 12.75) and 35.2 (22.45 + 12.75) 68% of the time. Hence, when someone scores around 9, we can say that the individual is 1 *SD* below the mean; a score of 35 is essentially 1 *SD* above the mean. Two standard deviations above the mean on the BDI-II would be about 48 (47.95, or 12.75 (2) + 22.45). Approximately 95% of individuals score between –2 and +2 *SD* units. Between –3 and +3 *SD* units encompasses 99% of the distribution (see Figure 5.1).

Understanding Standard Scores

Sometimes scores are expressed in standard deviation units as shown previously, known as *z scores*. A z score indicates how many standard deviations a score is from the mean. However, other methods are also used to convey the same information. For example, intelligence tests typically standardize scores with a mean of 100 and a standard deviation of 15. Rather than say that someone is 1 *SD* below or above the mean, researchers will say that the individual has scored an 85 (1 *SD* below the mean) or 115 (1 *SD* above

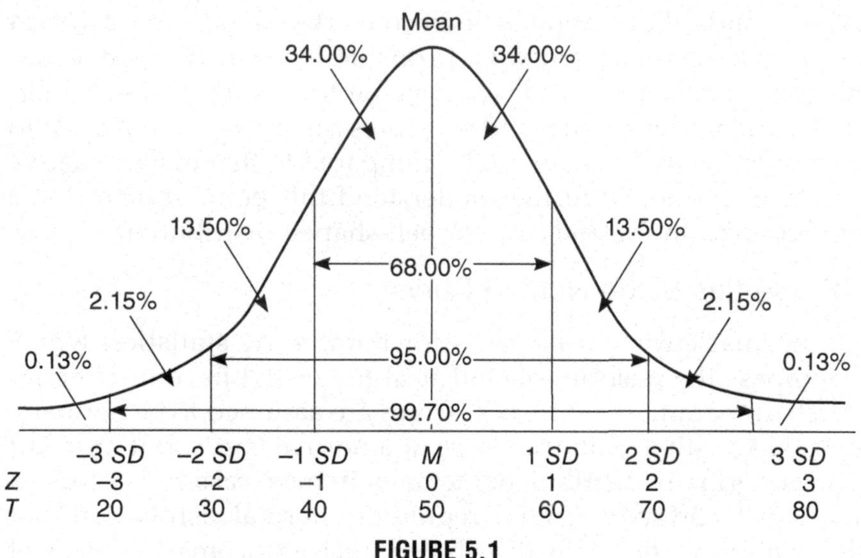

FIGURE 5.1
The 68-95-99 Rule With Standard Scores

Note. The *Z* score indicates how many standard deviations a score is from the mean. *T* scores are used with numerous psychological tests. *T* scores have a mean of 50 and a standard deviation of 10.

the mean). *T* scores are used with numerous psychological tests. *T* scores have a mean of 50 and a standard deviation of 10 (see Figure 5.1). Testing companies, such as those that administer the ACT, SAT, and Graduate Record Examination, use other types of standard scores. Converting raw scores to standard scores is not overly complicated:

$$z = \frac{X - \bar{X}}{\sigma},$$

where the *z* score is computed by subtracting the group mean from the raw score of an individual and dividing by the standard deviation. In our previous example of the BDI-II with a mean of 22.45 and a standard deviation of 12.75, an individual who scores 9 on the BDI-II would have a *z* score of about –1 *SD*, which would place this individual in approximately the 34th percentile for depressive symptoms:

$$z = \frac{X - \bar{X}}{\sigma} = \frac{9 - 22.45}{12.75} = -1.05$$

Standard scores are helpful for identifying where individuals or groups fall on the normal curve. Using the 68–95–99 rule, we can further break down the percentage to see how scores are interpreted (see Figure 5.1).

Notice that an individual who scores 2 *SD* below the mean is in about the 2.5 percentile; such scores, therefore, fall in the lowest 2.5%. A score that is 2 *SD* above the mean is almost in the 98th percentile, or the top 2%. Refer back to the example of an intelligence test with a mean of 100 and a standard deviation of 15. On such a test, a score of 100 (the mean) represents the 50th percentile; 85 (–1 *SD*) and 115 (+1 *SD*) represent the 16th and 84th percentiles, respectively; 70 (–2 *SD*) and 130 (+2 *SD*) represent about the 2nd and 98th percentiles, respectively. However, not all scores fit so nicely into the distribution. As previously noted, the BDI-II for individuals in outpatient counseling has a mean of 22.45 and a standard deviation of 12.75. The range of scores for the BDI-II is from 0 to 63. Hence, values can be computed for 2 or 3 *SD* above the mean on the BDI-II, but 2 *SD* below the mean on the BDI-II would result in a score less than 0, which is not possible.

Measures of Relationship

Measures of relationship refers to the extent to which a researcher can explain the relationship between two variables, often referred to as a *correlation*. The most common correlation coefficient is the *Pearson product–moment correlation coefficient*, or simply Pearson's *r*. Correlation coefficients range from –1 to +1 and are expressed in terms of direction and magnitude. The sign (+/–) refers to direction, whereas the value refers to magnitude. The closer a value is to –1 or +1, the stronger the relationship.

A positive correlation coefficient indicates that as values increase for one variable, the values for another variable will also increase. For example, clients who have higher levels of depression may be more likely to have disordered eating patterns. A negative correlation coefficient indicates that as values increase for one variable, the values for another variable will decrease. Clients who have higher self-esteem likely will have lower levels of depression.

The following guidelines may be helpful in interpreting correlation coefficients.

+/–.00–0.20	negligible
+/–.20–0.40	low
+/–.40–0.60	moderate
+/–.60–0.80	substantial
+/–.80–1.00	very substantial

Table 5.1 is a modified version of a table presented in the aforementioned study on the FRI (Balkin et al., 2014, p. 9). The descriptive statistics include average scores for the 200 participants who completed the FRI. The standard deviation indicates that some variability within each group was evident. In other words, individuals in the same group did not always answer similarly, often varying by 6 points, give or take. (Standard deviations range from 5.60 to 7.45.) These values, along with the correlation coefficients, may be helpful in verifying the results and replicating the study later.

The Nature of Hypothesis Testing

A conceptual understanding of the statistics discussed in the preceding sections provides the basis for understanding hypothesis testing. Statistical tests culminate in hypothesis testing and tend to be the primary focal point; a statistical test means nothing without the proper foundation for an experimental design.

Participant selection and assignment affect the extent to which the participants in a study are representative of the population of interest. *Assignment* refers to the process of placing individuals into experimental or control groups. The role of assignment and its potential effects on a study are discussed in Chapter 7.

Instrumentation refers to the validity of the measures for a particular study. The measures used in a study should align with the research questions. Strong psychometric properties are essential for instruments used in a research study. Scores that are inaccurate or inconsistent or the use of instruments for which validity evidence

TABLE 5.1

Descriptive Statistics and Correlations for the Forgiveness Reconciliation Inventory, Forgiveness Scale, and FLS

Scale or Subscale	Total (N = 200)		Clinical (n = 69)		Nonclinical (n = 131)								
	M	*SD*	*M*	*SD*	*M*	*SD*	1	2	3	4	5	6	7
1. Exploration	20.10	6.06	20.57	6.34	19.85	5.92	—	.46*	.47*	.42*	−.40*	−.41*	−.22
2. Role	17.55	6.21	20.15	6.52	16.18	5.60		—	.57*	.67*	−.42*	−.52*	−.20
3. Change	22.08	6.43	24.26	6.09	20.93	6.33			—	.68*	−.32*	−.50*	−.09
4. Outcome	20.47	6.95	22.25	7.45	19.52	6.51				—	−.44*	−.67*	−.23
5. Fsneg	33.56	7.91									—	.51*	.25*
6. Fspos	15.16	4.83										—	.32*
7. FLS	24.28	8.92											—

Note. Exploration, Role, Change, and Outcome represent the subscales of the Forgiveness Reconciliation Inventory; Fsneg = Forgiveness Scale Absence of Negative (N = 169); Fspos = Forgiveness Scale Presence of Positive (N = 169); FLS = Forgiveness Likelihood Scale (N = 170).

*p < .001.

is lacking will impact the generalizability of a study to the point that any results would be dubious.

Studies should be designed in a manner that limits the confounding effects of *extraneous variables*, or variables that influence a study but that were not actually included in the study. For example, a school counselor wants to evaluate a study skills program to raise scores for math achievement. The school counselor uses scores on a math achievement test that incorporates word problems. The school counselor does not take into account reading achievement, a variable that will have a confounding effect on this study. After all, a student with poor reading comprehension skills will have difficulty with word problems. So either reading comprehension needs to be considered in the study, or the design of the study might have a serious flaw. Similar problems may occur in clinical situations as well. For example, researchers may experience difficulty evaluating the effects of an intervention given the numerous variables that impact each individual differently. Recovery from trauma, for instance, may be affected by other variables, such as resilience, culture, previous history of psychosocial problems, and so forth. Hence, researchers need to develop thoughtful experimental designs that minimize threats to experimental validity (see Chapter 7).

With the proper foundation of selection and assignment, instrumentation, and design, researchers are prepared to collect data and conduct hypothesis testing. Statistical tests represent the tool(s) utilized to test hypotheses. Quantitative studies published in counseling journals usually indicate a research hypothesis, usually in the form of research questions or purpose statements. Statistical hypotheses, however, often do not appear in a research study. Statistical hypotheses represent the groups or relationships being investigated and use statistical notations to express these relationships. These relationships are represented through a null hypothesis, which indicates that all groups are equal or that no relationships exist, and an alternative hypothesis, which indicates that differences or relationships do exist. In hypothesis testing, the null hypothesis is tested. Hence, rather than test for differences, relationships, or effects, a researcher really is testing to see whether relationships or group differences do not exist. Although this may seem archaic and nonsensical, the method utilized today is an extension of scientific research used across numerous scientific disciplines. Before we elaborate on hypothesis testing, let's define some important concepts related to sources of error.

Types of Error

So far we have talked about error in terms of measurement, for example, using a mean to represent the group and needing to account for that error with the standard deviation or variance, and error that results because the measurement of constructs is so imperfect. However, another type of error results when we conduct statistical tests and make the wrong decision, which can happen for a variety of reasons, such as because scores in a sample are inaccurate representations of the population, mistakes were made in the calculations, instruments were not accurate measures of the construct, and so forth. Two primary types of error are Type I error and Type II error. Each of these is discussed in terms of the statistical definition followed by a more user-friendly definition. Further elaboration and examples of Type I and Type II error are provided later in the chapter.

Type I error occurs when a researcher rejects the null hypothesis when it should have been retained. Remember, rejecting the null hypothesis means that a relationship or significant difference exists. Put another way, a researcher makes a Type I error when he or she concludes that an actual relationship or difference exists when in fact it does not. So if a school counselor implements an antibullying program and concludes that the program made a positive impact in reducing school bullying when in fact occurrences of bullying remained the same, this would be a Type I error.

Type II error occurs when a researcher retains the null hypothesis when it should have been rejected. Remember, retaining the null hypothesis means that a relationship or significant difference does not exist. Put another way, a researcher makes a Type II error when he or she concludes that an actual relationship or difference does not exist when in fact it does. So if the school counselor concludes that the antibullying program did not make a positive impact in reducing school bullying when in fact occurrences of bullying actually decreased, this would be a Type II error.

Statistical Versus Practical Significance

Hypothesis testing is inherently tied to statistics and therefore represents a statement of probability. Statistical tests, then, are not indicative of meaningfulness but rather only identify whether group differences, relationships among variables, or phenomena or events occur outside the realm of chance. In other words, do differences between groups or relationships among variables occur simply because of luck, or given similar circumstances would they be replicated over and over again? When researchers indicate that a phenomenon is statistically significant, they are indicating that the event is probably not happening because of mere luck.

Whether a phenomenon is statistically significant is influenced by three primary factors: the actual magnitude of the result, the amount of error, and the sample size. The magnitude of the result is probably the easiest of the three to understand. In comparing groups, the larger the differences between the groups, the more likely it is that a statistically significant effect will be detected. In other words, as the difference between two mean scores increases, so does the likelihood of finding a statistically significant result.

With respect to the amount of error, keep in mind that the amount of error allowed in a study is a subjective decision on the part of the researcher. When researchers conduct an analysis, one goal is to make sure that a statically significant effect is not identified when one does not exist. In other words, researchers do not want to make a mistake in indicating a statistically significant result when in actuality the result is wrong or inaccurate. For example, a counselor wishes to compare clients who participated in group counseling and individual counseling and those who participated in individual counseling only on a scale that measures psychosocial distress (e.g., the CriSS). If the counselor indicates that the participants who received both group counseling and individual counseling had statistically significant lower levels of distress than clients who received individual counseling only, but the counselor's results were actually wrong, this would be a Type I error. In order to avoid making this type of error, researchers set stringent guidelines when conducting statistical tests by identifying an alpha (α) level. When a researcher reports statistical significance at $\alpha = .05$, the researcher is acknowledging a 5% chance of making a Type I error, or claiming that a study with a similar sample and effect would indicate the same results 95% of the time. When the probability of making a Type I error exceeds the alpha level, the result is not statistically significant. In other words, the researcher cannot ascertain that result is occurring outside the realm of chance. When alpha is smaller (e.g., $\alpha = .01$), the test is more stringent and the likelihood of detecting statistical significance decreases. When alpha is larger (e.g., $\alpha = .10$), the test is more amenable and the likelihood of detecting statistical significance increases. In counseling research, acceptable alpha levels are generally .05 or lower.

Sample size is the final issue affecting statistical significance and perhaps the easiest issue for the researcher to control. A primary reason for evaluating practical significance in conjunction with statistical significance has to do with the influence of sample size. When differences in magnitude between groups and level of significance are held constant, changes in sample size will affect *statistical power,* or the likelihood of detecting statistical significance if it actually exists. In order to understand the influence of sample size, a heuristic example comparing a sample to a population with a *z* test is utilized. Although the principles of the *z* test are foundational to quantitative research, many readers may not have been exposed to this procedure. So let us provide a conceptual explanation. A *z* test compares a sample mean to a population mean and accounts for error using the population standard deviation and the size of the sample,

$$z = \frac{\bar{X} - \mu}{\frac{\sigma}{\sqrt{n}}}$$

where $\bar{X} - \mu$ represents the sample mean minus the population mean and $\sigma \div \sqrt{n}$ represents the standard error of the mean using the population standard deviation divided by the sample size. The result of this computation is compared to a critical value indicating a .05 level of significance. In this example, a critical value of 1.96 is used, which is the standard value a researcher uses to indicate statistical significance with 95% confidence (i.e., at the .05 level of significance). The computation is not as important as understanding that parametric statistics essentially represent the same basic premise: A test of statistical significance is the ratio between effect (e.g., mean differences) and error:

$$\frac{\textit{effect}}{\textit{error}}$$

Essentially, a test of statistical significance translates to a fraction. The numerator represents mean differences, and the denominator represents error. When the numerator stays constant and the denominator increases (e.g., 1/4 to 1/8), the value decreases and statistical significance is less likely. In this example, error increased, and no differences were found. When the numerator increases and the denominator stays constant (e.g., 1/4 to 3/4), the value increases and statistical significance is more likely. In this example, mean differences increased and significant differences may be found.

In order to make this equation practical, assume that a researcher wants to look at the differences in depression among clients in a hospital setting and clients who receive outpatient counseling. In order to do this, the researcher administers the BDI-II to 36 clients, who have a mean score of 26. Recall that the population mean for outpatient clients on the BDI-II is 22.45 and that there is a population standard deviation of 12.75. At the .05 level of significance, the observed score from the z test will be compared to a critical value of 1.96 (taken from the z distribution table). In other words, in order for the researcher to conclude that the BDI-II scores for the clients in the hospital are significantly different from those in the population, the results of the z test would have to be greater than 1.96. Given the clients in the hospital and the known population parameters,

$$z = \frac{26 - 22.45}{\frac{12.75}{\sqrt{36}}} = 1.67$$

In this instance, when the researcher compares the z-test results to the critical value, there is no statistically significant difference between the sample and the population. Thus, the researcher concludes that the differences between BDI-II scores in the hospital sample and in the population are due to chance.

However, when the same criteria are used and the sample size is increased to 64,

$$z = \frac{26 - 22.45}{\frac{12.75}{\sqrt{64}}} = 2.23$$

Because a resulting z of 2.23 is greater than 1.96, the researcher concludes that the differences between BDI-II scores for clients in the hospital and for the population are significant. So even though differences between the groups do not change (the mean difference was 3.55 in both cases), the mere increase in sample size increases the likelihood of finding statistically significant differences. This not only highlights the importance of having an appropriate sample size to conduct research but also underlies the importance of reporting effect sizes in counseling research (Trusty, 2011; Trusty, Thompson, & Petrocelli, 2004), as statistical significance does not guarantee meaningful results.

Why does this happen in hypothesis testing? Notice that when the sample size increased, the error term (the denominator) decreased. When sample sizes are larger, error is smaller, as a larger sample size is a better estimate of a population than a smaller sample size. Theoretically speaking, a researcher will encounter less error by obtaining more participants from a target population; mathematically speaking, this concept is confirmed.

Simply because a result is statistically significant does not mean that such a phenomenon is meaningful. Meaningfulness is analogous to practical significance, which is an assessment of the extent to which group differences or relationships exist. Hence, a phenomenon can be statistically significant but not very meaningful. The important point here is that when counselors evaluate research, they must evaluate the results in light of both statistical and practical significance.

For example, the Centers for Disease Control and Prevention operates the Youth Risk Behavior Surveillance System. Its website provides an app that can evaluate greater or lesser risk between various demographic factors (Centers for Disease Control and Prevention, 2011). To illustrate the concepts of statistical and practical significance, we can use data from the website to evaluate whether males or females were at greater risk for abusing alcohol at age 13. In 2011, 3,668 ninth-grade youth (1,833 females and 1,835 males) were surveyed and asked whether they had drunk alcohol for the first time (other than a few sips) before age 13. A statistically significant difference between males and females was noted, $\chi^2(1, N = 942) = 7.87, p < .05$. Males ($n = 530$, 28.9%) were more likely than females ($n = 412$, 24.1%) to have drunk alcohol for the first time prior to age 13. Recall that statistical significance is merely a statement of probability. The result for this comparison is likely occurring outside the realm of chance. However, you will also recall that statistical significance is far more likely when the sample size is large, as is the case with this national sample of 3,668 ninth-grade youth. By examining the effect size, in this case a phi coefficient (ϕ), we can ascertain the meaningfulness of this effect. A phi coefficient is a type of correlation and can therefore be evaluated based on standards advanced by Jacob Cohen (1988). Cohen advanced the following guidelines for interpreting coefficients: .10 = small, .30 = medium, and .50 = large. For the comparison of males and females having their first drink prior to age 13, $\phi = .046$, a rather negligible effect. Although a statically significant effect is evident, the magnitude of the effect is not that meaningful. Focusing attention on the likelihood of males being more at risk than females for abusing alcohol is not advisable. The significance of this result is likely more a reflection of the large sample size than an actual effect.

Interpreting Statistical Tests and Assessing Practical Significance

Numerous types of statistical tests exist, but the reporting and interpretation of a statistical test is rather uniform. Balkin and Sheperis (2009) indicated the following:

> The reporting of statistical results follow this format: a Roman or Greek letter, followed by a number or pair of numbers in parenthesis, followed by a value, and concluded by a comparison to p [e.g., $F(3, 96) = 13.81, p < .001$]. While the presented numbers may look complex, they are really a summary statement of the research results. The Roman or Greek letter represents the type of test. In this case an F indicates that an [analysis of variance] was performed. The number(s) in parenthesis identifies degrees of freedom (i.e., an estimate of parameters or variability within a data set). The value after the equal sign is based on a calculation that incorporates changes in the dependent variable and error in measurement. The p-value indicates whether or not the result is statistically significant. (pp. 1–2)

Along with the report of a statistical test should be some evaluation of practical significance noted by the effect size. Most counseling journals require the reporting of the effect size. The effect size is typically reported in standard deviations units (e.g., Cohen's d), variance accounted for (e.g., R^2, ω^2, η^2, λ), or various correlation coefficients (e.g., r, ϕ), and an interpretation is generally provided indicating a small, moderate, or large effect using guidelines published by Cohen (1988, 1992). Hence, when evaluating counseling research, being aware of statistical significance, practical significance, and the influence of sample size is essential.

Chapter Summary

Major concepts in evaluating quantitative research were covered in this chapter. Constructs, as well as phenomena that are directly observable (e.g., sex, hair color, age), may be used as variables in a study. Variables may be discrete or continuous, depending on whether they are nominal, ordinal, interval, or ratio. Discrete variables, such as those variables measured on a nominal scale (e.g., sex, ethnicity), may be used for reporting frequencies and percentages, whereas continuous variables, such as interval or ratio variables (e.g., self-esteem, depression, coping), may often be scores or measures on which mathematical operations can be performed. Essential to measuring constructs and utilizing such measures in research is the validity of a measure, which is demonstrated through various types of evidence, both theoretical and quantitative.

Quantitative research is often associated with producing results generalizable to a target population. Parametric statistics are often utilized, but such tests should utilize populations that are based on a normal distribution. The normal curve enables easier understanding of interpreting scores for individuals, identifying relationships among variables, and distinguishing differences between groups.

Research questions may be addressed through hypothesis testing. Although hypothesis testing culminates in a statistical test, the generalizability of the results relies on a solid foundation of participants who are representative of a target population, the validity of the measures used in the study, and the design of the study. Detecting a statistically significant effect depends on the amount of error the researcher chooses for the study, the magnitude of the effect found in the study, and the sample size. Results of statistical tests are easily influenced by sample size, making the reporting and evaluation of practical significance (e.g., effect size) an essential element of understanding and evaluating quantitative research.

Suggested Activities

I. Read the following article:

Balkin, R. S., & Sheperis, D. S. (2009). *A primer in evaluating quantitative research for counseling professionals* (ACAPCD-26). Retrieved from https://www.counseling.org/resources/library/ACA%20Digests/ACAPCD-26.pdf

Select a quantitative research article from a counseling journal and see whether you can use the information in Balkin and Sheperis (2009) (a) to identify whether a statistically significant relationship was present, (b) to identify whether effect size is mentioned, and (c) to ascertain the importance of the findings.

II. Review the following articles:

Trusty, J. (2011). Quantitative articles: Developing studies for publication in counseling journals. *Journal of Counseling & Development, 89,* 261–267. doi:10.1002/j.1556-6678.2011.tb00087.x

Trusty, J., Thompson, B., & Petrocelli, J. V. (2004). Practical guide for reporting effect size in quantitative research in the *Journal of Counseling & Development*. *Journal of Counseling & Development, 82*, 107–110.

1. How is effect size reported?
2. Why is the reporting of effect size important to counseling research?

References

American Educational Research Association, American Psychological Association, & National Council on Measurement in Education. (2014). *Standards for educational and psychological testing*. Washington, DC: Author.

Balkin, R. S. (2014). *The Crisis Stabilization Scale manual and sampler set*. Menlo Park, CA: Mind Garden.

Balkin, R. S., Freeman, S. J., & Lyman, S. R. (2009). Forgiveness, reconciliation, and mechila: Integrating the Jewish concept of forgiveness into clinical practice. *Counseling and Values, 53*, 153–160. doi:10.1002/j.2161-007X.2009.tb00121.x

Balkin, R. S., Harris, N., Freeman, S. J., & Huntington, S. (2014). The Forgiveness Reconciliation Inventory: An instrument to process through issues of forgiveness and conflict. *Measurement and Evaluation in Counseling and Development, 47*, 3–13. doi:10.1177/0748175613497037

Balkin, R. S., & Sheperis, D. S. (2009). *A primer in evaluating quantitative research for counseling professionals* (ACAPCD-26). Retrieved from https://www.counseling.org/resources/library/ACA%20Digests/ACAPCD-26.pdf

Beck, A. T., Steer, R. A., & Brown, G. K. (1996). *BDI-II manual.* San Antonio, TX: Psychological Corporation.

Centers for Disease Control and Prevention. (2011). *High school YRBS*. Retrieved from https://nccd.cdc.gov/youthonline/App/Default.aspx

Cohen, J. (1988). *Statistical power analysis for the behavioral sciences* (2nd ed.). New York, NY: Psychological Press.

Cohen, J. (1992). A power primer. *Psychological Bulletin, 112*, 155–159.

Roid, G. H. (2003). *Stanford-Binet Intelligence Scales: Examiner's manual* (5th ed.). Itasca, IL: Riverside Publishing Company.

Trusty, J. (2011). Quantitative articles: Developing studies for publication in counseling journals. *Journal of Counseling & Development, 89,* 261–267. doi:10.1002/j.1556-6678.2011.tb00087.x

Trusty, J., Thompson, B., & Petrocelli, J. V. (2004). Practical guide for reporting effect size in quantitative research in the *Journal of Counseling & Development. Journal of Counseling & Development, 82,* 107–110.

Wechsler, D. (2008). *Wechsler Adult Intelligence Scale–Fourth Edition.* San Antonio, TX: Pearson.

Examining Relationships

Overview

This chapter focuses on correlational designs, including the type of research questions addressed in correlational research and the tools used to evaluate data using correlational analyses. Basic and advanced procedures are discussed, along with the type of analysis conducted, how it works, and what is commonly reported. The importance of evaluating statistical and practical significance is highlighted, along with important considerations when designing correlational research.

Why Conduct Correlational Research?

Correlational research is conducted when a researcher is interested in examining the relationship between or among a set of variables. As described in Chapter 4, correlational designs are the most popular types of quantitative research published in counseling journals. Different types of analytical strategies enable the researcher to use both discrete and continuous variables. Hence, correlational research is an adaptable strategy that may be used with a variety of measures and variables, from score scales to demographic labels. In a general sense correlational research is a building block on which many other research designs are based.

Elements of Correlational Research

Recall from Chapter 4 that true experimental designs include a manipulated independent variable and a dependent variable. In such a case, the dependent variable is continuous—that is, a measure of some type of phenomenon; the independent variable is discrete—that is, a nominal variable such as assignment to a group. Correlational research, in contrast, does not manipulate an independent variable and in most cases uses continuous variables. We discuss exceptions to this general rule later in the chapter.

Because the nature of correlational research differs from that of experimental research, given that no manipulation or comparison or treatment effect is assessed, different terms are used to describe the nature of the relationship between or among variables. *Criterion variables* take the place of the dependent variable(s) and represent what is being predicted. *Predictor variables* take the place of the independent variable(s) and refer to phenomena that relate to or predict the criterion variable. For example, when Balkin and Roland (2007) evaluated the relationship between therapeutic goal attainment and psychiatric symptoms for adolescents in crisis, two measures were used. Essentially, Balkin and Roland asked, "What is the extent of the relationship between therapeutic goal attainment and psychiatric symptoms for adolescents in crisis?" The researchers were attempting to investigate whether increases in therapeutic goal attainment would relate to decreases in symptom severity. The Clinician Problem Scale–Revised (Behavioral Health Outcome Systems, 2001) was a measure of symptom severity and represented the criterion variable. The Goal Attainment Scale of Stabilization (Balkin, 2014) had three subscales (problem identification, processing coping skills, and commitment to follow-up); these measures were the predictor variables. Notice that each of the measures used scores (i.e., continuous variables) to measure the extent of the relationship.

Most correlational research is based on an assumption of linearity—that there is essentially a direct relationship between the predictor variable(s) and the criterion variable(s). For example, we might hypothesize a linear relationship between disordered eating and depression. Individuals who show increases in eating disturbance will likely show increases in depression. However, not all relationships in counseling research are linear. There could be a curvilinear relationship between marital satisfaction and number of years married. In this hypothesis, couples who are newly married may have a high degree of marital satisfaction. As time goes on, they may experience a lull in marital satisfaction, but as even more time passes, the lull may dissipate, leading to a higher degree of marital satisfaction once again. Thus, the relationship between years married and marital satisfaction would be curvilinear (see Figure 6.1). In the following sections we highlight designs used in examining linear relationships in counseling research.

Correlational Analyses

Correlational designs may be univariate or multivariate in nature. A univariate design occurs when there is a single criterion variable and one or more predictor variables. The Balkin and Roland (2007) study referenced previously is an example of univariate correlational research, as there was only one criterion variable: psychiatric symptoms as measured by the Clinician Problem Scale–Revised. Pearson's *r*, simple regression, and multiple regression are examples of univariate correlational research.

Pearson's *r*

Pearson's *r*, also known as the Pearson product–moment correlation coefficient, was discussed in Chapter 5 and is an expression of a linear relationship between two variables. Table 5.1 shows that in a study by Balkin, Harris, Freeman, and Huntington (2014), the ex-

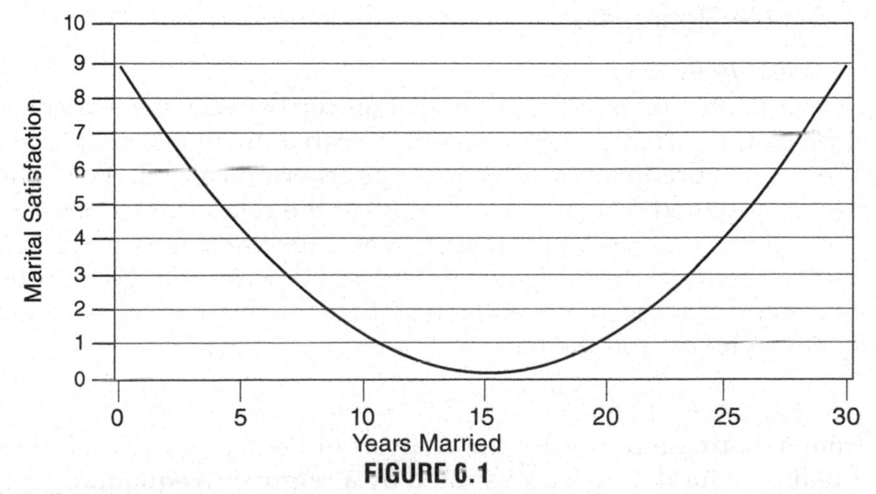

FIGURE 6.1
Nonlinear Relationship Between Marital Satisfaction and Years Married

tent to which a perpetrator expressed remorse or changed behavior was related to the extent to which the person harmed would seek to reconcile the relationship or remove himself or herself from the relationship ($r = .68$, $p < .001$). This is a rather strong correlation and denotes a linear relationship between the expression of remorse or change from the perpetrator and the decision to renegotiate the relationship from the victim. When correlation coefficients are presented in research, they are often accompanied by p values, which indicate whether the correlations are statistically significant. In this case the correlation is statistically significant.

Regression Procedures

Whereas Pearson's r is an exploratory statistic used to describe the linear relationship between two variables, regression includes procedures that involve examining a linear relationship between variables or sets of variables to establish a prediction model. In other words, values of a predictor variable or set of predictors are used to predict values of a criterion variable. Dimitrov (2009) explained, "Predictive research is on practical applications, not on causal explanations" (p. 144). Cause and effect are not established through correlational research. In counseling research, therefore, regression procedures are used to demonstrate theoretical relationships between or among values and can be helpful for understanding processes and applications related to the counseling profession.

Simple Regression

What Is It?

Simple regression tests the linear relationship between two variables: a predictor variable and a criterion variable. In simple regression there is one predictor variable and one criterion variable. As in the aforementioned example, we could test the relationship between the extent to which an individual who caused harm is perceived by the victim to have demonstrated remorse or change and the likelihood that the victim will renegotiate the relationship with the person who caused the harm.

How Does It Work?

Simple regression extends the analysis of Pearson's r to include a prediction model as demonstrated by a regression equation, $\hat{Y} = a + bX$, where $\hat{Y}$ represents the criterion variable being predicted, a represents a constant when the predictor (X) = 0, and b represents the beta weight or slope of the regression line (the amount of change in $\hat{Y}$ for each unit of change in X). Once again using the example from Balkin et al. (2014), we can examine the relationship between an offender's tendency to express remorse or change behavior (change) and the likelihood that the victim will choose to reconcile or not reconcile with the offender (outcome). To the extent that the victim feels that the perpetrator has not expressed intent to change or remorse, there is an increased likelihood that the victim will choose not to reconcile with the person who caused the harm. The regression equation is indicated by $\hat{Y} = 4.25 + .73X$. Scores on each of the scales (Change and Outcome) range from 6 to 30. Lower scores for change indicate that the victim perceives that the perpetrator has changed or expressed remorse, and higher scores represent a perceived lack of change or remorse; lower scores for outcome indicate that the victim is more likely to renegotiate a relationship with the person who caused the harm, and higher scores represent less of a likelihood. So a score of 6 on change (X), indicating that the victim perceives that the perpetrator has changed, leads to a predicted score of 8.63 on outcome, indicating a higher likelihood of renegotiating a relationship with the person who caused harm. For the regression equation, $\hat{Y} = 4.25 + .73X$, or $8.63 = 4.25 + .73(6)$. The closer the outcome score is to 30, the less likelihood there is of renegotiating the relationship. So a score of 25 on change, indicating that the victim perceives less change or remorse from the perpetrator, leads to the following predicted score: $22.5 = 4.25 + .73(25)$, or less likelihood of renegotiating the relationship.

What Gets Reported?

When simple regressions are reported in counseling research, we typically see the regression equation, often presented in a table. One key aspect of the regression equation is the slope (b), which in simple regression is also Pearson's r. Along with the regression equation are descriptive statistics (i.e., mean, standard deviation, Pearson's r) for each variable. In regression the F test is used to determine the significance of the relationship between the predictor and criterion variables. R^2 is presented to identify the amount of variance accounted for in the model and serves as a measure of effect size. R^2 ranges from 0 to 1. The closer the value is to 1, the more change in the predictor variable contributes to change in the criterion variable. In simple regression, R^2 is simply the squared value of Pearson's r. However, as more predictors are added to the regression (see "Multiple Regression"), R^2 becomes more complex.

Jacob Cohen (1988), a pioneer in reporting statistical power and effect size, categorized effect sizes into small, medium, and large effects. Cohen noted that these estimates were guidelines, not absolute principles. The importance of effect size is based on context as well as the magnitude of the value. Nevertheless, Cohen's guidelines for reporting R^2 are as follows:

Small: .02
Medium: .13
Large: .26

This means that large effects in multiple regression account for 26% of the variance in a model—more than one quarter of the variance. A large effect size may not seem that great. In our example of the relationship between change and outcome in Balkin et al.'s (2014) forgiveness research, the R^2 value was .465, accounting for nearly 47% of the variance in the model. This also means that about 53% of the variance in outcome is unaccounted for—we do not know what factors contribute to that. So when an effect size is considered large at 26%, 74% of the variance is not known. In other words, there is often far more that we do not understand about a phenomenon than we do understand.

Multiple Regression

What Is It?

Multiple regression is an extension of simple regression. Multiple regression is similar to simple regression in that they are both univariate procedures; that is, there is only one criterion variable. In multiple regression there are two or more predictor variables. Researchers use multiple regression to examine the linear relationship between a set of predictor variables and a criterion variable. For example, Davis, Balkin, and Juhnke (2014) examined the linear relationship between Quality of Relationships and Friendship (two scales on the Juhnke-Balkin Life Balance Inventory [JBLI]) and Interpersonal Relations (a scale on the Outcome Questionnaire–45 [OQ-45]). Quality of Relationships and Friendship were the predictor variables; Interpersonal Relations was the criterion variable.

How Does It Work?

Multiple regression extends the analysis of simple regression to include a model with multiple predictor variables demonstrated by a regression equation: $\hat{Y} = a + b_1X_1 + b_2X_2 \ldots$. In this case, there are multiple beta weights consistent with the number of predictor variables that are placed into the regression equation. The regression equation reported by Davis et al. (2014) was indicated by $\hat{Y} = 46.72 - .32X - .36X$.

Did you notice that the regression equation in this example appears slightly different from previous regression equations we have discussed? The beta weights are subtracted from the constant instead of added. The reason for this is that there is a negative relationship between the JBLI scales and the OQ-45 scale. Scales on the OQ-45 measure psychological distress. So higher values on Interpersonal Relations (the criterion variable) indicate more distress. However, on the JBLI higher scores indicate better life balance, so higher scores on the Friendship and Quality of Relationships scales have a linear relationship to lower levels of distress on Interpersonal Relations.

Because of the presence of additional predictor variables in multiple regression, counseling researchers need to be concerned with *multicollinearity*—high correlations between or among predictor variables. In other words, when there are two or more predictors and those predictors are highly correlated (e.g., .80 or above), the relationship between the predictors and the criterion variable is confounded, because the relationship between one of the predictors will be underestimated. A simple heuristic example involves college freshman grade point average and scores on aptitude tests, such as the ACT and SAT. If both SAT and ACT scores were used as predictors of grade point average, one of the predictors would be underestimated, because they are essentially measuring the same thing—aptitude. Because they measure the same construct, scores on the SAT and ACT would be highly correlated. Only one predictor would show a unique relationship with grade point average. The other predictor would be redundant. Although this seems somewhat confusing in the way the math works, the conceptual understanding is that researchers should avoid using predictors that are overly redundant or that measure the same construct. In other words, if a researcher wanted to evaluate the relationship between depression and disordered eating, he or she should use only one measure of depression, not multiple measures. Hence, counseling researchers need to be thoughtful about the predictors they use in a study to make sure that (a) the predictors make sense theoretically and (b) the predictors are not redundant.

What Gets Reported?

Recall that Davis et al. (2014) had Quality of Relationships and Friendship (the two JBLI scales) as predictor variables and Interpersonal Relations (a scale on the OQ-45) as the criterion variable. The purpose of this aspect of the study was to evaluate the extent of the relationship between Quality of Relationships and Friendship and the criterion variable, Interpersonal Relations.

In multiple regression there are two levels of reporting: (a) evaluation of the model and, if the model was statistically significant, (b) evaluation of the relationship of each predictor variable to the criterion variable. At each level statistical significance and practical significance (i.e., effect size) are reported. Statistical significance for the model is identified by an F statistic and p value; practical significance is identified by R^2, the amount of variance accounted for in the model.

> Statistically significant relationships were detected between the two JBLI scales, $F(2, 259) = 133.28, p \leq .001$, and the OQ-45.2 Interpersonal Relations scale. A large effect size was noted with approximately 51% of the variance accounted for in the model, $R^2 = .510$. Quality of Relationships and Friendship were significant predictors of Interpersonal Relations. (Davis et al., 2014, p. 190)

Notice that not only was the model statistically significant, but the effect size, according to Cohen's (1988) guidelines, was quite large. When a model is statistically significant, the contribution of each predictor variable is evaluated.

When the contribution of each predictor variable is assessed, researchers once again report both statistical significance and practical significance. Just because the model is significant does not mean that each predictor variable in the model is making a contribution. One possibility is that one of the predictors makes a significant contribution, but other predictor variables in the model do not. By examining the statistical and practical significance of each predictor variable, consumers of research can determine which variables are the most important. For example, Davis et al. (2014) reported that both Quality of Relationships and Friendship were significant predictors of Interpersonal Relations. Quality of Relationships uniquely accounted for 17% of the variance in the model; Friendship uniquely accounted for 21% of the variance in the model. The *unique amount of variance accounted for* in the model refers to variance that is not shared by either of the predictor variables; in this example, it is contributions to Interpersonal Relations that do not overlap with other predictor variables (see Figure 6.2). The unique contributions from each predictor variable are often

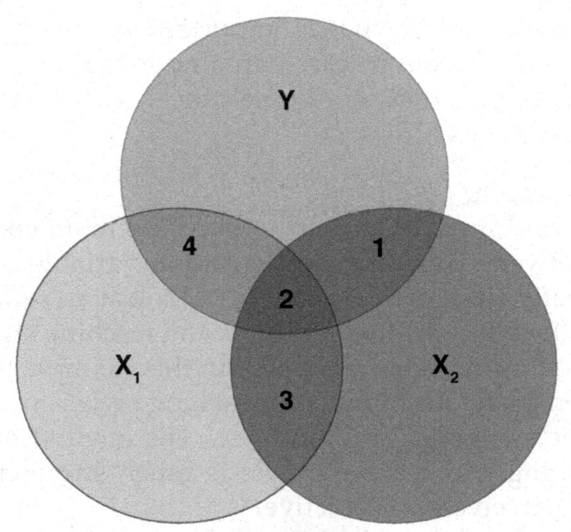

FIGURE 6.2
Shared and Unique Variance

Note. Y represents the criterion variable, in this case interpersonal relations. X_1 and X_2 represent the predictor variables, quality of relationships and friendship, respectively. Sections 1 and 4 represent unique variance quality of relationships and friendship contributions to interpersonal relations. Section 2 represents shared variance with interpersonal relations; Section 3 represents shared variance between quality of relationships and friendship but not with interpersonal relations. Predictor variables that bring in larger amounts of variance to the model tend to be more useful. Because sample size can influence statistical significance, a predictor variable could be found to have a statistically significant relationship with the criterion variable but not contribute much unique variance. In such cases, that predictor may not be as useful to the model.

reported as *structure coefficients* (*rs*) or *squared semipartial correlation coefficients* (sr^2). Whereas structure coefficients provide the unique amount of variance from what is predicted, squared semipartial correlation coefficients also consider error in the model and therefore are smaller than structure coefficients. More important is to understand that each of these terms represents an effect size (i.e., practical significance) of each predictor variable.

Other Procedures in Correlational Research

A few correlational strategies are commonly used in counseling research and may be helpful to understand at a conceptual level. Beyond what we discuss here are correlational designs that can be quite complex. A multivariate design includes two or more predictors and two or more criterion variables. Multivariate analyses include canonical correlation, path analysis, and structural equation modeling. In these cases, the complex relationships among variables are explored. What is important, however, is that the concepts of correlational research are understood. Here are some additional examples that will be helpful in understanding most correlational designs.

Moderation and Mediation

Moderation and mediation help to evaluate more complex relationships between predictor and criterion variables. *Moderation* essentially refers to an interaction. Let's look at an example of the relationship between professor ratings and teaching style (ranging from rigid to flexible; see Figure 6.3). In this example the relationship between professor rating and teaching style is moderated by the professor's physical attractiveness. The relationship between professor rating and teaching style is much stronger when the professor is perceived as attractive.

In *mediation,* another variable is used to explain the relationship between a predictor variable and criterion variable. In other words, the relationship between a predictor variable and a criterion variable

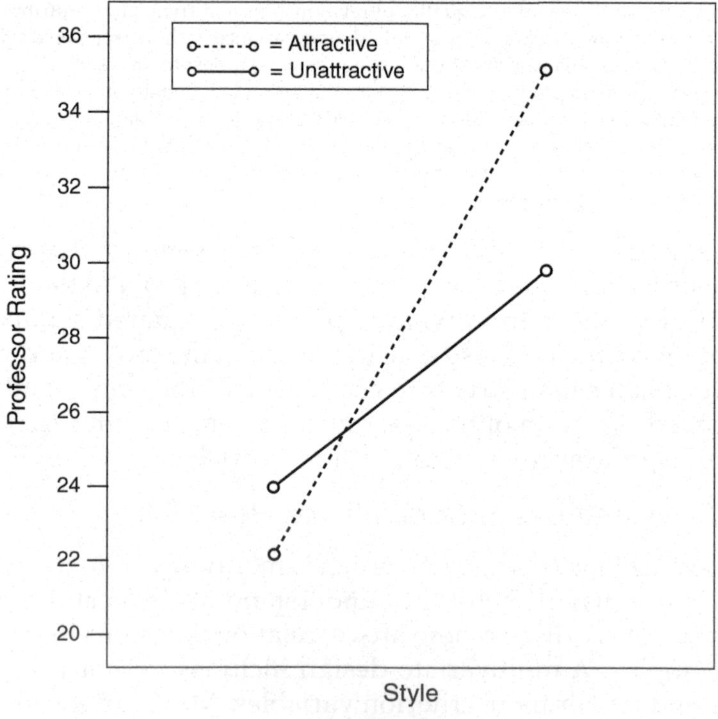

FIGURE 6.3
Plot of Moderation in Regression

is weakened when a third variable is controlled for in the model. Balkin, Perepiczka, Sowell, Cumi, and Gnilka (2016) examined the relationship between individuals' perceptions of someone who had harmed them and the extent to which they would renegotiate a relationship with the offender. The relationship between perceptions of the offender and renegotiating the relationship was mediated by the extent to which the offender expressed remorse or changed behavior (see Figure 6.4). Thus, when remorse or change in the offender was controlled (i.e., perceived as equal for all participants), the relationship between the individuals' perceptions of the offender and renegotiating the relationship was weakened. In other words, when remorse or change was introduced into the model, the relationship between clients' exploration of perceptions related to the perpetrator and the renegotiation of the relationship was reduced. Why? Because the extent to which an offender expresses remorse or changes behavior affects the relationship between individuals' perceptions of the offender and renegotiating the relationship.

Chi-Square Test for Association

When two variables are categorical, researchers may be interested in whether there is a relationship between them; to find out, they conduct a *chi-square test for association.* For example, consider the relationship between receiving community-based interventions and recidivism (Lancaster, Balkin, Garcia, & Valarezo, 2011). Adjudicated youth were categorized into two groups: those who received

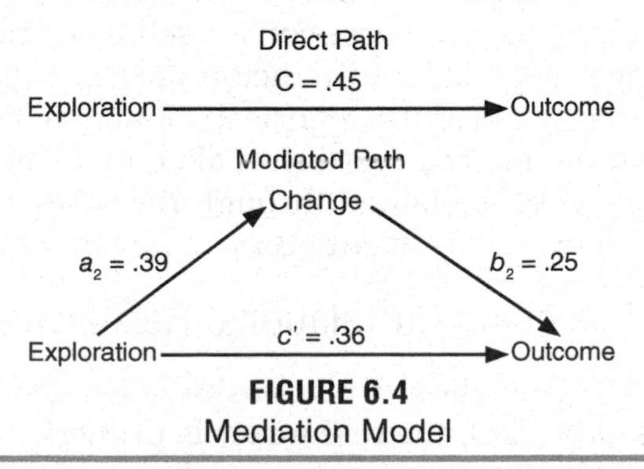

FIGURE 6.4
Mediation Model

Note. Adapted from "The Forgiveness Reconciliation Model: An Empirically Supported Process for Humanistic Counseling," by R. S. Balkin, M. Perepiczka, S. M. Sowell, K. Cumi, and P. B. Gnilka, 2016, *Journal of Humanistic Counseling, 55*, p. 61. Exploration is the predictor variable; outcome is the criterion variable; change is a mediator. C = total effect of independent variable on dependent variable; *a* = independent variable to mediator; *b* = mediator on dependent variable; *c'* = direct effect of independent variable on dependent variable; $a \times b$ = indirect effect of independent variable on dependent variable through mediator.

community-based intervention services and those who did not. In addition, the youth were identified as those who reoffended within a 2-year time period and those who did not reoffend. Hence, all variables were categorical. A statistically significant effect was noted in recidivism rates across the treatment and control groups indicative of a small to moderate effect size, $\chi^2(5, N = 240) = 14.64$, $p = .012$, $\phi = .25$. Hence, there was a relationship between recidivism and receiving community-based treatment. Some key points to identify in the results should be highlighted. In a study such as this, the null hypothesis would indicate that there is no relationship between treatment intervention and recidivism. The test of statistical significance was a chi-square test; the p value was indeed less than .05 (reported at .012), indicating that there was less than a 5% of chance that the results were due to Type I error. In addition, the effect size was noted by a phi coefficient (ϕ). Phi coefficients for effect size are interpreted similarly to Pearson's r and are used to denote the magnitude of the relationship between categorical variables. In general, correlation coefficients at or below .10 are considered low, those at .30 are considered moderate, and those at or greater than .50 are considered large. In this case, the coefficient of .25 denotes a small to moderate relationship (Cohen, 1988).

Logistic Regression

Often counseling researchers are interested in categorical outcomes: Did the client relapse or not? Did the student score proficient or not? In these cases, the dependent variable is *dichotomous* (i.e., there are only two options). Logistic regression is used when the dependent variable is dichotomous and the predictors are generally continuous (they can be dummy coded if categorical). Similar to the chi-square test for association, logistic regression also uses a chi-square (χ^2) and effect size can be explained through the interpretation of an *odds ratio*—the odds of one event occurring over another.

Designing Correlational Research

Two key components should be considered when designing a correlational study. First, the researcher is primarily interested in the relationships between or among variables. Second, and noting exceptions of chi-square and logistic regression, the variables in the study are generally continuous. Categorical variables can be used when they are dummy coded, but because correlational research in the counseling field is often concerned with measuring constructs, variables tend to be continuous.

One distinct advantage of correlational research is that information can be collected all at once. Although multiple instruments may be used to collect data, data are often collected one time. The lack of repeated measures enables researchers to keep data anonymous, which often helps in the institutional review board process.

The criterion variable represents the phenomenon of interest the researcher wishes to predict or examine how it is influenced by the predictors. Predictor variables represent measures that likely influence the criterion variable. Similar to experimental research, correlational research focuses on the relationship or influence a set of variables (predictors) has on another variable or set of variables (criterion). Put another way, criterion variables represent what the researcher determines is likely to be influenced; predictor variables represent what the influential factors might be.

Correlational research follows general rules, and counseling researchers often limit themselves to the exploration of linear relationships. Careful testing of the assumptions that govern correlational designs is important and should not be overlooked or summarily dismissed. Because correlational research is highly dependent on the valid, consistent, and accurate reporting of constructs, measures should be carefully selected. The reliability of scores and the selection and valid administration of instruments should be noted in the Methods section of a study. Reliability estimates from the scores of the normative sample should be evaluated along with reliability estimates from the scores of the sample used in the current study. In this way, readers can note the appropriateness of the measure and the sample considered for investigation.

Most important, when researchers decide to conduct correlational research, they should select their criterion and predictor variables based on theory. A fatal flaw in correlational research is exploring a relationship in which there is no viable connection. Correlations can be spurious—that is, highly related but not theoretically linked. Vigen (2015) appropriately identified the fact that correlation is not causation by showing spurious correlations between theoretically irrelevant variables, such as marriage rates in Kentucky and people who drowned falling out of a fishing boat ($r = .95$). Hence, counseling researchers must first and foremost be well versed in the constructs of interest. In other words, they should be knowledgeable about the literature so that the connections made between or among variables make sense theoretically and statistically. Simply put, correlational research without a strong theoretical connection does not make a viable contribution to the literature.

Chapter Summary

When presenting results of correlational research, the statistical and practical significance of both the model and, if significant, each predictor variable should be reported. Such information provides an explanation of whether a meaningful prediction or relationship is present and what variables might be contributing to that relationship.

Model tests for simple and multiple regression include the *F* test and, in the case of multiple regression, the *t* test for evaluating the statistical significance of each predictor variable. An evaluation of practical significance in simple and multiple regression includes the calculation of R^2 to address the amount of variance accounted for in the model and sr^2 to evaluate the unique contribution of each predictor variable. When researchers evaluate the extent of the relationship between categorical variables, chi-square (χ^2) is used, with the phi coefficient (ϕ) serving as a measure of practical significance. In the case of logistic regression, the odds ratio may be used to evaluate practical significance.

Despite the emphasis on statistical and practical significance, more important is the theoretical relationship when evaluating the association between or among variables. Correlational research is inherently tied to theory. As correlational research does not evaluate causation, a theoretical connection between or among variables lends credibility to the statistical tests associated with this design.

Suggested Activities

I. A number of articles cited in this chapter used correlational designs, including the following:

Balkin, R. S., Harris, N., Freeman, S. J., & Huntington, S. (2014). The Forgiveness Reconciliation Inventory: An instrument to process through issues of forgiveness and conflict. *Measurement and Evaluation in Counseling and Development, 47,* 3–13. doi:10.1177/0748175613497037

Balkin, R. S., Perepiczka, M., Sowell, S. M., Cumi, K., & Gnilka, P. B. (2016). The forgiveness-reconciliation model: An empirically supported process for humanistic counseling. *Journal of Humanistic Counseling, 55,* 55–65. doi:10.1002/johc.12024

Balkin, R. S., & Roland, C. B. (2007). Re-conceptualizing stabilization for counseling adolescents in brief psychiatric hospitalization: A new model. *Journal of Counseling & Development, 85*, 64–72. doi:10.1002/j.1556-6678.2007.tb00445.x

Davis, R. J., Balkin, R. S., & Juhnke, G. A. (2014). Validation of the Juhnke-Balkin Life Balance Inventory. *Measurement and Evaluation in Counseling and Development, 47*, 181–198. doi:10.1177/0748175614531796

Lancaster, C., Balkin, R. S., Garcia, R., & Valarezo, A. (2011). An evidence-based approach to reducing recidivism in court-referred youth. *Journal of Counseling & Development, 89*, 488–492.

Pick one of these articles or find your own and identify the following:

1. Which variables or measures were correlated?
2. How is the illustration of the relationships important to counseling?
3. What is meant by "correlation is not causation"? Apply this axiom to the findings in the research.

References

Balkin, R. S. (2014). *The Crisis Stabilization Scale manual and sampler set*. Menlo Park, CA: Mind Garden.

Balkin, R. S., Harris, N., Freeman, S. J., & Huntington, S. (2014). The Forgiveness Reconciliation Inventory: An instrument to process through issues of forgiveness and conflict. *Measurement and Evaluation in Counseling and Development, 47*, 3–13. doi:10.1177/0748175613497037

Balkin, R. S., Perepiczka, M., Sowell, S. M., Cumi, K., & Gnilka, P. B. (2016). The forgiveness-reconciliation model: An empirically supported process for humanistic counseling. *Journal of Humanistic Counseling, 55*, 55–65. doi:10.1002/johc.12024

Balkin, R. S., & Roland, C. B. (2007). Re-conceptualizing stabilization for counseling adolescents in brief psychiatric hospitalization: A new model. *Journal of Counseling & Development, 85*, 64–72. doi:10.1002/j.1556-6678.2007.tb00445.x

Behavioral Health Outcome Systems. (2001). *Clinician ratings of patient symptoms and role functioning* [Internal report]. New York: Author.

Cohen, J. (1988). *Statistical power analysis for the behavioral sciences* (2nd ed.). New York, NY: Psychology Press.

Davis, R. J., Balkin, R. S., & Juhnke, G. A. (2014). Validation of the Juhnke-Balkin Life Balance Inventory. *Measurement and Evaluation in Counseling and Development, 47*, 181–198. doi:10.1177/0748175614531796

Dimitrov, D. M. (2009). *Quantitative research in education: Intermediate and advanced methods.* New York, NY: Whittier.

Lancaster, C., Balkin, R. S., Garcia, R., & Valarezo, A. (2011). An evidence-based approach to reducing recidivism in court-referred youth. *Journal of Counseling & Development, 89*, 488–492. doi:10.1002/j.1556-6676.2011.tb02846.x

Vigen, T. (2015). *Spurious correlations: Correlation does not equal causation.* New York, NY: Hachette.

Examining Differences Between Groups

Overview

This chapter focuses on examining differences between groups, also referred to as *between-groups designs.* Between-groups designs are often used either to identify how a treatment or intervention differs between groups, such as those who receive an intervention and those who do not, or to describe how groups vary across a particular domain or construct, such as gender differences when processing issues of forgiveness. Experimental design is highlighted in this chapter. The design of a study is the foundation for establishing the extent of differences that may or may not exist between groups. Particular attention is paid to the procedures counseling researchers use to establish that the differences found between groups are valid. Basic and advanced procedures are discussed, along with the type of analysis conducted, how it works, and what is commonly reported. The importance of evaluating statistical and practical significance is highlighted, along with important considerations when designing between-groups studies.

Why Conduct Between-Groups Analyses?

Between-groups analyses are conducted when a researcher is interested in examining or identifying differences between or among groups. Between-groups analyses include one or more independent variables (IVs) and a single dependent variable (DV) for univariate analysis, known as an *analysis of variance,* or two or more DVs for multivariate analysis, known as a *multivariate analysis of variance.*

Between-groups analyses are a special case of regression. Most of the analyses discussed in this chapter are special cases of correlational research. When researchers inquire about whether there are differences between groups, they are essentially suggesting a relationship between the IV and the DV. Let's take a look at a heuristic example to make this clearer.

A Heuristic Example

A researcher is interested in examining pilot data for a research study to determine whether there are differences between males and females in scores on the Alcohol Use Disorders Identification Test (AUDIT; Babor, Higgins-Biddle, Saunders, & Monteiro, 2001). As this is only a pilot study (and a heuristic example), we will focus on the data of 12 individuals—six males and six females who were court ordered to an alcohol education class because of an arrest for driving under the influence. Scores for males and females on the AUDIT are in Table 7.1.

There are two primary ways to address this research question:

1. What is the extent of the relationship between sex (i.e., male or female) and AUDIT score for participants in an alcohol education class?
2. What is the extent of the differences in AUDIT scores between males and females in an alcohol education class?

TABLE 7.1
AUDIT Scores for Males and Females

Participant	AUDIT Score
Male	20
Male	18
Male	21
Male	18
Male	23
Male	20
Female	18
Female	16
Female	20
Female	19
Female	21
Female	20

Note. AUDIT = Alcohol Use Disorders Identification Test.

Let's look more closely at the analytical strategies for answering each of these research questions.

The first research question evaluates the relationship between the predictor variable (sex) and the criterion variable (AUDIT score) and would be answered using simple regression by dummy coding the sex variable so that males are labeled with a 0 and females are labeled with a 1. When these scores are run with regression, we see that there is no significant relationship between sex and AUDIT scores, $F(1, 10) = 0.882$, $p = .370$, $R^2 = .081$.

The second research question evaluates differences in AUDIT scores (the DV) between males and females (the IV). When the differences between mean scores of males and females are evaluated using analysis of variance, we see that there is no significant difference in AUDIT scores between males and females, $F(1, 10) = 0.882$, $p = .370$, $\eta^2 = .081$.

So you probably notice that with the exception of the label for effect size, these scores are exactly the same. Why? Because the math is the same. When researchers are exploring differences between groups, they are examining a special case of relationships between or among variables. This can have important considerations in counseling research, especially in multicultural counseling research. For example, when school districts evaluate test scores based on students' ethnicity, the same math used to explore these differences would be used to examine whether ethnicity is a predictor of achievement test scores. The nature and underlying philosophy of such studies is discriminatory and is known as *construct-irrelevant variance*, the examination of a construct with variables that are not theoretically associated with the construct (American Educational Research Association, American Psychological Association, & National Council on Measurement in Education, 2014). In this case, there is no theoretical connection between student ethnicity and achievement, yet school districts are very focused on differences in standardized achievement test scores based on ethnicity.

Elements of Between-Groups Analyses

In order to understand experimental design, and more specifically between-groups analyses, researchers should consider the variables included in such studies and experimental validity, or the extent to which influences that affect a study limit generalizability. In addition to focusing on these concepts, in this chapter we address models of experimental design. The models, along with the nature of the variables, experimental validity, random assignment, and statistical control, form the blueprint of an experimental design and play an important role in the generalizability of results. Essential to understanding between-groups analyses is the nature of the variables included in the design. Identifying the IVs and DVs of a study is confusing to most graduate students in counseling. As both IVs and DVs are described here, be attentive to the descriptors used for each. Briefly, the IV is a discrete variable, categorical in nature. The IV defines the group(s) being studied. The DV is typically a continuous variable, usually some type of measure.

IVs

Recall from Chapter 4 that IVs are used in both experimental (i.e., true experimental, quasi-experimental) research and nonexperimental, explanatory research. True experimental designs include a manipulated IV and random assignment. In quasi-experimental research, the IV is manipulated, but there is no random assignment. In explanatory, nonexperimental research, such as studies in which comparisons by sex or ethnicity are made, groups are compared, but there is no manipulation of an IV. In such cases manipulating the IV is not possible, as participants cannot be randomly assigned to a group.

Hence, some IVs are manipulated and randomly assigned, as in a true experimental design; some IVs are manipulated but not randomly assigned, as in a quasi-experimental design. For example, if a researcher wanted to evaluate differences between treatment and control groups, in which some individuals receive counseling services and others are on a waitlist, the IV would be *group* or *condition* and would have two levels: treatment and control. Often in counseling research, researchers are interested in comparing demographic factors or groups that are intact rather than randomly assigned. For example, many measures compare scores from clinical and nonclinical populations. Davis, Balkin, and Juhnke (2014) recruited participants receiving counseling services and professionals and community members not receiving counseling services to develop and validate the Juhnke-Balkin Life Balance Inventory (JBLI). Because participants could not be randomly assigned to receive counseling services, as individuals who did not desire counseling services could never be assigned to receive counseling, this was an explanatory, nonexperimental design. In this case the IV was *group* or *condition* and had two levels: receiving counseling services and not receiving counseling services. An IV can have more than two levels that may or may not be randomly assigned. For example, treatment modality can have four levels (e.g., individual counseling, group counseling, individual and group counseling, no counseling) that may or may not be randomly assigned, or ethnicity can have many levels (e.g., White, African American/Black, Asian, Latino[a], Native American, biracial, multiracial) that are not randomly assigned. The concept of levels within an IV can be confusing. One IV (e.g., treatment condition, sex, ethnicity) will have two or more levels. A common mistake among beginning researchers is that they think they have two or more IVs when in fact they have levels within one IV. Keep in mind that *levels* refers to groups or conditions within a single IV.

DVs

In experimental design, the DV represents a measure of outcome variable. In counseling research DVs are often continuous variables that measure some psychological construct. For example, Davis et al. (2014) evaluated differences between clinical (i.e., adult participants who were currently in counseling) and nonclinical (i.e., adult participants not currently in counseling) participants with respect to their scores on the JBLI. Each of the subscale scores on the JBLI represented a DV, whereas the group (clinical or nonclinical) represented the IV. Notice that the continuous scores, in this case scores on each of the 10 subscales of the JBLI (e.g., Positive Orientation, Global Health, Quality of Relationships), function as DVs.

Although DVs are typically continuous in nature, they do not have to be. Lancaster, Balkin, Garcia, and Valarezo (2011) examined differences in recidivism rates between court-referred adolescents who received counseling through a community-based program (the treatment group) and adjudicated youth who had not received such services (the control group). In this study, the IV was the group designation (treatment vs. control group), and the DV was the time until reoffense (no reoffending in 2 years, reoffended within 3 months, reoffended within 6 months, reoffended within 12 months, reoffended within 18 months, or reoffended within 24 months). Notice that the DV in this case was not an exact number of months (i.e., a continuous variable) but rather was measured using one of six categories. So in this case the DV was a discrete (i.e., categorical) variable like the IV.

If both IVs and DVs can be categorical, how do you determine the difference? Remember that the DV is a measure, outcome, or effect. Such information is often the product of an instrument (e.g., the Forgiveness Reconciliation Inventory [FRI], JBLI) or some type of measured outcome (e.g., how long until an adolescent reoffends, did the client relapse [yes/no]?).

Experimental Validity

With an understanding of the variables involved in experimental and explanatory nonexperimental research, we move on to the concept of *experimental validity,* which focuses on influences within the study (known as *internal experimental validity*) and outside of the study (known as *external experimental validity*). The generalizability of a study—that is, the notion that the findings are applicable to a population of interest—is dependent on experimental validity. Campbell and Stanley (1966) outlined seminal concepts related to experimental validity, and an overview of these concepts follows.

Internal Experimental Validity

Internal experimental validity addresses whether any change in the DV was a result in change in or manipulation of the IV. In the previous example of Lancaster et al. (2011), who compared recidivism rates between adolescents who were court referred to a community-based counseling intervention and adolescents who were not, internal experimental validity addresses whether differences in recidivism rates can be attributed to actual differences between the treatment and control groups. The reason why recidivism rates may differ between treatment and control groups is quite logical. Participants in counseling typically may be less likely to reoffend. Indeed, Lancaster et al. found differences between treatment and control groups with respect to recidivism rates:

> For youth who received counseling services (i.e., treatment group), 60% did not reoffend during the 24-month period when data were gathered. For youth who received counseling services and reoffended, one half of the youth who reoffended (20% of the treatment group) did so within 3 months. Youth who did not reoffend after 3 months were not likely to reoffend within 2 years after completing the program. Only 20% of the treatment group reoffended after 3 months. For the control group, approximately 46% of the youth did not reoffend. For the 54% of the control group youth who did reoffend, approximately 42% of them reoffended within 1 year . . . Adolescents in the treatment group were more likely to avoid reoffending within a 2-year time period or reoffend within 3 months. Adolescents in the control group were more likely to reoffend between 6 months and 24 months. (p. 491)

Taken alone, the group differences could not be used to establish that the treatment and control groups truly differed across recidivism rates. However, later in the chapter we present evidence of internal experimental validity to demonstrate the efficacy of the counseling intervention.

To understand the limitations of making comparisons between groups, Campbell and Stanley (1966) identified threats to internal experimental validity. Addressing each of these threats is critical to providing evidence that differences in scores on the DV truly may be attributed to the IV or the groups being compared.

Maturation refers to change that occurs in participants over time. Such changes could include developmental, emotional, or physiological changes or even fatigue due to participating in the study (LaFountain & Bartos, 2002).

History refers to events outside of the study that can affect participants. The key to understanding history effects is knowing that the results of a study could be invalid if an event occurred outside of the study and affected participants in one group but not the other.

Testing is a common threat when a measure is administered two or more times—known as a *testing effect*. When researchers administer a measure to participants repeatedly, they run the risk of overexposing the participants, which can affect the validity of the administration. Participants can learn to make responses, especially when they become too familiar with the administration of an instrument or implementation of an intervention.

Instrumentation refers to the accuracy, consistency, and utility of an administered measure. When measures lack evidence for valid use for measuring a construct or population, or when scores on measures are inaccurate or inconsistent, the results of a study may be questionable or invalid.

Statistical regression occurs when a measure is administered more than once and the scores on the measure are at the lowest or highest end. Consider for example a study by Lenz, Perepiczka, and Balkin (2013), in which doctoral students in counseling received repeated measures related to their attitude toward statistics. Participants were administered the Attitudes Towards Statistics Scale (Wise, 1985):

> The [Attitudes Towards Statistics Scale] evaluates attitudinal perceptions of engaging with statistics coursework . . . The 29-item instrument with a 5-point Likert-type response design evaluates perceptions ranging from 1 (*strongly disagree*) to 5 (*strongly agree*).

> The [Attitudes Towards Statistics Scale] total score used in this study includes 14 negatively scored items and yields a minimum score of 29 and a maximum score of 145 with higher scores representing more positive attitudes toward statistics and lower scores indicating a more negative outlook. (Lenz et al., 2013, p. 29)

If participants score at the very low end (e.g., around 29), indicating a negative attitude toward statistics, scores may improve more easily; furthermore, scores cannot decrease, creating what is known as a *baseline effect*. However, if students' perceptions of statistics are high at the onset of the study (e.g., scores around 145), it is unlikely that scores will decrease; this is known as a *ceiling effect*.

Selection bias occurs when two or more groups in a study are unequal across the phenomenon of interest or the characteristics of the groups are so vastly different that differences in the DV cannot necessarily be attributed to group differences. Selection bias can be avoided by making sure that the groups are equivalent and that participants have similar characteristics at the onset of the study.

Mortality refers to participants not completing a study. Missing or incomplete data are common in counseling research. In particular, when asked to complete a series of measures with numerous items, participants often leave measures incomplete or skip items. In addition, ethical guidelines indicate that participants have the right to withdraw from a study at any time. When a number of participants withdraw from a study or data are incomplete, counseling researchers should identify whether the data collected and reported truly are representative of the population of interest.

Addressing Threats to Internal Experimental Validity

Experimenter bias occurs when the researcher predisposes participants to an intervention or response. Experimenter bias is likely to occur when researchers implement the intervention in addition to collecting the data and evaluating the results. Counseling researchers should be attentive to treatment fidelity and the ethical implementation of a study.

Random assignment. The concept of random assignment, which was introduced in Chapter 4, has been mentioned repeatedly throughout this chapter. Random assignment is the process of randomly designating individuals to groups. When an experimental study includes random assignment, the study is considered a true experimental design; otherwise, the study is quasi-experimental. The advantage of random assignment is that extraneous variables are theoretically dispersed equally between or among the groups. In other words, characteristics of participants that could affect the study are dispersed equally between or among groups so that they do not affect the results. In their study on students' attitudes toward statistics, Lenz et al. (2013) used random assignment to ensure equivalent treatment and control groups.

However, there are times when participants cannot be randomly designated to groups because the focus of the comparison is not a phenomenon that can be randomly assigned or the groups are intact. Such was the case in Lancaster et al.'s (2011) study of recidivism among adolescents, in which equality of the groups was established through statistical control, not random assignment.

Statistical control. Statistical control occurs through either controlling for inequality between groups at the onset of the study or matching traits of participants between groups. When researchers are able to identify which variables could impact a study, known as *covariates,* and random assignment is not possible, they have two choices. First, they could use a regression procedure to adjust scores on the DVs based on what the predicted DV would be if all participants scored equally across the covariate. Of course, this is based on a prediction model, which does not actually represent data as collected; rather, data are adjusted. In cases like this, the covariate must be a continuous variable. Second, they could match participants across characteristics. Although this can ensure group equivalence across participant characteristics, random sampling may be compromised.

In their study of recidivism among adolescents, Lancaster et al. (2011) could not randomly assign participants to a treatment versus control group. Rather, participants in the community-based intervention program were court ordered. In order to determine the effectiveness of the program, Lancaster et al. matched participants with adjudicated youth who were not court referred based on characteristics that could theoretically influence the results: geographic area, sex, age, ethnicity, and severity of offense. There may have been other factors as well that were not controlled, such as living environment or socioeconomic status. When random assignment is not used, a study will have limitations due to the infeasibility of controlling for every conceivable extraneous variable. Nevertheless, Lancaster et al. accounted for potential differences across important demographic variables. No significant differences in recidivism rates were noted between the treatment and control groups across sex, age, ethnicity, or severity of offense.

External Experimental Validity

External experimental validity refers to the extent to which an intervention or treatment may be extended to a variety of settings or environments. Experimental studies may utilize procedures or interventions that are artificial or settings that are unrealistic.

One thing researchers must consider is the *artificiality of the setting*. Consider the nature of psychiatric hospitalization, which often occurs in settings in which clients are placed in locked or secure units with several hours of individual and group counseling each day. Clients may have difficulty implementing the coping skills learned in psychiatric hospitalization because of the differences in support and structure or the artificiality of the setting. The psychiatric hospital setting is quite different from the pressures clients may experience in the real world, and interventions in psychiatric hospital settings may not be generalizable to the real world. Hence, external experimental validity could be compromised, even if the study were conducted under rigorous experimental conditions, such as the use of random assignment. Counseling researchers need to consider the setting in which a study is conducted and determine whether it compromises or limits generalizability of the findings.

Interference of prior treatment can affect the outcome of a study. If clients in one group are more predisposed to a past history of treatments or interventions, results could be corrupted by this past experience. Ensuring group equivalence with respect to prior history of treatment is important to generalizing results.

Another threat to external experimental validity may be the *artificiality of a treatment or intervention*. Even if a treatment or intervention is deemed effective in an experimental study, the complexity of the intervention could impact the client's ability to generalize the treatment to real-world settings. What occurs in counseling may be difficult to replicate outside of counseling. In addition, the treatment or intervention may interact with other aspects of experimental validity, including selection, testing, and implementation.

Researchers must also consider any possible *interaction of selection and treatment*. The use of random sampling in counseling research is limited because of the dependence on volunteer participants and intact groups rather than groups that are randomly assigned. As a result, the generalizability of findings may be limited to populations that are similar to the participants in the study. Providing demographic information on the participants is important to addressing broader contexts of generalizability.

Earlier we mentioned that the presence of a pretest can affect the results of a study (known as a *testing effect*). An *interaction between testing and treatment* occurs when a testing effect not only affects the outcome of the study but affects each of the groups differently. Once again, random assignment is a preventive measure against this threat.

Another possible interaction is an *interaction of treatment implementation.* When a researcher implements a treatment or intervention, the procedure needs to be consistent, particularly if it is implemented multiple times or across different participants or groups. If treatment fidelity is compromised, the findings cannot be generalizable. Hence, treatment implementation must be unchanging and replicated consistently throughout the study and across all participants.

To further understand the impact of threat to experimental validity, let's consider Lancaster et al.'s (2011) study on the effects of a community-based intervention program for court-referred youth. Recall that because random assignment was not possible in this study, threats to internal and external experimental validity could have impacted the generalizability of the findings.

To make their study procedure viable and provide evidence of generalizability, Lancaster et al. (2011) had to eliminate the threats to experimental validity that did not impact the study. Random assignment was not possible, so group equivalence was a concern. However, testing, instrumentation, and statistical regression were not viable threats in this study. No pretest was administered, and no formal instrument was utilized. Rather, records were reviewed to identify whether subsequent offenses were recorded after the initial arrest. Because there was no measure, statistical regression was not an issue.

Experimental Design Models

Experimental validity is a cornerstone of generalizability and experimental design. With this in mind, and with an understanding of statistical control and random assignment, we turn our attention to experimental design models. The models we explore can be implemented with true experimental designs; quasi-experimental designs; and explanatory, nonexperimental research. The strongest scenario for experimental design, though not always possible, is the utilization of true experimental designs, as random assignment ensures group equivalence. As we discuss each of the models, consider its limitations if a true experimental design is not used. A true experimental design will have three key aspects: random assignment, a manipulated IV, and a measure of effect or change. In addition, keep in mind that although classic experimental design examines the effect of an intervention between a treatment group and a control group, often in counseling research the control group will be another comparison group. In other words, one group receives an intervention and another group receives a different type of intervention (comparison group) as opposed to no intervention (control group).

Posttest-Only Control Group Design

The posttest-only control group design is among the simplest, as only one outcome measure is required. Quite simply, two equivalent groups are compared. One group receives a treatment or intervention. The other group does not. The effect after the implementation of the intervention is measured to determine the extent of the differences between the treatment group and control group. The process of a posttest-only control group design can be expressed as follows:

Treatment group ⟶ Intervention ⟶ Outcome measure
Control group ⟶ No intervention ⟶ Outcome measure

The Lancaster et al. (2011) study was a quasi-experimental posttest-only design. One measure (reoffenses) was examined between two groups (a group that received services in a community-based court-referred program and a control group); random assignment did not occur in the study, opening up threats to experimental validity. Because random assignment was not possible in this study, participants in the treatment group were matched with individuals in the control groups using demographic variables (e.g., sex, age, severity of offense) that could influence the results of the study.

Random assignment is an important component of the posttest-only control group design to demonstrate group equivalences at the onset of the study. When random assignment is not used, evidence of controlling for influential variables, as in the Lancaster et al. (2011) study, should be demonstrated. Without random assignment or evidence of statistical control, this design should not be used. If group equivalence is not tenable, another design should be selected.

Pretest–Posttest Control Group Design

The pretest–posttest control group design is an appropriate design in quasi-experimental research. A pretest can be incorporated into the design to establish group equivalence at the onset of the study. This is followed by one group receiving a treatment or intervention and the control or comparison group not receiving an intervention or receiving a different intervention. The effect after the implementation of the intervention is measured to determine the extent of the differences between the treatment group and control group. The process of a pretest–posttest control group design can be expressed as follows:

Treatment group → Pretest → Intervention → Posttest
Control group → Pretest → No intervention → Posttest

Balkin, Tietjen-Smith, Caldwell, and Shen (2007) studied the effects of exercise and depression on young adult women. Depression was measured using the Beck Depression Inventory–II (BDI-II; Beck, Steer, & Brown, 1996). The study took place on a college campus with students enrolled in an aerobics class, weight training (an anaerobic class), and no exercise (control group). Because students enrolled in the classes (or did not enroll in the case of the control group), random assignment was not used. To establish group equivalence at the onset of the study, researchers administered the BDI-II prior to participants beginning their class. Six weeks after the onset of the classes, the BDI-II was administered again to see whether exercise and the type of exercise affected measures of depression.

Although this design does not require random assignment, when random assignment is used, the pretest serves as an additional measure of group equivalence. The drawback of the use of the pretest is the introduction of a testing effect. After the repeated administration of an instrument, participants can become wise to the measure, which could compromise the authenticity of responses.

Solomon Four-Group Design

The Solomon four-group design is perhaps the crème de la crème of experimental design. In this design a pretest is introduced, but the testing effect is controlled. As in the previous design, some participants receive a treatment and some do not. However, in the Solomon four-group design, the treatment group and control group are further divided into those who receive a pretest and those who do not. The process of a Solomon four-group design can be expressed as follows:

Treatment group → Pretest → Intervention → Posttest
Treatment group → No pretest → Intervention → Posttest
Control group → Pretest → No intervention → Posttest
Control group → No pretest → No intervention → Posttest

Kimbrough, Balkin, and Rancich (2007) evaluated the effects of yoga and memory using a Solomon four-group design. Participants were randomly assigned to four groups: (a) a treatment group that received instruction in inverted yoga positions, a short-term memory pretest, and a short-term memory posttest; (b) a treatment group that received instruction in inverted yoga positions, no short-term memory pretest, and a short-term memory posttest; (c) a control group that did not receive yoga instruction but did receive a short-term memory pretest and a short-term memory posttest; and (d) a control group that did not receive yoga instruction, did not receive a short-term memory pretest, and did receive a short-term memory posttest. From this design, researchers can establish group equivalence by examining the pretest scores of (a) and (c). If there are no statistically significant differences in the pretest scores, groups can be considered equivalent. Furthermore, researchers can establish whether there is a testing effect by examining the posttest scores of (a) and (b) and of (c) and (d). If there are no statistically significant differences between the groups, no testing effect is evident. Finally, posttest scores can be examined for the treatment and control groups to determine whether inverted yoga positions affect short-term memory.

Explanatory, Nonexperimental Designs

As mentioned earlier in this chapter, not all designs that compare groups are considered experimental. Some IVs, including demographic variables such as sex, ethnicity, marital status, and so forth, cannot be randomly assigned. When comparisons are made between groups on a construct for which no formal manipulation occurred and groups could not be randomly assigned, the study is known as an explanatory, nonexperimental study (Johnson, 2001). For example, when Davis et al. (2014) compared individuals who did and did not receive counseling services across life balance domains, group assignment was not random and no intervention was conducted. Rather, a measure (the JBLI) was used to make comparisons between the two groups. This comparison was made to lend further evidence to the validation of the JBLI; as a standalone study, this comparison would be problematic because of the lack of random assignment and statistical control. These limitations need to be addressed when conducting explanatory, nonexperimental research.

Components for Evaluation

The type of statistical analysis chosen to compare groups will depend on the nature of the comparison, the number of groups being compared, the number of DVs included in the study, and the presence of covariates in the study. The primary purpose of the statistical tests covered in this chapter is to evaluate the extent of differences between groups. Researchers need to be aware of not only whether a statistically significant difference exists between groups but also the magnitude of the difference. Recall from Chapter 5 that statistical significance is driven in part by sample size. Thus, it is possible to have a statistically significant effect that is minimal in magnitude (i.e., unimportant), which can occur when the study has a large sample size.

What Are the Statistical Tests for Comparing Groups?

The various technical requirements and formulae for these statistical tests are briefly covered here, but the computation and techniques are outside the scope of this chapter. What follows is a brief overview of these statistical tests, how they are computed, and what is reported.

z Test

The *z* test is used to test whether a statistically significant difference exists between a sample and a known population mean. The *z* test is based on the assumption of a normally distributed population in which both the population mean and population variance are known. (Note that we use *variance* here as a general term to denote error in the mean, as in variance, standard deviation, etc.) In a *z* test the sample used in the study should be sufficiently large (e.g., greater than or equal to 30). Because both the population mean and variance must be known to use a *z* test, this statistical test is rarely used in counseling research.

A *z* test might be used in a school counseling environment if a school counselor wished to know whether a particular cohort of students had significantly different tests scores on a standardized test (i.e., a test for which the population mean and variance were known). In addition, any of the designs and models discussed previously could be implemented to determine significance from a population.

t Test

The *t* test comes in two forms. The *one sample* t *test* is used to test whether a statistically significant difference exists between a sample and a hypothesized mean. It differs from the *z* test in that the population mean or variance is unknown. It can be used if a particular sample is evaluated against a specific score. For example, many instruments (e.g., the Substance Abuse Subtle Scale Inventory-2 and the Crisis Stabilization Scale) use standard scores, with 50 representing the average. A counselor using one of these measures for group counseling may wish to evaluate the group against the standardized mean (50) to see whether a group scores significantly higher or lower on any of the domains.

The *independent-samples* t *test* is used to evaluate significant differences between two means. In this case two means are compared, and the variances of each group are used to identify whether the scores of one group differ significantly from those of the other. Once again, take a look at Davis et al. (2014), in which two group means were compared using *t* tests. A group receiving counseling services was compared to a group not receiving counseling services across life balance domains as measured by the JBLI. Five life balance domains were identified as having statistically significant differences between the clinical and nonclinical groups. The clinical group exhibited lower levels of life balance in the areas of positive orientation, quality of relationships, substance use, career satisfaction, and friendships.

An additional note about the *t* test, which is not necessarily important to understanding the concept behind it but is kind of fun to know if you are a stats geek, concerns the history behind the *t* test. You will likely see the *t* test referred to as *Student's* t *test.* Most statistical tests are referred to by the person(s) who developed them. So who was Student?

Student was Sir William Sealy Gosset, a noted statistician employed by Guinness Brewery who devoted time to determining the best barley varieties for creating beer. Gosset could not use statistics based on population parameters (e.g., the normal curve), the tool used at the time. So he developed the *t* distribution to approximate the distribution of the normal curve depending on the sample size. The normal curve for smaller sample distributions is somewhat more leptokurtic (i.e., a broader bell-shaped curve) than that for larger samples, which more closely resembles the normal curve (see Figure 7.1). Hence, an adjustment for sample, referred to as *degrees of freedom,* is used to make approximations of samples to a normal distribution.

But why was the *t* test named "Student's *t* test" as opposed to "Gosset's *t* test"? Guinness Brewery did not want its competitors (i.e., other breweries) to know that it was employing statisticians to gain a competitive edge in producing the ultimate beer. So Guinness had Gosset publish under a pseudonym—hence the name Student.

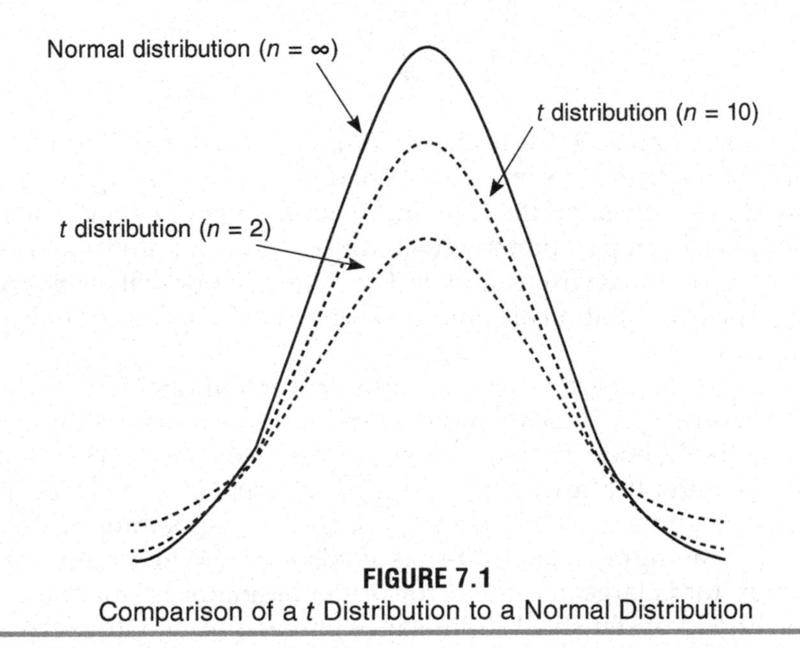

FIGURE 7.1
Comparison of a *t* Distribution to a Normal Distribution

F Test

The *F* test refers to a family of tests used to evaluate mean differences between two or more groups in univariate and multivariate designs. The *F* test is an extension of the *t* test in that it can be used to compare two or more groups, can extend to multivariate analysis (i.e., more than one DV), and can extend to covariates.

We see an example of the *F* test from Balkin, Harris, Freeman, and Huntington (2014), who evaluated clinical and nonclinical groups on the subscales of the FRI. Like in the previous example using the JBLI, only two groups were compared. However, the *F* test was necessary because the evaluation was multivariate in nature—Balkin et al. (2014) used four DVs. Balkin et al. (2014) noted that the clinical group had significantly higher scores on the FRI domains than the nonclinical group, indicating that the "the clinical group identified more negative feelings or attributes toward those that harmed them" (p. 8).

How Do They Work?

Although computations of various statistical tests can be complex, including elements of probability, calculus, and matrix algebra, the essential comparison, whether it is between-groups designs discussed in this chapter, within-groups designs discussed in Chapter 8, or correlational designs discussed in Chapter 6, can be summarized using a simple, basic formula:

$$\frac{effect}{error}$$

Recall from Chapter 5 that in this formula *effect* refers to mean differences; *error* refers to some established or computed variance or standard error term. So the numerator will generally show some mathematical computation in which means are compared, such as subtracting one mean from another. The denominator will generally show some computation of combined error that looks at variability within each group.

This equation operates as any ratio or fraction operates. If the effect or numerator is small and the error or denominator is large, then the likelihood of statistical significance *decreases*. Think of it conceptually: If a researcher has a lot of error in a measure or instrument, there is less likelihood of finding something different and meaningful. The antithesis is also true. When the effect or numerator is large and the error or denominator is small, then the likelihood of statistical significance *increases*. Again, think of it conceptually: If a researcher has a small amount of error in a measure or instrument, there is more likelihood of finding something different and meaningful.

What Gets Reported?

The reporting of statistical results for a between-subjects design is fairly standard. Means, standard deviations, and sample size for each group need to be presented. When tests are conducted (e.g., z test, t test, F test), the reporting of statistical results follows this format: a Roman or Greek letter, followed by a number or pair of numbers in parentheses, followed by a value, concluding with a comparison to a p value. For example, when reporting results between clinical and nonclinical groups on the FRI, Balkin et al. (2014) reported "$\lambda = .885$, $F(4, 195) = 6.22$, $p < .001$" (p. 8).

Although the numbers presented may look complex, they are really a summary statement of the research results. The Roman or Greek letter represents the type of test. In this case, the F indicates that a multivariate analysis of variance was performed. The number(s) in parentheses identifies the *degrees of freedom*, an estimate of parameters or variability within a data set. The value after the equals sign is based on a calculation that incorporates changes in the DV and error in measurement. The p value indicates whether the result is statistically significant (Balkin & Sheperis, 2009). From this result, we can deduce that an F test resulted in a statistically significant difference between the two groups across the four FRI subscales.

The Results section of a study should address both statistical and practical significance. For example, Balkin et al. (2014) used lambda (λ) to denote the effect size and explained the following: "A moderate effect size was noted, accounting for 11.5% of the variance in the model" (p. 8). Hence, in a research article both a measure of effect size and interpretation of the effect size should be offered.

Designing a Between-Groups Study

Several important concepts have been addressed that pertain to experimental design and explanatory, nonexperimental design. Regardless of whether a counselor plans to conduct research, an ability to identify the concepts related to between-groups studies is pertinent to addressing whether or not the differences between groups are important. In other words, counselors should be cautious in integrating counseling strategies and techniques that do not emanate from strong designs. An examination of group differences using a simple statistic, such as a *t* test, is much more meaningful when the design is sophisticated, such as including random assignment and thereby controlling for extraneous variables. Studies that use sophisticated statistical procedures may actually be less rigorous if the design is flawed. Thus, the design of the study is far more important to identifying empirically supported treatments than the statistic. In designing a between-groups study, researchers should consider the following blueprint:

1. *Identify your research hypotheses or research questions.* Between-groups designs establish whether the extent of differences between groups is due to mere chance or whether there could be a more established rationale for such differences.
2. *Identify the DV(s).* What construct or phenomenon is being studied? How is it being measured? Counseling researchers need to make sure that any measure that is utilized is a valid measure of the construct or phenomenon of interest. In between-groups design, the DV is generally a score measured as an interval, quasi-interval, or ratio variable.
3. *Identify the IV(s).* What groups are being compared? Some group comparisons include a treatment or intervention; others do not. In some group comparisons both groups receive a measure and the scores are compared, with the only difference

being the group to which participants were assigned. Keep in mind two important considerations: (a) For studies in which groups are not randomly assigned (i.e., quasi-experimental studies), the results will have limitations related to internal experimental validity; and (b) for studies in which the IV is not manipulated and random assignment is not possible because of the comparison of innate factors (e.g., sex, ethnicity) or the design is explanatory, nonexperimental, group equivalence needs to be assessed at the onset of the study.

4. *Consider the appropriate model for the research.* If a decision is made to use a pretest, consider the advantages (e.g., establishment of group equivalence) and disadvantages (e.g., testing effect) of doing so. The absence of random assignment does not necessarily mandate a pretest if other methods can be used to demonstrate statistically that the groups are equivalent.
5. *Identify the statistical test(s) to be used in the study.* An established statistical analysis includes both statistical and practical significance. Furthermore, results need to be explained beyond whether the results are significant. The extent to which the results are meaningful needs to be highlighted and may in fact be more important in the communication of the results. Remember that statistical significance is driven in part by sample size; reflecting on the magnitude of the significance lends further credibility to the findings.

A well-designed study integrates participants, IVs and DVs, established measures, and a well-orchestrated procedure to collect data. The true meaningfulness of the study, which culminates from a statistical test, is only as good as the established structure. Counseling researchers grounded in the practitioner-scholar model recognize that without a solid structure, as evidenced by the design of the study, even the most sophisticated statistics are flawed and contribute very little to established practice. Between-groups studies are the foundation on which empirically supported treatments are published. Counselors are strongly encouraged to pay close attention to experimental design.

Chapter Summary

In this chapter we expanded on the experimental designs (preexperimental, quasi-experimental, and true experimental) introduced in Chapter 4 and introduced the many facets of experimental validity. We explained how experimental validity can be threatened, the role of random assignment, models of experimental design, and the role of comparison groups and pretesting. In counseling research, random assignment is not always possible. Hence, quasi-experimental designs or explanatory, nonexperimental designs may incorporate other methods of addressing threats, such as matching participants between groups on specific characteristics or using a covariate that is theoretically linked with what is being measured or investigated.

We also revisited some statistical concepts of effect and error introduced in Chapter 5 and applied these concepts to evaluate differences between groups. Reporting both statistical significance and practical significance is essential to addressing both the probability of the results (i.e., statistical significance) and the overall meaningfulness of the findings (i.e., practical significance; effect size). Regardless of the level of sophistication of an analysis or statistical procedure, a study is only as good as its foundation. A well-designed study supersedes the sophistication of a statistical analysis, and consumers of research should focus on the representativeness of the participants, the identified IVs and DVs, and the use of established measures and a well-designed procedure to collect data in addition to the overall results of the study.

Suggested Activities

I. Review the following article:

Lancaster, C., Balkin, R. S., Garcia, R., & Valarezo, A. (2011). An evidence-based approach to reducing recidivism in court-referred youth. *Journal of Counseling & Development, 89,* 488–492. doi:10.1002/j.1556-6676.2011.tb02846.x

1. Random assignment was not used in this study. Why do you think that is?
2. How did the authors address the lack of random assignment?
3. How would the results of the study have been limited without the processes implemented?

II. Review the following article:

Johnson, B. (2001). Toward a new classification of nonexperimental quantitative research. *Educational Researcher, 30*(2), 3–13. doi:10.3102/0013189X030002003

1. What is Johnson's concern with the use of the term *causal-comparative?*
2. How do you differentiate between a quasi-experimental design and an explanatory, nonexperimental design? What are the similarities and differences?

References

American Educational Research Association, American Psychological Association, & National Council on Measurement in Education. (2014). *Standards for educational and psychological testing.* Washington, DC: Author.

Babor, T. F., Higgins-Biddle, J. C., Saunders, J. B., & Monteiro, M. G. (2001). *AUDIT: The Alcohol Use Disorders Identification Test: Guidelines for use in primary care* (2nd ed.). Retrieved from http://apps.who.int/iris/bitstream/10665/67205/1/WHO_MSD_MSB_01.6a.pdf

Balkin, R. S., Harris, N., Freeman, S. J., & Huntington, S. (2014). The Forgiveness Reconciliation Inventory: An instrument to process through issues of forgiveness and conflict. *Measurement and Evaluation in Counseling and Development, 47,* 3–13. doi:10.1177/0748175613497037

Balkin, R. S., & Sheperis, D. S. (2009). *A primer in evaluating quantitative research for counseling professionals* (ACAPCD-26). Retrieved from https://www.counseling.org/resources/library/ACA%20Digests/ACAPCD-26.pdf

Balkin, R. S., Tietjen-Smith, T., Caldwell, C., & Shen, Y. (2007). The relationship of exercise and depression among young adult women. *Adultspan Journal, 6,* 30–35. doi:10.1002/j.2161-0029.2007.tb00027.x

Beck, A. T., Steer, R. A., & Brown, G. K. (1996). *BDI-II manual.* San Antonio, TX: Psychological Corporation.

Campbell, D. T., & Stanley, J. C. (1966). *Experimental and quasi-experimental designs for research.* Boston, MA: Houghton Mifflin.

Davis, R. J., Balkin, R. S., & Juhnke, G. A. (2014). Validation of the Juhnke-Balkin Life Balance Inventory. *Measurement and Evaluation in Counseling & Development, 47,* 181–198. doi:10.1177/0748175614531796

Johnson, B. (2001). Toward a new classification of nonexperimental quantitative research. *Educational Researcher, 30*(2), 3–13. doi:10.3102/0013189X030002003

Kimbrough, S., Balkin, R. S., & Rancich, A. (2007). The effect of inverted yoga positions on short-term memory. *Athletic Insight: The Online Journal of Sport Psychology, 9*(2). Retrieved from http://athleticinsight.com/Vol9Iss2/YogaMemory.htm

LaFountain, R. M., & Bartos, R. B. (2002). *Research and statistics made meaningful in counseling and student affairs.* Pacific Grove, CA: Brooks/Cole.

Lancaster, C., Balkin, R. S., Garcia, R., & Valarezo, A. (2011). An evidence-based approach to reducing recidivism in court-referred youth. *Journal of Counseling & Development, 89,* 488–492. doi:10.1002/j.1556-6676.2011.tb02846.x

Lenz, A. S., Perepiczka, M., & Balkin, R. S. (2013). Evidence for the mitigating effects of a support group for attitudes toward statistics. *Counseling Outcome Research and Evaluation, 4,* 26–40. doi:10.1177/2150137812474000

Wise, S. L. (1985). The development and validation of a scale measuring attitudes toward statistics. *Educational and Psychological Measurement, 45,* 401–405. doi:10.1177/001316448504500226

Examining Differences Within Groups and Single-Case Research Designs

Overview

This chapter focuses on examining differences when the same participants are used to test the effects of an intervention or phenomenon. Because the same participants are used at each observation (two or more observations), within-subjects design is often referred to as *repeated measures design*. Hence, within-subjects designs are used to evaluate changes over time or differences that occur across the same group of participants.

Single-case research design (SCRD) is discussed, as this type of research may be extended to program evaluation (see Chapter 13) and provide empirical support for efficacious interventions in counseling. In addition, design components of both within-subjects design and SCRD are highlighted. Basic and advanced procedures are discussed, along with the type of analysis conducted, how it works, and what is commonly reported. The importance of evaluating statistical and practical significance is highlighted, along with important considerations in designing within-subjects and SCRD studies.

Finally, perceptions of various populations and changes over time are often assessed in survey and longitudinal research. An overview of these methods is provided.

Why Conduct Within-Subjects Research?

Within-subjects research is conducted when a researcher wishes to know how a set of participants changed over time or across repeated measures of a construct. In counseling, such designs are commonly used to find out whether significant changes over time have occurred as a result of an intervention. In a within-subjects design, each participant is evaluated across each level of the independent variable. This is a major difference from between-subjects design. Recall that in a between-subjects design, members of one group may receive a different treatment from another group or no treatment at all. In within-subjects designs, all members of a single group receive the same intervention or exposure. Both between- and within-subjects designs have in common a measurable dependent variable. Let's take a look at an example.

Lenz, Del Conte, Lancaster, Bailey, and Vanderpool (2014) conducted a mixed-methods study on adolescents in partial psychiatric hospitalization. As part of the study, Lenz et al. were interested in evaluating change from intake to discharge using the Symptom Checklist–90–Revised (SCL-90-R; Derogatis, 1996): "To what degree is [partial hospitalization program] treatment associated with change in the severity of mental health symptoms from admission to discharge?" (p. 4). Participants were 35 adolescents. Thus, there was only one group. Each participant was administered the SCL-90-R at admission and at discharge. We have now identified both the independent and dependent variables. The independent variable is time of administration of the SCL-90-R at admission and at discharge. The dependent variable is score on the SCL-90-R for each participant.

Elements of Within-Subjects Research

The components of between-subjects/groups designs can be applied to within-subjects designs. In the previous example, the dependent variable, score on the SCL-90-R, is continuous. The independent variable is discrete and refers to the time point when the dependent variable is administered. Time of an administration serves as a common independent variable in repeated measures designs. In this example, admission and discharge are the time points in which the SCL-90-R, the dependent variable, was measured. Other examples of this design could include pretest/posttest and follow-up administrations of a measure or instrument.

However, the independent variable in within-subjects research is not limited to time. The nature of within-subjects research is that the participants are being measured across a common phenomenon. Take for example a school counselor who wishes to monitor the progress of a number of students receiving responsive services in the school.

The school counselor wants to take into account various perspectives on student behavior and uses the Child Behavior Checklist (Achenbach & Rescorla, 2001), which is to be completed by the parent, the teacher, and the student. Each of these three ratings is of the same phenomenon—the student's behavior. Hence, this would also be a repeated measures design, as the student, the teacher, and the parent are all rating the same observation. In this case, the independent variable would be the rater, and the dependent variable would be the Child Behavior Checklist score from each rater.

Mixed Design

Some of the experimental design models mentioned in Chapter 7 may be used to evaluate between-groups differences, within-subjects differences, or both simultaneously, referred to as *mixed designs.* Other common names for this type of design include *split-plot analysis of variance* or *between-groups analysis with a within-subjects effect*. In a mixed design, researchers can examine differences across time as well as differences between groups. Both the pretest–posttest control group design and the Solomon four-group design offer these options. Let's look at the following example to address the complexities of this design.

Carlson, Barden, Daire, and Greene (2014) examined the efficacy of a relationship education program with couples. They used a pretest–posttest control group design to evaluate differences in relationship satisfaction across time (at the beginning and end of the program) while also examining differences between males and females and treatment versus control groups. The study had the following components:

1. Heterosexual couples (N = 113) were randomly assigned to treatment and control groups. The treatment group received the relationship education program; the control group was placed on a waitlist.
2. Demographic information was collected from males and females across treatment and control groups.
3. Participants (in both the treatment and control groups) were administered scales at intake and at the conclusion of the program (approximately 4–6 weeks after intake).

Carlson et al. were able to evaluate differences between intake and program completion for both treatment and control groups and account for differences between males and females. Thus, the within-subjects analysis accounted for differences between intake and program completion, and the between-groups analyses accounted for differences between males and females and differences between treatment and control groups.

SCRD

The majority of tools in quantitative methods are based on large data procedures. In other words, using statistics to provide evidence of relevant relationships or effective interventions requires collecting large amounts of data to produce generalizable results. The reality, however, is quite different. Counselors generally do not acquire large amounts of data. The focus of a treatment or intervention tends to be individuals or small groups. Counselors are more likely to conduct individual, couples, family, and small-group sessions. Hence, it is more difficult for counseling researchers to gather large amounts of data to conduct research than it is for educational researchers, who often use data based on classrooms, schools, and districts.

SCRD may be a more natural fit for counseling research. SCRD does not require large numbers of participants in randomized groups to demonstrate the efficacy of a treatment or intervention. Rather, SCRD takes advantage of the practices commonly used by counselors to provide care—individual and small-group sessions (Balkin, 2013). In addition, Lenz (2013, 2015) noted the historical recognition of SCRD in providing evidence for empirically supported treatments.

In SCRD there may be one or more participants, but the measure of each participant stands alone. For example, Ikonomopoulos, Smith, and Schmidt (2015) provided data on eight participants in an SCRD. However, the analysis includes evaluating each case without the context of the other cases. In other words, SCRDs evaluate whether interventions work on an individual level, but if the intervention is working and is evaluated across multiple individuals, then it may be viewed as efficacious. Figure 8.1 provides data on one of the cases from Ikonomopoulos et al. The figure shows the scores of a participant in a juvenile boot camp facility on the Global Severity Index of the Brief Symptom Inventory (BSI; Derogatis, 1993) during two phases of the study: the baseline phase (B) and the treatment phase receiving narrative therapy (T). An explanation of these phases of the study is provided later in the chapter.

The essential element of SCRD is a focus on the presence of a functional relationship between the baseline measures and measures

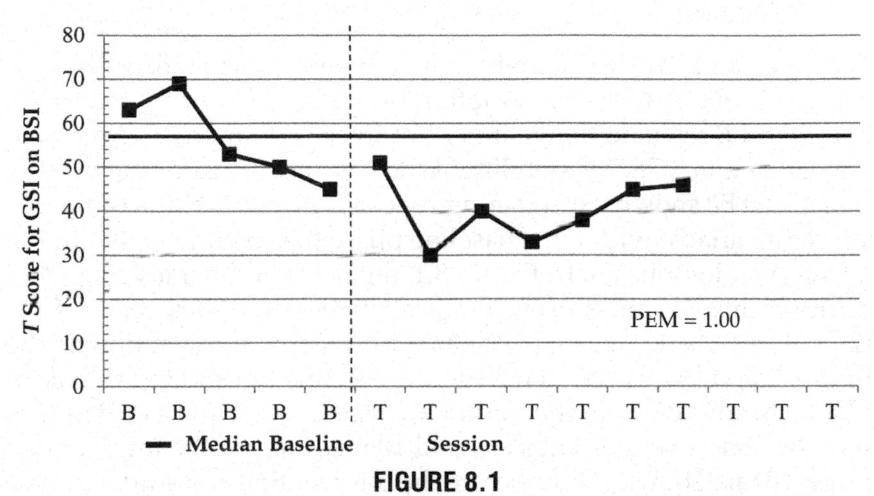

FIGURE 8.1
A Case Example of an A-B Design From Ikonomopoulos et al. (2015)

Note. GSI = Global Severity Index; BSI = Brief Symptom Inventory; PEM = percentage of data exceeding the median; B = baseline; T = treatment.

of the intervention and follow-up procedures as opposed to a focus on statistical significance (O'Neill, McDonnell, Billingsley, & Jenson, 2011). "Hence, such analyses are less dependent on sophisticated statistics and easily understood by the practitioners" (Balkin, 2013, p. 259). SCRD may be viewed as a special case of within-subjects design, as "participants serve as their own comparison" through the analysis of baseline scores on a dependent variable contrasted with scores on the same dependent variable from a treatment or intervention (Lenz, 2015, p. 387). Much like within-subjects designs described earlier, the treatment or intervention serves as the independent variable, and scores on either baseline or treatment/intervention measures serve as the dependent variable.

Design Models

Within-subjects designs and SCRDs share common elements with respect to experimental design. What follows is a discussion of basic design elements, followed by further explication of more advanced models for within-subjects designs and issues specific to SCRDs.

Phases of treatment in within-subjects designs include a baseline or pretreatment phase (A) and a treatment phase (B). For more complex designs, additional treatment conditions (C, D, etc.) can be added.

A-B Design

The most basic design model for within-subjects designs is the A-B design. In the A-B design, *A* refers to the baseline or pretreatment phase and *B* refers to the treatment or intervention phase. An essential element in SCRD is stability of the baseline measure (Ray, 2015), which can be shown by obtaining repeated measurements of the dependent variable within the baseline phase (i.e., before the treatment or intervention phase). In Figure 8.1, a participant in a juvenile boot camp facility is scored using the Global Severity Index (GSI) of the BSI before (A) and during (B) a narrative therapy intervention. In the figure, *B* and *T* are used to refer to the baseline (A) and treatment (B) phases, respectively. In the figure, the results of a typical A-B design with five baseline measures (A) and 10 measures in the intervention phase (B) are shown. Thus, before the intervention was initiated, five baseline measures were obtained, which helps to demonstrate the stability of the measure over time. When only a single measure is used as a baseline, a serious limitation can be the accuracy of the baseline measure, especially in SCRDs.

However, traditional within-subjects research designs utilize means to repeatedly measure a group or changes over time. Looking again at Lenz et al. (2014), we see that they also used an A-B design. However, they used a single measure in the initial phase and then a single measure at discharge. A legitimate criticism of this design is that the use of a single measure prior to treatment may not meet Ray's (2015) criteria for demonstrating stability in the baseline measure, which is typically done in SCRD. To address this critique of counseling research, and keeping in mind the practitioner-scholar model, the following points should be noted:

1. Repeated baseline measures are not always practical in counseling research. Delaying counseling may not be in the best interest of the client. Consider for example a counselor who wishes to evaluate suicide interventions. Obtaining multiple baseline measures prior to initiating treatment would be highly deplorable and unethical. Lenz et al. (2014) evaluated adolescent clients in need of partial hospitalization (i.e., intensive crisis services). Obtaining a single measure for baseline was practical and ethical.
2. Within-subjects designs utilize group means. When the sample size is sufficient, outliers can be minimized or possibly eliminated. Hence, the use of group means when the sample size is sufficient provides stability in the measure not possible in SCRD.

A-B-A Design

Often researchers want to know the effects of an intervention or treatment after it concludes. An A-B-A design assesses change after the treatment or intervention is over, such as in a study in which participants receive a preassessment (A), a treatment (B), and a follow-up after treatment has been completed (A). Ikonomopoulos et al. (2015) were able to obtain measures for some of their participants after the completion of the narrative therapy intervention. Figure 8.2 shows the results of one participant in the A-B-A design. The figure shows the scores of this participant in a juvenile boot camp facility on the Global Severity Index of the BSI during three phases of the study—the baseline phase (B), the treatment phase receiving narrative therapy (T), and the withdrawal phase (W)—constituting an A-B-A design.

More Complex Designs

Within-subjects designs can grow in complexity. Treatments can be removed and reintroduced (e.g., A-B-A-B-A-B). Or, as mentioned earlier, more than one treatment can be introduced: In an A-B-A-C-A design, B could represent Treatment 1 and C could represent Treatment 2.

When more than one treatment is introduced, researchers need to be aware of *sequencing* effects; that is, the order of the interven-

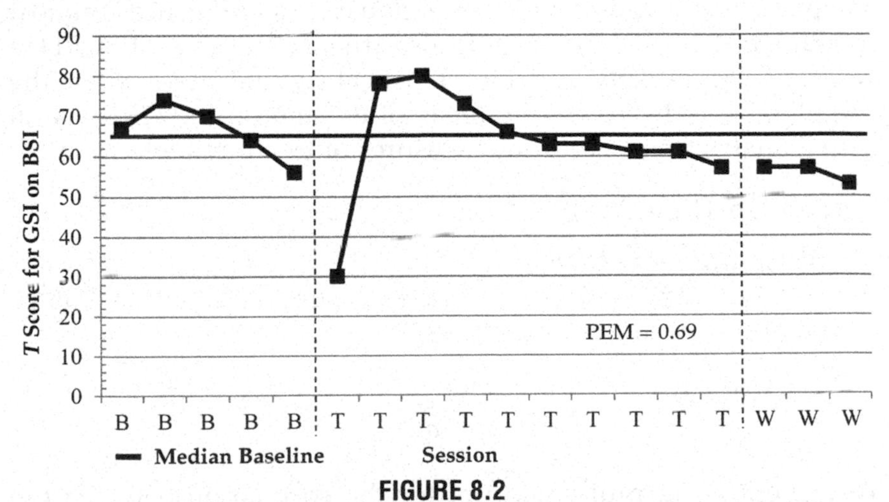

FIGURE 8.2

A Case Example of an A-B-A Design From Ikonomopoulos et al. (2015)

Note. GSI = Global Severity Index; BSI = Brief Symptom Inventory; PEM = percentage of data exceeding the median; B = baseline; T = treatment; W = withdrawal.

tions could confound the results. One way to address this concern is to *counterbalance* the design so that equal numbers of participants receive the treatments in a different or opposite order (Lane, n.d.).

Components for Evaluation

Components for evaluating within-subjects designs differ from those for evaluating SCRDs, as within-subjects designs often rely on statistical tests and SCRDs rely on both visual analysis and measures of effect size (ES).

What Are the Statistical Tests?

Within-Subjects Designs

The two main statistical tests used in within-subjects designs are the paired-samples *t* test (also known as the *dependent* t *test*) and the *F* test. Both of these tests may be referred to as *repeated measures tests,* as they take into account the fact that each participant was measured more than once and the comparison of the scores is based on the measure of each observation rather than a comparison of two groups.

SCRDs

As discussed in Chapter 5, statistical significance can be manufactured if the sample size is large enough. Essentially, when the sample size in a study is very large, statistical significance is almost guaranteed. But the opposite is also true. In the case of SCRD, a researcher is unlikely to detect statistical significance because the sample size is 1. Hence, the focus of evaluation in SCRDs is on visual analysis and reporting measures of treatment effect.

How Do They Work?

Within-Subjects Designs

The conceptual formula for repeated measures is similar to that for evaluating between-groups effects:

$$\frac{\textit{effect}}{\textit{error}}$$

However, the formulas account for the correlation between the measures of each participant. In other words, repeated measures tests must account for the fact that each participant is completing a measure more than once. However, the basic concepts of identifying statistically significant differences between or among the repeated measures remain the same as identified in Chapter 7.

SCRDs

A number of different ESs are used in SCRDs to demonstrate the efficacy of an intervention or change over time, some of which are covered in this chapter. We focus here on ES measures that are more widely used in counseling research and are easy to calculate. Interested readers are encouraged to review Vannest and Ninci (2015) for more specific information related to ES in SCRD.

Percentage of nonoverlapping data (PND). PND (Scruggs, Mastropieri, & Casto, 1987) is likely among the simplest ESs to calculate and among the most popular used in SCRD (Vannest & Ninci, 2015). To calculate PND, take the most extreme score in the baseline as the reference point; the percentage of scores that do not overlap the baseline score serves as PND. Although Ikonomopoulos et al. (2015) used the percentage of data exceeding the median (PEM), the data presented in Figure 8.1 can be used to compute PND. Ikonomopoulos et al. used the BSI, on which higher scores represent an increase in symptoms. Of the baseline scores on the Global Severity Index of the BSI in Figure 8.1, the most extreme is 43. Seven scores in the intervention phase were documented, and one score (the first measure in the intervention phase) overlapped with the PND baseline score (43). Hence, PND = 6/7 = .86. Although PND is among the most widely used measures of ES in SCRD, keep in mind that an outlier in the baseline phase can misrepresent the results. Hence, PND is only a good measure when the baseline measures appear stable.

Keep in mind that the most extreme score can be at the high end or low end. This is important, as the researcher needs to ascertain whether the highest score or the lowest score represents the most conservative estimate of progress. In this example, a score of 43 on the Global Severity Index represented the lowest score. However, should a researcher use a different measure, the highest score could be the most extreme score. For example, higher scores on the Juhnke-Balkin Life Balance Inventory (Davis, Balkin, & Juhnke, 2014) represent a healthier life balance. Therefore, the highest score would be used and individuals scoring higher than the most extreme score would be noted.

PEM. PEM (Ma, 2006) is very similar to PND, except the determination of the baseline is based on the median score as opposed to the most extreme score. In this regard PEM is less influenced by outliers in the baseline phase, but if the baseline scores are not stable using PEM is not advisable (Vannest & Ninci, 2015). Ikonomopoulos et al. (2015) used PEM to provide evidence of the efficacy of narrative therapy when working with adolescents in a boot camp program. In Figure 8.1, none of the scores exceed the median, and hence PEM = 7/7 = 1.00. For the data in Figure 8.2, Ikonomopoulos et al. computed PEM as the percentage of data points exceeding the median in the intervention and withdrawal phases: 9/13 = .69.

Nonoverlap of all pairs (NAP). NAP (Parker & Vannest, 2009) compares each data point in the baseline phase to each data point in subsequent phases (e.g., intervention, withdrawal). Thus, in an A-B design, as in Figure 8.1, each data point in A is compared to each data point in B. If a data point in B exceeds a data point in A, the researcher records 1. For data points for which B does not exceed A, 0 is recorded. Ties can be ignored or coded as 0.5. Figure 8.1 shows five baseline (A) scores and seven intervention scores (B). Hence, there are 35 score comparisons to be made (5 × 7 = 35). Table 8.1 shows 35 scores. There is one tie, so that score is ignored, producing a total of 34 scores; 31 out of the 34 scores indicate progress equating to a NAP of 31/34 = .91. A strength of this approach is that all of the data are used, as opposed to a single score in the baseline or a median score (Vannest & Ninci, 2015).

What Gets Reported?

Within-Subjects Designs

Once again, the concepts identified in Chapter 7 apply here as well. The Results section of a study should address both statistical and practical significance. Means, standard deviations, and sample size for the group need to be presented. When tests (e.g., *t* tests, *F* tests) are conducted, the reporting of statistical results follows this format: a Roman or Greek letter, followed by a number or pair of numbers in parentheses, followed by a value, concluding with a comparison

TABLE 8.1
Nonoverlapping Pairs From Figure 8.1 (Ikonomopoulos et al., 2015)

	Phase B						
Phase A	51	30	40	32	39	43	44
61	1	1	1	1	1	1	1
70	1	1	1	1	1	1	1
52	1	1	1	1	1	1	1
50	0	1	1	1	1	1	1
43	0	1	1	1	1	Tie	0

to a *p* value. For example, Lenz et al. (2014) reported results for the SCL-90-R, noting both statistical significance using a dependent *t* test and practical significance using Cohen's *d*. Table 8.2 show the results as reported by Lenz et al., who noted statistical significance by indicating an asterisks and an interpretation of ES (p. 8).

SCRDs

ESs can demonstrate the meaningfulness of an effect and intervention, which is important to establishing effective counseling practice (Trusty, 2011; Trusty, Thompson, & Petrocelli, 2004). The importance or magnitude of an effect is always subjective, depending on the study and importance placed on the findings. However, Lenz (2013) summarized typical guidelines for interpreting ESs:

- .90 and greater indicate very effective treatments
- .70 to .89 represent moderate effectiveness
- .50 to .69 are debatably effective
- less than .50 are regarded as not effective

Similar to previous examples covered in this text, counseling researchers should report both quantitative findings and an interpretation of the findings.

TABLE 8.2

Reliability Coefficients and Comparisons of Admission and Discharge Assessments for Symptom Checklist–90–Revised and the Relational Health Indices–Youth Subscales

		Admission		Discharge			
Variable	α	*M*	*SD*	*M*	*SD*	*t*	ES
SCL-90-R							
Anxiety	.86	41.82	8.22	37.89	5.77	2.48**	.55
Depression	.94	45.02	9.65	38.03	8.38	2.79**	.77
Hostility	.78	43.36	6.30	39.84	5.26	2.77**	.60
Interpersonal Sensitivity	.87	43.84	7.86	40.46	6.36	1.92	.47
Obsessive-Compulsive	.82	45.59	7.39	40.89	5.88	2.51**	.70
Paranoid Ideation	.75	44.16	5.20	40.08	5.14	3.61**	.78
Phobic Anxiety	.79	44.23	5.68	42.92	4.38	1.00	.25
Psychoticism	.90	45.86	9.74	39.19	7.55	2.73**	.76
Somatization	.87	48.30	9.54	43.32	8.35	2.18*	.56
RHI-Y							
Friend	.93	17.73	4.22	19.88	3.50	2.31*	.55
Mentor	.88	16.01	3.90	19.50	8.61	2.10*	.52
Community	.73	16.37	3.26	16.64	4.67	0.31	.06

Note. ES = Cohen's *d* effect size interpreted as small (ES ≥ .20), medium (ES ≥ .50), and large (ES ≥ .80). SCL-90-R = Symptom Checklist–90–Revised (Derogatis, 1996); RHI-Y = Relational Health Indices–Youth (Liang, Tracy, Kenny, Brogan, & Gatha, 2010).
$^*p \le .05$. $^{**}p \le .01$.

Survey and Longitudinal Research

As much of within-subjects designs addresses changes over time, focusing on survey and longitudinal studies seems appropriate, as the intent of such research is similar. *Survey and longitudinal research* refers to studies conducted to understand changes over time in particular populations or differences in respondents who share specific qualities. Although survey and longitudinal research are presented together here because of their similarities in structure, they are not necessarily the same. Longitudinal research requires at least two specific data collection periods and can include many more over a longer period of time. Survey research can be completed in one administration or can be longitudinal in nature.

For example, Reiner, Dobmeier and Hernández (2013) surveyed counselor educators to understand their perspectives on counselor identity, recognition, and professional advancement. Participants were members of the Association for Counselor Education and Supervision. All members of the association were solicited (N = 1,334) and 378 responded, yielding a response rate of approximately 30%. Obtaining an adequate response rate in survey research can be a challenge. With a poor response rate, generalizability to the population of interest is questionable.

Panel, cohort, and trend studies are types of longitudinal studies. Some longitudinal research may use between-groups analyses, as opposed to analyses more consistent with within-subjects designs, or data may be presented descriptively or graphically to demonstrate differences in responding groups or demographic characteristics.

Panel Studies

A *panel study* is the classic within-subjects design as described in the aforementioned Lenz et al. (2014) article. Lenz et al. had a single group of participants who completed measures at two different time points. The key here is that the respondents were the same across two different points in time. The same sample is evaluated repeatedly over time. In longitudinal research, the participants in a panel can be followed repeatedly, sometimes over years. Repeated measures designs of this nature are extremely powerful. Rather than comparing a participant's scores to scores of other participants, researchers compare each of the focal participant's scores with his or her other scores. This means that each participant serves as a control, making individual differences within the group obsolete

(Lane, n.d.). However, findings from panel studies can be difficult to generalize because of internal threats of experimental validity, such as mortality and testing effects. In the case of mortality, research studies often experience attrition, in which participants drop out of the study or the researcher loses contact with them and is no longer able to follow up. Repeated administrations of a measure could result in participants being overly familiar with the items, which could result in response bias. In addition, there is a lack of experimental control. Taken alone, the differences in scores between discharge and admission cannot account for change related to the partial hospitalization program in which Lenz et al.'s adolescents participated. The passage of time could have resulted in a decrease in symptom severity. However, Lenz et al. included a qualitative component to the study in which participants were interviewed. Thus, by examining both quantitative and qualitative findings, the researchers could further substantiate the benefits of the program.

Cohort Studies

Cohort studies study a specific population with a common characteristic over time. The distinguishing characteristic between cohort and panel studies is that the population remains the same in the cohort study, but the participants are different at each administration. In other words, the respondents share similar characteristics but vary over two or more administrations. For example, if a counselor wanted to look at changes in the way adolescents perceive social media in a panel study, he or she would survey the same students year after year. In a cohort study, each new 10th-grade class, for example, would be surveyed each year. Note that the population is the same, but the participants differ.

Trend Studies

Trend studies are similar to cohort studies in that they evaluate a specific population over time, but in trend studies having a constant common characteristic is not necessary. Although the population is the same, the location or region from which the participants are recruited may vary. For example, when the Centers for Disease Control and Prevention (2011) administers the Youth Risk Behavior Survey, the participants and representatives from various regions may be quite different. As participants in trend studies may have little in common, obtaining a large, representative sample is extremely important to producing generalizable findings.

Designing Research Studies to Address Trends and Change Over Time

Each of the aforementioned designs—within-subjects designs, SCRD, surveys, and longitudinal studies—may be used to describe populations, trends, treatment efficacy, and changes over time. Within-subjects designs and SCRD may often include fewer participants, which may result in exclusion from publication in many academic journals because of limitations in generalizability due to small sample sizes and threats to experimental validity. Such studies can be strengthened with the addition of mixed designs (e.g., the addition of a between-subjects element), experimental control (e.g., random assignment, counterbalancing), or mixed methods (e.g., the addition of a qualitative component).

Survey research and longitudinal studies require larger sample sizes, and these can be difficult to obtain. Response rates for Internet research in counseling tend to be low, and the expense of mailing out surveys tends to make the use of such methods less prevalent in counseling research. Furthermore, the adequacy of survey development requires particular attention. Item clarity and the validity and reliability of the measures are extremely important considerations in survey research (see Chapter 12). The following considerations should be noted when designing research studies to address trends and change over time:

1. The stability of the measure is extremely important to developing baseline scores that are meaningful and provide an accurate representation of the construct of interest for the participants.
2. The importance of the validity and reliability of the measures cannot be overstated. Part of the foundation of studies in counseling research is based on the psychometric properties of the instruments utilized in the studies. The use of instruments for which the theoretical underpinnings are lacking or methods for establishing validity are in question leads to research studies that are not generalizable or do not contribute to the counseling literature.
3. Participant selection is an important consideration and contributes to both the generalizability and limitations of a study. Justification of the design and sample size and explanations of solicitation are essential to demonstrating trends and change over time.
4. When a study includes an intervention or treatment, the fidelity of the approach needs to be demonstrated (Ray, 2015). That is, the consistency of the intervention needs to be documented.

How was the treatment implemented? Were the providers of the treatment adequately trained? Was the method of implementation consistent over time, and how was that evaluated? The Methods section of a study should include details on the implementation of interventions and strategies.

Chapter Summary

Within-subjects designs use repeated measures to detect changes or effects over time or from different perspectives. For example, a child's behavior may be evaluated over different time points at Weeks 1, 3, and 5; or a child's behavior could be evaluated from the perspectives of the teacher, parent, and counselor. The common element is the use of multiple measures over a common individual or group. In the case of surveys, obtaining information and describing a group, which is hopefully generalizable to the population of interest, is the primary goal. Surveys may be an initial snapshot or may be used to conduct longitudinal research.

The unit of observation can be participants in a group (or in the case of a mixed design, groups) or a series of individuals (as in SCRD). The analytical process for within-subjects designs is similar to what was addressed in Chapter 7 for between-groups designs. However, SCRD uses unique tools based on visual analysis and ES to determine treatment efficacy and changes over time. The implementation of repeated measures designs may be time consuming because of their longitudinal nature. In addition, researchers need to be vigilant with respect to treatment fidelity and the selection of valid measures that are designed to be used repeatedly over the course of a study.

Suggested Activities

I. Review the following article:

Reiner, S. M., Dobmeier, R. A., & Hernández, T. J. (2013). Perceived impact of professional counselor identity. An exploratory study. *Journal of Counseling & Development, 91,* 174–183. doi:10.1002/j.1556-6676.2013.00084.x

1. What was the construct of interest related to the population studied? What did the researchers want to learn from this survey?
2. Do you believe the results of this study to be generalizable? Why or why not?

3. If this study were to be expanded into a longitudinal study, how could it be done? Would it fit as a panel, cohort, or trend study? Explain your answer.

II. The *Journal of Counseling & Development, 93*(4), highlighted the use of SCRD. Review the issue and consider the following:

1. What do you believe are the advantages and disadvantages of SCRD?
2. Should SCRD be used more often in counseling research? Explain your answer.

References

Achenbach, T. M., & Rescorla, L. A. (2001). *Manual for the ASEBA School-Age Forms and Profiles*. Burlington, VT: University of Vermont, Research Center for Children, Youth, and Families.

Balkin, R. S. (2013). From the editor. *Journal of Counseling & Development, 91,* 259–260. doi:10.1002/j.1556-6676.2013.00093.x

Carlson, R. G., Barden, S. M., Daire, A. P., & Greene, J. (2014). Influence of relationship education on relationship satisfaction for low-income couples. *Journal of Counseling & Development, 92,* 418–427. doi:10.1002/j.1556-6676.2014.00168.x

Centers for Disease Control and Prevention. (2011). *Youth Risk Behavior Surveillance System (YRBSS).* Retrieved from www.cdc.gov/yrbs

Davis, R. J., Balkin, R. S., & Juhnke, G. A. (2014). Validation of the Juhnke-Balkin Life Balance Inventory. *Measurement and Evaluation in Counseling & Development, 47,* 181–198. doi:10.1177/0748175614531796.

Derogatis, L., R. (1993). *BSI: Administration, scoring, and procedures for the Brief Symptom Inventory* (3rd ed.) Minneapolis, MN: National Computer Systems.

Derogatis, L., R. (1996). *SCL-90-R: Symptom Checklist–90–Revised: Administration, scoring, and procedures manual*. Bloomington, MN: NCS Pearson.

Ikonomopoulos, J., Smith, R. L., & Schmidt, C. (2015). Integrating narrative therapy within rehabilitative programming for incarcerated adolescents. *Journal of Counseling & Development, 93,* 460–470. doi:10.1002/jcad.12044

Lane, D. M. (Ed.). (n.d.). *Online statistics education: An interactive multimedia course of study*. Retrieved from http://onlinestatbook.com

Lenz, A. S. (2013). Calculating effect size in single-case research: A comparison of nonoverlap methods. *Measurement and Evaluation in Counseling and Development, 46,* 64–73. doi:10.1177/0748175612456401

Lenz, A. S. (2015). Using single-case research designs to demonstrate evidence for counseling practices. *Journal of Counseling & Development, 93,* 387–393. doi:10.1002/jcad.12036

Lenz, A. S., Del Conte, G., Lancaster, C., Bailey, L., & Vanderpool, E. (2014). Evaluation of a partial hospitalization program for adolescents. *Counseling Outcome Research and Evaluation, 5,* 3–16. doi:10.1177/2150137813518063

Liang, B., Tracy, A. J., Kenny, M. E., Brogan, D., & Gatha, R. (2010). The Relational Health Indices for Youth: An examination of reliability and validity aspects. *Measurement and Evaluation in Counseling and Development, 42,* 255–274. doi:10.1177/0748175609354596

Ma, H. H. (2006). An alternative method for quantitative synthesis of single-subject research: Percentage of data points exceeding the median. *Behavior Modification, 30,* 598–617. doi:10.1177/0145445504272974

O'Neill, R. E., McDonnell, J. J., Billingsley, F. F., & Jenson, W. R. (2011). *Single case research designs in educational and community settings.* Upper Saddle River, NJ: Pearson.

Parker, R. I., & Vannest, K. J. (2009). An improved effect size for single case research: Nonoverlap of all pairs (NAP). *Behavior Therapy, 40*(4), 357–367. doi:10.1016/j.beth.2008.10.006

Ray, D. C. (2015). Single-case research design and analysis: Counseling applications. *Journal of Counseling & Development, 93,* 394–402. doi:10.1002/jcad.12037

Reiner, S. M., Dobmeier, R. A., & Hernández, T. J. (2013). Perceived impact of professional counselor identity. An exploratory study. *Journal of Counseling & Development, 91,* 174–183. doi:10.1002/j.1556-6676.2013.00084.x

Scruggs, T. E., Mastropieri, M. A., & Casto, G. (1987). The quantitative synthesis of single-subject research: Methodology and validation. *Remedial and Special Education, 8*(2), 24–33. doi:10.1177/074193258700800206

Trusty, J. (2011). Quantitative articles: Developing studies for publication in counseling journals. *Journal of Counseling & Development, 89,* 261–267. doi:10.1002/j.1556-6678.2011.tb00087.x

Trusty, J., Thompson, B., & Petrocelli, J. V. (2004). Practical guide for reporting effect size in quantitative research in the *Journal of Counseling & Development*. *Journal of Counseling & Development, 82,* 107–110. doi:10.1002/j.1556-6678.2004.tb00291.x

Vannest, K. J., & Ninci, J. (2015). Evaluating intervention effects in single-case research designs. *Journal of Counseling & Development, 93,* 403–411. doi:10.1002/jcad.12038

Synthesizing Research Results Using Meta-Analysis

A. Stephen Lenz

Overview

So far you have reviewed several important ways in which counseling researchers can model relationships between constructs and identify the degree to which interventions or programs are associated with therapeutic effects. In this chapter, I review a research strategy that systematically identifies and integrates available research on a grand scale to answer the fundamental questions of what works, for whom, how, and under what circumstances. The purpose of this chapter is to orient you to the general activities associated with completing a systematic review of empirical literature in the context of meta-analysis. In this discussion, you will begin to understand how foundational concepts, inherent processes, and prudent interpretation of findings contribute to an even-handed depiction of relationships between predictive variables or interventions and associated outcomes. After this, future directions in the meta-analysis and limitations are reviewed.

Why Conduct a Meta-Analysis?

Previous conceptualizations of evidence-based practice in medicine, education, and the helping professions placed a heavy emphasis on the results of individual studies that used statistical significance testing to determine the merit of an intervention or program. For example, Chambless and colleagues (1996, 1998) considered only two well-designed experiments to be necessary for designation as an evidence-based practice. By contrast, contemporary conceptualizations of evidence-based practice (Tolin, McKay, Forman, Klonsky, & Thombs, 2015; Wampold, Lichtenberg, & Waehler, 2002) have called for the consideration of all available evidence together using systematic and quantifiable methodology for review. *Meta-analysis* refers to a statistical method of quantitatively summarizing the results from primary studies to yield a more precise estimate of intervention effects that has greater statistical power, reflects greater diversity in population samples, and thus is more generalizable. These summaries of individual studies are done in a manner that accounts for threats to internal validity, the influence of sample size, statistical power, and reporting bias. With a more comprehensive, quantifiable depiction of the relationship between an intervention and outcomes of interest, stakeholders such as policymakers, third-party payers, school districts, mental health agencies, and individual practitioners can make informed decisions about which interventions may best suit their population.

All meta-analyses are intended to answer two types of research questions: those related to the mean effect across all eligible studies for synthesis and those related to the participant and study variables that influence the mean effect. Example research questions related to the mean effect include the following:

- "To what degree is [the Coping Cat program] effective for decreasing the severity of anxiety symptoms compared to no-treatment or viable alternative counseling interventions?" (Lenz, 2015, p. 53)
- "What is the comparative effectiveness of different types of outpatient treatment for adolescents with substance use disorders?" (Tanner-Smith, Wilson, & Lipsey, 2013, p. 146)

In each case, the results of individual primary studies are being combined to yield an overall mean effect. Example research questions related to exploring how participant and study characteristics influence the mean effect include the following:

- "To what degree do treatment effect size estimates yielded from clinician-based versus self-report measures differ?" (Lenz & Williams, 2014, p. 77)

- "What differences between the characteristics of the participant samples, the treatment programs, and the study methods are related to those changes in substance use?" (Tanner-Smith et al., 2013, p. 146)

Although these may appear to be simple enough to understand, the elements of a meta-analysis that are addressed in this chapter are systematic, thorough, and place an emphasis on precision and practicality.

Elements of a Meta-Analysis

Whether you are conducting your own meta-analysis or just reviewing a research report, some common elements are regarded as necessary for inspecting the rationale, method, results, and implications of a study. In the same way that one would expect reporting in primary studies to promote replication through transparency, meta-analysts regard some elements of their work to be essential for putting the findings in context and determining the potential of the results to influence practice, programming, and policy within counseling settings. Reference guides such as the *Preferred Reporting Items for Systematic Reviews and Meta-Analyses* (PRISMA; Moher, Liberati, Tetzlaff, Altman, & The PRISMA Group, 2009) and *Meta-Analysis Reporting Standards* (American Psychological Association, 2009) have emerged as helpful resources for practitioners and researchers that provide depictions of standardized components. In this section, I review some of the universal elements that characterize systematic reviews and meta-analyses, with particular attention to those elements related to developing the methodology and reporting results.

Reporting Elements of Methodology

Every meta-analysis is born out of a defensible purpose to synthesize previous study results. Once this need is established and related research questions have been developed, a systematic approach to searching for relevant research reports that contain the type of information that supports the expressed intent can begin. Broadly speaking, meta-analysts focus their attention on methodological details associated with (a) establishing eligibility criteria for studies to be included in and excluded from the analysis; (b) developing a search strategy; (c) coding relevant data, which allows for the computation of individual and aggregate effect sizes; and

(d) completing analyses that estimate treatment effects, precision of estimates, and moderator variables. It should be noted that the features of each of these methodological characteristics are predicated on the type of data with which a researcher is working. For example, strategies that intend to aggregate single-group, pre/post contrasts, or between-groups contrasts will vary considerably from those that are inspecting associations between variables. With this assumption in mind, each of these methodological components is introduced and briefly discussed in the context of exploring clinical phenomena relevant to counseling practice.

Establishing Eligibility Through Inclusion and Exclusion Criteria

Part of any good meta-analytic plan involves establishing the type of studies that can help address your research questions. Several authors (Cooper, 2010; Erford, Savin-Murphy, & Butler, 2010; Lipsey & Wilson, 2001) have depicted general recommendations for study criteria; however, these recommendations can be summarized generally as being related to characteristics of either the study (design features, sample characteristics, time frame, type of publication, cultural considerations) or the intervention and related outcomes (interventions of interest and related variables).

Study Characteristics

When identifying which studies to include in or exclude from their meta-analysis, researchers often begin with some important information related to study characteristics. *Design features* refers to the general degree to which a study's parameters fit with the type of questions guiding the study. For example, if a researcher is interested in exploring the effectiveness of an intervention, the results of single-case research designs or between-groups designs may be of interest; by contrast, if a researcher is exploring associations between two or more constructs, predictive designs would be of interest.

Sample characteristics refers to broad demographic characteristics of the sample, such as age, gender, and ethnic identity, but also more specific features of interest, such as diagnostic category, setting (e.g., school, the community, inpatient facilities), or education level.

It is also helpful for researchers to specify the time range of included studies to increase the relevance of their findings to the contemporary sociopolitical contexts within which counselors work. For example, although motivational approaches to treating substance use disorders are longstanding, Lenz, Rosenbaum, and Sheperis (2016) limited their investigation of motivational enhancement therapy to a 20-year time frame from 1995 to 2014 because of procedural developments associated with Project MATCH, which has become the gold-standard reference for the intervention.

Researchers are also required to identify the publication type that is of interest in answering their research questions. Most systematic reviews are completed with the assumption that a comprehensive and exhaustive effort was made to include data reported from varied sources, including published journal articles, books, treatment manuals, dissertations, theses, data repositories, technical reports, unpublished manuscripts, and conference proceedings. Any decision not to find and include data from these sources should be identified and justified.

Finally, *cultural considerations* refers to broader cultural identity and linguistic concerns that may interfere with including reported data in a way that is accurate. For example, many meta-analysts exclude primary studies that would prove difficult to translate, that are not culturally homogeneous with the rest of the sample of studies, or in which representation of constructs is not equivalent across cultures. Once these basic study characteristics have been identified and defined, researchers can proceed to depicting the intervention and related outcome characteristics that will complete the picture of studies to be included in their analyses.

Characteristics Related to Interventions of Interest and Related Variables

Meta-analyses can have a scope that varies from narrow (dialectical behavior therapy) to broad (cognitive behavior therapies), and thus researchers are encouraged to specify characteristics related to the interventions that are under investigation. For example, Lenz, Hall, and Smith (2016) investigated the effectiveness of an 8-session mindfulness-based cognitive therapy protocol (Segal, Williams, & Teasdale, 2002). Although several applications of the original protocol by Segal et al. (2002) have been made, Lenz, Hall, and Smith (2016) specified this approach as the strategy of interest based on the justification that the majority of trainings, certifications, and primary research studies were grounded in the original 8-session approach.

Finally, researchers should identify and operationalize any related variables that are hypothesized to be influenced by the intervention of interest. Related variables can be continuous (such as scores on a standardized inventory) or categorical (such as the proportion of individuals who relapse after a follow-up interval vs. those who do not). In this example, Lenz et al. (2016) defined their variable of interest as the severity of depression symptoms based on *Diagnostic and Statistical Manual of Mental Disorders, Fourth Edition, Text Revision* (American Psychiatric Association, 2000) or *Diagnostic and Statistical Manual of Mental Disorders, Fifth Edition* (American Psychiatric Association, 2013) criteria at treatment termination and follow-up intervals.

Search Strategy

Once a meta-analyst has established what types of studies are eligible for inclusion through inclusion and exclusion criteria, he or she can move forward with establishing a systematic search strategy. In an effort to develop a representative population of studies, researchers are interested in putting together an approach for locating studies that is thorough, recursive, and exhaustive of available resources. Often this requires multiple searches that move from exploratory in nature to more extensive and targeted. Furthermore, based on guidelines for reporting in the PRISMA and Meta-Analysis Reporting Standards, a certain degree of document accounting should take place so that the process is transparent and replicable. A multitude of strategies have been recommended for identifying studies for inclusion (White, 2009); however, the strategies that are contemporarily used are associated with (a) electronic database searches, (b) journal-specific searches, (c) repository searches, (d) footnote chasing, and (e) consultation. In each case, the strategy implemented is intended to obtain all available published reports (white paper literature) as well as those unpublished documents (gray literature) that may contribute to a more accurate depiction of treatment effect or relations between variables.

Database Searches

With myriad databases available for researchers to access, Reed and Baxter (2009) suggested that selection of which ones to query should be based on disciplinary scope, access, date, language, and country and the degree to which it includes unpublished work. Each bibliographic database has a target discipline within its scope of coverage that should be considered by researchers. For example, databases such as PsycINFO and Academic Search Complete both contain behavioral and mental health documents; however, Academic Search Complete also contains abstracts for documents in related fields, such as ethnic and cultural studies, women's studies, and theology, which may extend the yield of a search. Given the complications of a pay-for-access system of publication abstracting and indexing, researchers should also consider whether they have access to a database; what time frame is covered in their access; whether that access includes documents from another language or country; and whether the access includes unpublished documents such as dissertations, theses, or government reports. In the event that someone cannot access a particular database or access is limited, searching target journals by hand or pursuing another means may be a prudent alternative. When conducting any search, it is a good idea to use search terms and variations of search terms that target your topic, population of interest, and intervention. For example, when completing a meta-analysis of the effectiveness of trauma-focused cognitive behavior therapy for treating the symptoms of posttraumatic stress disorder, Lenz and Hollenbaugh (2015) used the search strings "TF-CBT" and "trauma" to identify the topic, intervention, and dependent variable; variations included "trauma-focused CBT" and "PTSD" and "posttraumatic."

Journal-Specific Searches

Completing a search for candidate articles requires a certain familiarity with your topic and the types of publication outlets in which research reports may typically be found. Often researchers choose to pursue flagship journals of the related profession (e.g., *Journal of Counseling & Development* for counseling), specialty publications (e.g., *Counseling Outcome Research and Evaluation* for outcome research), and topic-specific periodicals (e.g., *Journal of Aggression, Maltreatment & Trauma* for trauma interventions) to promote a broad, recursive yield of candidate articles. Journal-specific searches are an important part of any systematic search strategy because not every database has full access to journals relevant to your topic, or databases may have limited access. With increased access to peer-reviewed publications, searching specific journals for candidate articles can be done easily online or using a more traditional, hand-search approach in a library.

Repository Searches

Repository searches are those that access any of the many data storage and management resources available to researchers. Often these open-source, free repositories contain collections of published and unpublished studies along with relevant commentary regarding quality and implications. For example, Lenz (2015) searched the Substance Abuse and Mental Health Services Administration's National Registry of Evidence-Based Programs and Practices. Unlike these broad-reaching government resources, some repositories have a more narrow focus, such as those operated by the National Center for Education Statistics and the National Child Stress Network. Specific to meta-analyses, the Campbell Collaboration and Cochran Collaboration have developed and maintained repositories of meta-analyses and systematic reviews addressing topics such as mental health intervention, public health policy, social welfare programming, and educational activities.

Footnote Chasing

Footnote chasing refers to the adroit usage of article footnotes or previous authors' reference lists to identify relevant research reports for inclusion in an analysis (White, 2009). White (2009) noted that the strength of this approach lies in the almost immediately accessible identification of primary studies related to the study topic. After all, it is easier to comb through a series of reference lists than the hundreds of results returned from a single database search. Common sources of footnote chasing include primary studies that have been identified for inclusion, educational or treatment manuals, and reference lists of related meta-analyses.

Consultation

Meta-analysts are rarely topic experts on the majority of primary studies that contribute to a meta-analysis; therefore, it is important that they consult with experts who may be. Ideal targets for consultation are typically individuals who have developed or pioneered the particular intervention meta-analysts are investigating, general topic experts, or colleagues with in-depth knowledge of the content area. For example, when completing a meta-analysis of the Coping Cat program, Lenz (2015) contacted the developer of the program as well as those pioneers who had modified the program for Canadian and Australian applications. In each of the three cases, communication with these individuals provided guidance and support to either identify additional studies or attest that there were no additional studies that they could provide.

Data Collection and Coding Processes

Once meta-analysts have collected their population of studies (*N*) and applied their inclusion and exclusion to define their sample (*k*), they can proceed to coding the data that will support reporting and analysis. Several authors (Erford et al., 2010; Lipsey, 2009; Lipsey & Wilson, 2001; Whiston & Li, 2011) have recommended guidelines for what data should be coded and to what end; however, the broad categories of interest to meta-analysts include bibliographic information, data needed to compute effect sizes, and study descriptors that support subgroup and moderator analyses. Bibliographic data include all of the aspects associated with reporting an American Psychological Association–style reference, including author names, publication titles, and page numbers. Data needed to compute effect sizes can take several forms depending on the type of research question the meta-analyst is attempting to answer, but most often this information will help researchers compute standardized values for mean gain, mean difference, proportion difference, logged odds ratio, or product–moment *r*. (You will learn more about effect sizes, what data are required to compute them, and when each is indicated in the next section, but now it is sufficient to understand that like in other aspects of a meta-analysis, accurately identifying and coding this information is critical to accurately depicting treatment effects.) Finally, meta-analysts are interested in coding study descriptors such as sample size, study quality, important demographic characteristics, and intervention features. With these three categories of information accounted for, meta-analysts can transparently document which studies they have included in their analyses and proceed to answering questions related to aggregated mean effect sizes across all studies and for whom, how, and under what circumstances the mean effect applies to the broader population represented by the sample of included studies.

When coding data from primary studies, meta-analysts are encouraged to use a coding guide that depicts the target bibliographic, effect size, and study descriptor data of interest. In addition, it is recommended that more than one person identify, code, and document the target data and enter this information independently into a general data management system such as Microsoft Excel or one specific to meta-analysis, such as Comprehensive Meta-Analysis or Mix 2.0. The use of a coding guide and multiple coders promotes consistency, accuracy, and computation of interrater reliability, all of which increase the internal validity of a study.

Estimates of Treatment Effect and Precision

Although testing statistical significance is valuable, it is also limited (a) because of the influence that sample size has on results and (b) because of the tendency of consumers of research to regard p values as the chances that a null hypothesis is false, interpreting small p values as generalizable to larger populations and regarding findings in a binary reject/do not reject manner that can obscure the merit of an intervention or relationship (Valentine, Aloe, & Lau, 2015). As an alternative, meta-analysts rely on the use of effect size metrics to depict the value of associations between interventions and outcomes as well as between criterion and predictor variables. *Effect size* is a broad term referencing a class of metrics that depict the magnitude of change among scores associated with an intervention and the direction in which that change occurs (Ellis, 2010; Thompson, 2007). Several authors (Ellis, 2010; Lipsey & Wilson, 2001; Trusty, Thompson, & Petrocelli, 2004) have suggested that the beauty of estimations of effect size is that they standardize the findings of primary studies regardless of differing types of measures, variables, and populations in a way that is easily conceptualized by individuals who may not have advanced statistical training. When researchers use effect size estimates, they not only promote an even-handed estimation of the efficacy of an individual study but also promote the aggregation of results across studies to yield a mean effect size that can be generalized to a larger population under the right circumstances.

The myriad effect sizes available to researchers can be grouped into two classes: those that represent differences within and between groups (the d family) and those that depict association between variables (the r family). Both classes of effect sizes have potential for depicting meaningful relationships that can inform counseling practice. The d family of effect sizes can be implemented with continuous outcomes such as scores on a standardized anxiety inventory and result in common metrics such as Cohen's d, Hedges's g, or probability of superiority. Those d family metrics that depict dichotomous outcomes, such as whether a participant will report the criteria for major depressive disorder at follow-up, are represented by metrics including risk difference, risk ratio, and odds ratio. The r family of effect sizes is indicated for estimating the degree of correlation (e.g., Pearson's r, Kendall's τ, Spearman's ρ) and proportion of variance (Cohen's f, η^2, R^2). It should be noted that not all effect size metrics are created equal, and decisions regarding which one is most appropriate for a study should be based on the characteristics and type of variables under inspection.

The magnitudes of the effect sizes of primary studies can be distorted by the influence of sample size and sampling error, and as a result effect size metrics can be either biased or unbiased in their depiction of magnitudes (Erford et al., 2010; Lipsey & Wilson, 2001). When a biased effect size, such as Cohen's *d* ($d = M_1 - M_2 / S_p$), is used, a study with a small sample (e.g., $N = 20$) that has a greater degree of inherent sampling error would yield the same estimate of treatment effect as one with a very large sample ($N = 220$) with much less random error. Therefore, meta-analysts typically use unbiased effect sizes, such as Hedges's $g = d \times (1 - [3/4N - 9])$, to estimate individual study outcomes as a standard of practice. Likewise, meta-analysts also attempt to account for each study's contribution within the combined grand mean effect size formula by weighting individual study effect sizes ($w = 2n / 4[1 - r] + ES^2$) to adjust for the degree of sampling error associated with sample size (Borenstein, Hedges, Higgins, & Rothstein, 2009; Erford et al., 2010). Subsequently, the sum of individual weighted effect sizes is divided by the sum weights to yield a mean effect size estimate. In a meta-analysis, it is common to report the effect size estimates of individual studies as well as the aggregated grand mean visually and narratively, respectively.

Confidence Intervals

Although an effect size estimate reveals information about the magnitude of a treatment effect or relationship between variables, it does not provide any information related to how precise and defensible that estimation is. Thus, meta-analysts are compelled to compute and report the confidence intervals that surround their individual and mean effect sizes (Borenstein et al., 2009; Shadish & Haddock, 2009). Confidence intervals are grounded in the standard error estimates of an effect size and are therefore influenced by sample size to depict relationships with sampling error. For example, a study with 20 participants will almost certainly have a much larger confidence interval than one with 220 participants. Furthermore, researchers in the social sciences and counseling in particular tend to compute their estimates to reflect 95% or 99% degrees of certainty. For example, Lenz, Taylor, Fleming, and Serman (2014) used 95% confidence intervals to evaluate the effectiveness of dialectical behavior therapy for treating eating disorders and related depression symptoms, whereas Whiston, Tai, Rahardja, and Eder (2011) used 99% confidence intervals to examine school counseling interventions on a range of outcomes. The larger the confidence interval value, the wider researchers can expect their intervals to be. When meta-analysts present effect sizes and their confidence intervals, a more accurate depiction of treatment effect can be considered.

Prediction Intervals

Although effect sizes and confidence intervals provide meta-analysts with important information about interventions and relationship among constructs, they do not provide an indication of the distribution of true effects around the mean effect size (Borenstein et al., 2009). Whereas confidence intervals communicate information about the precision of the mean effect, prediction intervals illustrate the dispersion of effect sizes in a manner analogous to the Gaussian curve associated with population samples in a primary study. With this information, meta-analysts can provide an estimate of the parameters within which an effect size could be expected to occur.

Additional Analyses

As mentioned previously, all meta-analyses are intended to address not just which interventions work or which variables covary on average but also who the mean effect best represents and under what circumstances. When the effect sizes in a sample of studies are evenly distributed or relatively similar, then the sample of studies is said to be homogeneous, and the mean effect can be considered characteristic of the demographic and clinical variables represented in the sample. Conversely, when homogeneity cannot be assumed and a sample of studies is regarded as heterogeneous, meta-analysts are compelled to complete additional analyses of variables that may moderate the mean effect. Exploring these moderator variables assists in depicting for whom, how, and under what circumstances an intervention may be most indicated. Two strategies for exploring moderators of mean effects are subgroup analysis and metaregression.

Subgroup Analysis

Subgroup analysis is in many ways analogous to analysis of variance for primary studies, which was discussed in previous chapters. When used in a meta-analytic context, subgroup analysis allows researchers to inspect the mean effect for categorical subgroups in a sample of studies. Some categories of interest with a documented history of influencing effect size include study quality (randomized trials vs. quasi-experiments), domicile (domestic vs. international), and treatment setting (inpatient vs. outpatient). For example, Lenz, Henesy, and Callender (2016) evaluated the degree to which a treatment program was effective for treating co-occurring posttraumatic stress disorder and substance use disorders. In their analyses, the treatment was inspected across the mean effects for the categorical types of trauma (e.g., sexual assault, domestic violence) represented in a sample of studies. Although there are a few strategies for completing subgroup analyses, a general rule of thumb suggests that in the absence of overlap between confidence intervals for subgroups, a statistically significant difference between the categories of studies represented will be detected (Borenstein et al., 2009).

Metaregression

In the same way that subgroup analyses help meta-analysts explain the influence of categorical variables on the mean effect size, metaregression illustrates predictive associations with continuous study variables. By weighting individual studies within a predictive model, meta-analysts are able to compute an R^2 value that explains the proportion of variance in the mean effect size that can be accounted for. Examples of continuous variables that are of interest to meta-analysts include publication year, mean age of primary study samples, and percentage of men versus women in primary study samples. For example, Lenz, Hall, et al. (2016) detected a statistically significant metaregression model ($R^2 = .36$) depicting that the mean age of participants was negatively associated with decreases in depression symptoms following the completion of an 8-session mindfulness-based cognitive therapy intervention. Although metaregression is a wonderful addition to the meta-analyst's toolbox, it is often limited by its notoriously underpowered nature, requiring a minimum of 10 studies per variable in the regression model (Borenstein et al., 2009).

Reporting and Interpreting Meta-Analysis Results

Several authors have reported on the type of data that should be reported from a meta-analysis (Borenstein et al., 2009; Moher et al., 2009; Rubin & Bellamy, 2012). Some variation will always exist due to the types of analyses associated with the research questions; however, at a basic level some common elements have emerged. In this section, I discuss reporting and interpreting meta-analytic results, particularly those that support practical inferences from data that can guide counselor decision making.

Mean Effect, Confidence Intervals, and Prediction Intervals

As mentioned in the previous section, meta-analysts are charged with depicting mean effect sizes, identifying estimates of precision for the mean effect through confidence intervals, and predicting how true effects are dispersed through a population of studies. Some important things to consider when interpreting mean effect sizes include identifying the direction of the value (positive or negative) and situating the values in context. A negative effect size (e.g., –.75) indicates a decreased occurrence compared to another treatment; conversely, a positive effect size (e.g., .75) indicates an increased occurrence. In addition, consumers of meta-analytic research are encouraged not to become fixated on the size of a mean effect but instead always consider the practical context and clinical implications of their findings. When considering this point, Ellis (2010) suggested that small effects may prompt bigger outcomes, small effects can accumulate into larger ones over time, and large effects may apply to too few people to make much of an impact.

Figure 9.1 depicts a hypothetical intervention outcome scenario in which the mean Hedges's *g* effect size is –.55 with an associated 95% confidence interval ranging from a lower limit of –.66 to an upper limit of –.44 and a prediction interval ranging from a lower limit of –.73 to an upper limit of –.37. In this scenario, the mean effect size of –.55 suggests that the hypothetical intervention outperformed the alternative treatment to the degree of about 55% of 1 *SD*. The small-size confidence interval and prediction interval bands surrounding the mean effect size indicate that the researcher can be fairly confident in the precision of the detected mean effect. What is not depicted in this plot but which is important to note is that the mean effect size also has a standard deviation, referred to as *tau* (τ), just like the mean in a primary study, that influences the distribution of true effects across studies. For this hypothetical data set, the findings would be reported as yielding a mean effect size of –.55, 95% confidence interval [–.66, –.44], $p < .01$, $\tau = .08$. Furthermore, inspection of the prediction interval indicates that the range of possible effect sizes that can be expected from studies of the intervention to comparison intervention treatment falls between –.73 and –.37. When looking solely at the numbers we cannot tell much of what this means to clients or students, but if we apply context a better picture forms. For example, what if this intervention were associated with symptoms of major depressive episodes?

Summary Tables and Visual Displays

The use of summary tables and visual displays such as forest plots is a cornerstone of meta-analytic study reporting because of their ability to collate large amounts of data succinctly and enable the

Study and Statistics

Study	Hedges's *g*	*SE*	95% CI	*p*
Study 20	–0.12	0.25	[–0.36, 0.61]	.620
Study 19	–0.12	0.30	[–0.71, 0.48]	.700
Study 18	–0.14	0.34	[–0.80, 0.53]	.690
Study 17	–0.31	0.42	[–1.14, 0.52]	.460
Study 16	–0.36	0.31	[–0.96, 0.24]	.240
Study 15	–0.39	0.48	[–1.34, 0.55]	.420
Study 14	–0.40	0.24	[–0.87, 0.06]	.090
Study 13	–0.46	0.23	[–0.90, 0.02]	.040
Study 12	–0.46	0.39	[–1.22, 0.29]	.230
Study 11	–0.47	0.21	[–0.87, –0.06]	.020
Study 10	–0.54	0.16	[–0.86, –0.21]	.000
Study 9	–0.57	0.26	[–1.07, –0.07]	.030
Study 8	–0.58	0.40	[–1.36, 0.19]	.140
Study 7	–0.59	0.18	[–0.94, –0.24]	.000
Study 6	–0.61	0.29	[–1.19, –0.03]	.040
Study 5	–0.63	0.32	[–1.27, –0.00]	.050
Study 4	–0.64	0.19	[–1.01, –0.26]	.000
Study 3	–0.66	0.14	[–0.94, –0.38]	.000
Study 2	–0.78	0.17	[–1.11, –0.46]	.000
Study 1	–1.00	0.18	[–1.35, –0.65]	.000
Mean	–0.55	0.06	[–0.66, –0.44]	.000

Hedges's *g* and 95% CI

–2.00 –1.00 0.00 1.00 2.00

Favors Intervention — Favors Comparison

FIGURE 9.1

Forest Plot Example of Effect Sizes (ESs), Confidence Intervals (CIs), and *p* Values in Studies

Note. Forest plot of Hedges's *g* ESs, 95% CIs, and *p* values for studies evaluating the effectiveness of an intervention versus alternative treatment for decreasing symptoms of depression. *SE* = standard error.

identification of patterns that may otherwise go unnoticed (Anzures-Cabrera & Higgins, 2010; Beretvas, 2010; Derzon & Alford, 2013). Summary tables in meta-analyses commonly depict descriptive characteristics of individual studies that are helpful for placing them into context with one another while also providing information that is relevant to moderator analyses. For example, Lenz, Bruijn, Serman, and Bailey (2014) provided information related to length of treatment, treatment setting, sample size, mean participant age, ethnic identity, and type of comparison group. This information not only aided in characterizing the population of studies in their analyses but also provided important information that was used in understanding the heterogeneity of the mean effect size. Other summary tables, such as those depicted by Whiston et al. (2011), document important statistical information for readers to consider.

With study characteristics accounted for through summary tables, meta-analysts are compelled to illustrate their findings using visual aids such as *forest plots* to depict information related to mean effect size, confidence intervals, and prediction intervals. Forest plots such as the one depicted in Figure 9.1 were named to be congruent with the idiom "See the forest for the trees" because their depiction of individual and mean effect sizes helps consumers of research consider the bigger picture that exists within the universe of studies rather than take a short-sighted view by focusing on just one or a few studies (Borenstein et al., 2009). It is common practice to depict the effect size, confidence intervals, and *p* values for individual studies and the mean effect. Individual studies are marked by their bibliographic identifier, with a shape (line, square, circle) to indicate the effect size and confidence intervals indicated by whiskers on either side of the effect size indicator. Mean effect sizes and confidence intervals, such as the values depicted in Figure 9.1, are indicated by a diamond spanning the range of values; a horizontal line through the mean effect diamond represents the prediction interval.

Heterogeneity Among the Sample of Studies

It is expected that the many studies included in a meta-analysis will have differing results. Therefore, meta-analysts compute and report estimates of the degree to which similar and dissimilar results influence the mean effect size. When there is little variation among the studies, meta-analytic results are regarded as homogeneous, and secondary inspection of subgroups and metaregression may not be warranted. By contrast, when there is considerable variation among the studies, the meta-analytic results are regarded as heterogeneous, and secondary analyses are warranted.

Two common strategies for estimating the degree of heterogeneity among studies are inspecting Cochran's Q and the inconsistency index (I^2). As a rule of thumb, when Q values are statistically significant and greater than degrees of freedom (the number of studies in an analysis minus 1), heterogeneity may be suspected (Borenstein et al., 2009; Lipsey & Wilson, 2001). In addition, when I^2 is near or greater than 50%, the dispersion of effect sizes may be considered problematic (Erford et al., 2010; Higgins, Thompson, Deeks, & Altman, 2003). Taken together, these two metrics support inferences about the degree to which heterogeneity among individual studies may influence a mean effect size; however, it is important to note that meta-analysts cannot rely solely on these numbers, and they should always be considered in the context of the number of studies, the size of the effect, and the strength of evidence they are associated with. In the sample of studies depicted in Figure 9.1 ($k = 20$, $df = 19$), $Q = 21.52$, $p = .30$, and $I^2 = 11.72$. In this example, Q is not less than the degrees of freedom, yet it is far from being statistically significant, and the I^2 value is far from 50. When these facts are combined with the medium-size sample of studies and the robust mean effect with small confidence intervals, it is likely that we can prudently regard the mean effect as having little influence from heterogeneity among studies.

Risk of Bias Among the Sample of Studies

Every meta-analytic report should evaluate the degree to which the results have been influenced by biases related to reporting outcomes of primary studies. This *publication bias* can create a scenario in which the available literature for a meta-analysis is systematically unrepresentative of the actual treatment effectiveness. Although several strategies are available to help counselors identify the presence and impact of publication bias, two of the most common approaches are examining funnel plots and computing fail-safe N (N_f).

Figure 9.2 is a funnel plot of the hypothetical intervention outcome data depicted in Figure 9.1. Funnel plots are simple scatterplots that situate individual effect sizes in reference to the mean effect size on the abscissa (x-axis) and their related standard error values on the ordinate (y-axis). When plotted values are generally symmetrical around the mean effect size, the distribution of studies is considered to be devoid of bias. Conversely, when plotted values are skewed, aligned heavily on one side of the mean effect size, or notably situated outside of the funnel, bias is said to be present. Because funnel plots are considered exploratory in nature, statistically based methods such as computing N_f are a standard of practice (Sutton, 2009). N_f was developed to estimate the number of new studies with null findings that would be required to negate the mean effect size. For example, in the hypothetical intervention outcome study depicted in Figures 9.1 and 9.2, $N_f = 656$, suggesting that 656 studies with null results would be needed to bring the value of the mean effect size to a value greater than zero and outside of the range of statistical significance. Although this number is apparently high, there are no proportional guidelines for consumers of research to consider (Sutton, 2009).

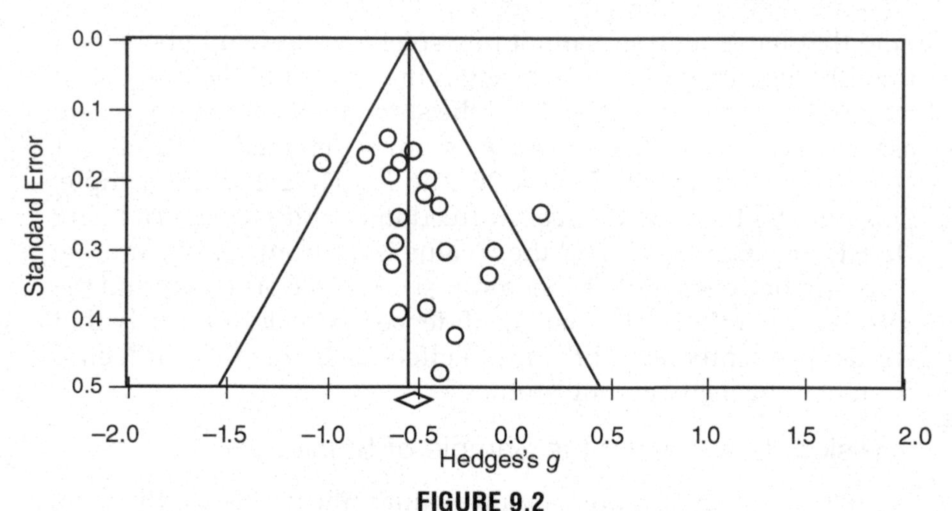

FIGURE 9.2
Funnel Plot of Individual Studies' Hedges's *g* Effect Sizes and Related Standard Errors

Considerations for Interpreting Meta-Analysis Results

Meta-analyses provide a systematic and even-handed approach to summarizing and synthesizing research within counseling and related fields. Consequently, the results of strong, well-developed studies can be used by stakeholders such as policymakers, third-party payers, school districts, mental health agencies, and individual practitioners to make decisions about which interventions work best for whom, how, and under what circumstances. Despite this tremendous potential, it is important to acknowledge that, like primary studies, meta-analyses are also limited in their ability to detect true effects. In fact, when the use of appropriate statistical methods is controlled, a meta-analysis is only as meritorious as its constituent studies are rigorous. Therefore, meta-analyses that include studies with the most rigorous evaluative designs are generally regarded as more useful and trustworthy than those that include quasi-experimental or preexperimental designs. Furthermore, meta-analyses are limited in their potential to depict true effects when the number of studies is small, the sample sizes of included studies are small, and outcome variables are assessed on disparate scales of measurement (e.g., continuous vs. categorical). Finally, it can be tempting to stay critical scrutiny of an intervention's worth following review of the magnitude and direction of a mean effect size; however, this is considered a short-sighted and unadvisable approach to making informed decisions. Because meta-analyses often include such diverse samples, a degree of heterogeneity among the effect sizes that contribute to the mean effect is anticipated. Thus, the utility of meta-analytic results may lie in the subgroup and metaregression analyses that explain variations in effect across sample characteristics.

Chapter Summary

As an emerging counselor or counselor educator, you are required by the *ACA Code of Ethics* (American Counseling Association, 2014) to be an active consumer of research findings. This chapter is intended to support that activity whether you are reviewing studies completed by others or embarking on an empirical endeavor yourself. With an understanding of the purpose and types of questions that meta-analyses are suited to answer, you can proceed to evaluating and designing studies using some of the critical elements discussed in this chapter. In particular, this chapter will support your ability to critically appraise methodological considerations, interpret effect sizes, and understand the ways in which moderating variables influence heterogeneity. With these considerations in mind, you will be well suited to starting to situate research findings within their sociopolitical context and matching interventions to individuals using an evidence-supported approach.

Suggested Activities

I. Review the following article:

   Lenz, A. S., Taylor, R., Fleming, M., & Serman, N. (2014). Effectiveness of dialectical-behavioral therapy for treating eating disorders. *Journal of Counseling & Development, 92*, 26–35. doi:10.1002/j.1556-6676.2013.00127

   1. What type of studies were included in the analysis? Why do you think the authors chose to include some types of studies but not others?
   2. Look at the mean effect sizes depicted in Tables 2 and 3. How effective was dialectical behavior therapy for reducing disordered eating and the symptoms of depression?
   3. To what population do the results of this study most apply? Why do the results apply to some individuals but not others?

II. What are some strengths of a well-designed meta-analysis? Even the best designed meta-analyses have limitations. Identify and describe some of those limitations.

References

American Counseling Association. (2014). *ACA code of ethics.* Alexandria, VA: Author.

American Psychiatric Association. (2000). *Diagnostic and statistical manual of mental disorders* (4th ed., text rev.). Washington, DC: Author.

American Psychiatric Association. (2013). *Diagnostic and statistical manual of mental disorders* (5th ed.). Washington, DC: Author.

American Psychological Association. (2009). *Publication manual of the American Psychological Association* (6th ed.). Washington, DC: Author.

Anzures-Cabrera, J., & Higgins, J. P. T. (2010). Graphical displays for meta-analysis: An overview with suggestions for practice. *Research Synthesis Methods, 1,* 66–88. doi:10.1002/jrsm.6

Beretvas, N. (2010). Meta-analysis. In G. R. Hancock & R. O. Mueller (Eds.), *The reviewer's guide to quantitative methods in the social sciences* (pp. 255–264). New York, NY: Routledge.

Borenstein, M., Hedges, L. V., Higgins, J. P., & Rothstein, H. (2009). *Introduction to meta-analysis.* West Sussex, England: Wiley.

Chambless, D. L., Baker, M. J., Baucom, D. H., Beutler, L. E., Calhoun, K. S., Crits-Christoph, P., . . . Woody, S. R. (1998). Update on empirically validated therapies, II. *The Clinical Psychologist, 51,* 3–16.

Chambless, D. L., Sanderson, W. C., Shoham, V., Johnson, S. B., Pope, K. S., Crits-Christoph, P., . . . McCurry, S. (1996). An update on empirically validated therapies. *The Clinical Psychologist, 49,* 5–18.

Cooper, H. W. (2010). *Research synthesis and meta-analysis: A step-by-step approach* (4th ed.). Thousand Oaks, CA: Sage.

Derzon, J. H., & Alford, A. A. (2013). Forest plots in Excel: Moving beyond a clump of trees to a forest of visual information. *Practical Assessment, Research & Evaluation, 18*(7). Retrieved from http://pareonline.net/getvn.asp?v=18&n=7

Ellis, P. D. (2010). *The essential guide to effect sizes: Statistical power, meta-analysis, and the interpretation of research results.* Cambridge, England: Cambridge University Press.

Erford, B. T., Savin-Murphy, J. A., & Butler, C. (2010). Conducting a meta-analysis of counseling outcome research: Twelve steps and practical procedures. *Counseling Outcome Research and Evaluation, 1,* 19–43.

Higgins, J. P. T., Thompson, S., Deeks, J. J., & Altman, D. G. (2003). Measuring inconsistency in meta-analyses. *BMJ, 327,* 557–560.

Lenz, A. S. (2015). A meta-analysis of the Coping Cat program for decreasing severity of anxiety symptoms among children and adolescents. *Journal of Child and Adolescent Counseling, 1,* 51–65. doi:10.1080/23727810.2015.1079116

Lenz, A. S., Bruijn, B., Serman, N., & Bailey, L. (2014). Effectiveness of cognitive processing therapy for treating post-traumatic stress disorder. *Journal of Mental Health Counseling, 36,* 360–376.

Lenz, A. S., Hall, J., & Smith, L. B. (2016). Meta-analysis of group mindfulness-based cognitive therapy for decreasing symptoms of acute depression. *Journal for Specialists in Group Work, 41,* 44–70.

Lenz, A. S., Henesy, R., & Callender, K. (2016). Effectiveness of Seeking Safety program for co-occurring PTSD and substance use. *Journal of Counseling and Development, 94,* 51–61. doi:10.1002/jcad.12061

Lenz, A. S., & Hollenbaugh, M. H. (2015). Meta-analysis of trauma-focused cognitive behavioral therapy for treating PTSD and co-occurring depression among children and adolescents. *Counseling Outcome Research and Evaluation, 5,* 18–32. doi:10.1177/2150137815573790

Lenz, A. S., Rosenbaum, L., & Sheperis, D. (2016). Meta-analysis of randomized controlled trials of motivational enhancement therapy for reducing substance use. *Journal of Addictions & Offender Counseling, 37,* 66–76. doi: 10.1002/jaoc.12017

Lenz, A. S., Taylor, R., Fleming, M., & Serman, N. (2014). Effectiveness of dialectical-behavioral therapy for treating eating disorders. *Journal of Counseling & Development, 92,* 26–35. doi:10.1002/j.1556-6676.2013.00127

Lenz, A. S., & Williams, R. T. (2014). Comparative efficacy between self-report and clinician administered assessments of posttraumatic stress disorder symptoms across seven studies. *Counseling Outcome Research and Evaluation, 5,* 75–88. doi:10.1177/2150137814550523

Lipsey, M. (2009). Identifying interesting variables and analysis opportunities. In H. Cooper, L. V. Hedges, & J. C. Valentine (Eds.), *The handbook of research synthesis and meta-analysis* (pp. 147–158). New York, NY: Russell Sage Foundation.

Lipsey, M. W., & Wilson, D. (2001). *Practical meta-analysis.* Thousand Oaks, CA: Sage.

Moher, D., Liberati, A., Tetzlaff, J., Altman, D. G., & The PRISMA Group. (2009). Preferred reporting items for systematic reviews and meta-analyses: The PRISMA statement. *PLoS Med, 6*(6), e1000097. doi:10.1371/journal.pmed.1000097

Reed, J. G., & Baxter, P. M. (2009). Using reference databases. In H. Cooper, L. V. Hedges, & J. C. Valentine (Eds.), *The handbook of research synthesis and meta-analysis* (pp. 73–102). New York, NY: Russell Sage Foundation.

Rubin, A., & Bellamy, J. (2012). *Practitioners guide to using research for evidence-based practice* (2nd ed.). Hoboken, NJ: Wiley.

Segal, Z. V., Williams, J. M. G., & Teasdale, J. D. (2002). *Mindfulness-based cognitive therapy for depression: A new approach to preventing relapse.* New York, NY: Guilford Press.

Shadish, W. R., & Haddock, C. K. (2009). Combining estimates of effect size. In H. Cooper, L. V. Hedges, & J. C. Valentine (Eds.), *The handbook of research synthesis and meta-analysis* (pp. 257–278). New York, NY: Russell Sage Foundation.

Sutton, A. J. (2009). Publication bias. In H. Cooper, L. V. Hedges, & J. C. Valentine (Eds.), *The handbook of research synthesis and meta-analysis* (pp. 435–452). New York, NY: Russell Sage Foundation.

Tanner-Smith, E. E., Wilson, S. J., & Lipsey, M. W. (2013). The comparative effectiveness of outpatient treatment for adolescent substance abuse: A meta-analysis. *Journal of Substance Abuse Treatment, 44,* 145–158. doi:10.1016/j.jsat.2012.05.006

Thompson, B. (2007). Effect sizes, confidence intervals, and confidence intervals of effect sizes. *Psychology in the Schools, 44,* 423–432. doi:10.1002/pits.20234

Tolin, D., McKay, D., Forman, E., Klonsky, E., & Thombs, B. (2015). Empirically supported treatment: Recommendations for a new model. *Clinical Psychology: Science and Practice, 22,* 317–338. doi:10.1111/cpsp.12122

Trusty, J., Thompson, B., & Petrocelli, J. V. (2004). Practical guide for reporting effect size in quantitative research in the *Journal of Counseling & Development. Journal of Counseling & Development, 82,* 107–110.

Valentine, J. C., Aloe, A. M., & Lau, T. S. (2015). Life after NHST: How to describe your data without "p-ing" everywhere. *Basic and Applied Social Psychology, 37,* 260–273. doi:10.1080/01973533.2015.1060240

Wampold, B. E., Lichtenberg, J. W., & Waehler, C. A. (2002). Principles of empirically supported interventions in counseling psychology. *The Counseling Psychologist, 30,* 197–217. doi:10.1177/0011000002302001

Whiston, S. C., & Li, P. (2011). Meta-analysis: A systematic method for synthesizing counseling research. *Journal of Counseling & Development, 89,* 273–281.

Whiston, S. C., Tai, W. L., Rahardja, D., & Eder, K. (2011). School counseling outcome: A meta-analytic examination interventions. *Journal of Counseling & Development, 89,* 37–55.

White, H. D. (2009). Scientific communication and literature retrieval. In H. Cooper, L. V. Hedges, & J. C. Valentine (Eds.), *The handbook of research synthesis and meta-analysis* (pp. 51–72). New York, NY: Russell Sage Foundation.

Qualitative Research Designs

Qualitative research—but why, you might ask? Or you might be thinking, "I've seen 'Other comments' at the end of surveys. Isn't that qualitative research?" No, not in the slightest, I (David M. Kleist) say! But before we get into a discussion of the philosophies undergirding qualitative methods, we need to prepare ourselves for the qualitative transition.

So far Rick has done an exceptional job of detailing a wide array of quantitative methods that you can utilize and understand as professional counselors. The world of quantitative methods is organized by a way of knowing, of understanding the world around us, people, and relationships, which is embedded in a paradigm far different from the ways of knowing in qualitative research. I suggest you sit quietly in a chair. Now think of all you have learned from Rick about positivism, empiricism, deductive reasoning, the distilling of human experience into quantifiable understanding, Pearson coefficients, *F* ratios, standard error of measurement, analyses of variance, multivariate analyses of variance, and so on. "Ommmmmm. Ommmmmm. Ommmmm." Think of all of the wonderful knowledge of quantitative research you have learned . . . and now let it drift on by and move aside, temporarily, to allow space for a new world and way of knowing, of understanding the world, people, and relationships. "Ommmm . . . ommmm . . ."

Okay, what on earth am I asking you to do? How silly is this? Well, it's quite serious actually. You see, quantitative and qualitative research are distinct ways of understanding the world and producing knowledge through research. Both have value for you in your role as practitioner-scholar. However, there are important differences. The two forms of research actually use different parts of the brain (e.g., Carmichael, 2011; Pink, 2006). Even more exciting, in my view, is the notion Daniel Pink (2006) put forth, that the tendencies of right brain thinking—the inventiveness, storytelling, meaning making, creativity, and holistic thinking that are required for qualitative research—will be at the forefront of advancements in a variety of professions moving forward. Will counseling as a profession be among them? Well, only if we provide a balance in what professional counselors learn as the means to generate knowledge and research impacting the process of counseling. My hope for you over the next two chapters is to have an open mind, to allow yourself to embrace a way of knowing and producing research to which you probably have had little exposure during your education so far. I hope that when you have completed these chapters you see many places and ways for integrating qualitative research into your role as professional counselor.

References

Carmichael, S. (2011, October 28). *Lou Rosenfeld—beyond user research* [Podcast]. Retrieved from https://www.uie.com/brainsparks/2011/10/28/lou-rosenfeld-beyond-user-research-live/

Pink, D. H. (2006). *A whole new mind: Why right-brainers will rule the future.* New York, NY: Penguin Group.

Fundamental Concepts in Qualitative Research

Overview

This chapter will introduce you to some of the key philosophies, concepts, and ideas surrounding the rich research traditions of qualitative research. Essential components of the various qualitative traditions are discussed to create a foundation for the discussion of specific qualitative methods and procedures in Chapter 11.

Let's get started. As Rick has said to students, and me (David), "A MANOVA is a MANOVA is a MANOVA." In quantitative research and statistics, it is not possible to alter much in the different philosophies of knowledge that exist. Quantitative research is firmly grounded in positivism, or postpositivism today. Postpositivists believe that reality cannot be directly known, that we as humans construct understanding of the real world that exists outside of ourselves. Knowledge from research can only be probabilistically known through the use of the methods Rick so clearly described in the previous chapters. ("Oh, but remember, let these thoughts float on by for now!") Here is the pathway to constructivism and an overlap of philosophy that can connect quantitative and some qualitative research approaches.

Some qualitative approaches are firmly embedded in postpositivist philosophy that underlies all of quantitative research. However, that is only the beginning for qualitative research. In the next two chapters we will look not only at qualitative methods that are embedded in postpositivist ways of knowing and producing knowledge but also at qualitative methods that are grounded in an array of philosophical stances toward the world that impact all facets of research. Hold onto your seats here, as we will be examining how the philosophical stances of critical theory and constructivism (also known as interpretivism), which will be viewed along a continuum reaching to social constructivism (connected to postmodernism or the participatory action paradigm), inform qualitative research methods (Lincoln, Lynham, & Guba, 2011). So when we talk later about grounded theory, for example, we will not be able to say, "Grounded theory is grounded theory is grounded theory." We will learn to embrace the oft-used phrase "It depends," which I use with my students. How a grounded theory research study is designed depends on your philosophical stance as a researcher. You see, postpositivist grounded theory is different from constructivist grounded theory or a blend of constructivist and postmodern grounded theory. The use and understanding of grounded theory will depend on your philosophical stance toward knowledge or knowing. Yes, we are about to enter a wide-open world of qualitative research possibilities that requires that you be very aware of yourself and your views of reality. Your philosophical stance has a clear impact on how you conduct, design, and understand qualitative research and its knowledge products.

I am sure I have only made your day more confusing and muddied the research waters even further. You thought you knew what research was, is, and can be after reading the first nine chapters of this book. Hang in there. Be open to new ideas to research, just like you are asked to be open to new ideas about people and the world around you as you develop as a counselor. Remember to breathe . . .

The varied philosophical stances that can impact qualitative research are not clear cut, nor are they universally agreed on by counselors, counselor educators, or qualitative research methodologists. We are talking philosophy here, so we have to (to use another oft-used phrase) "embrace ambiguity." I structure my discussion of the philosophies impacting qualitative research around the stances of two of the most preeminent scholars on qualitative research—Yvonne Lincoln and Egon Guba—along with a new colleague, Susan Lynham (Lincoln et al., 2011). All three are qualitative research methodologists by training and have spent their careers applying qualitative methods to social and educational inquiry.

I must insert a disclaimer here: The reality is, qualitative research is relatively new to the counseling profession. There are many potential reasons for this, and their discussion is beyond the scope of this chapter, but between 1994 and 1997 only three qualitative studies were published in the *Journal of Counseling & Development* versus 57 between the years 2006 and 2009 (Erford et al., 2011). In my specific field of counselor education and supervision, the first formal qualitative study was not published in the Association for Counselor Education and Supervision's journal, *Counselor Education and Supervision,* until 1995 (Kleist, 2013). Over the past 20 plus years the counseling profession has come to see the value of qualitative research, a form of research that has been firmly embedded in sociological and educational research for well over 50 years (Bogdan & Biklen, 2007). In my assessment, the profession of counseling is still getting comfortable with qualitative research, its place, and its impact on our roles and actions as professional counselors and has for the most part viewed qualitative research through a postpositivist paradigm.

Postpositivism

Postpositivism has grown out of the positivist position that Rick described in Chapter 1. When discussing this position, or stance, I will do my best to avoid philosophical babble and instead describe what you, as a practitioner-scholar, would look like adopting this stance when understanding and conducting qualitative research. In line with this philosophical stance toward knowledge and research, as a counseling practitioner you believe that the world exists beyond yourself as a person. You move through your counseling day believing that there is a single reality, or truth, for your work with a client. Your understanding of the client comes from your direct interaction and observation of your client. The words you use to understand your client, or diagnostic terms, are linked to real mental heath problems (or disorders) that have been identified through research. How you help your client is also informed by research on how to work with clients diagnosed with various mental health problems. Yes, you have created a therapeutic climate for change based on your relationship with your client, but how you have done so is, again, informed by research on how best to develop therapeutic relationships. You believe you can understand your client's situation, though you acknowledge that full, complete, and static understanding is probably not possible. To best work with your client you try to be as objective as possible. You know you bring your own subjectivity to the relationship, including values and beliefs, but your job is to keep them in check, to not allow them to influence your work with clients. You may use self-disclosure with clients but keep it to a minimum and really only if research supports its use. The counseling process is relational, but your overarching management of it depends on research-based evidence on the process of change and its stages, with you as the counselor ultimately holding more responsibility for counseling's outcome. Counseling terminates as a joint decision but one that is highly informed by your marking client change via an array of assessment tools. Your ethical treatment of clients and the entire counseling process is ever present, but your worries are quelled by your following the evidence-based treatment procedures that guide your role as professional counselor.

Now transition into the scholar side of your role as practitioner-scholar adopting a postpositivist stance toward research and knowledge. What is your process for understanding research and its production? As a professional counselor utilizing and producing knowledge to inform practice, you again believe in the existence of mental health problems, like depression or eating-disordered behavior (e.g., bulimia), and understand the value in learning directly from individuals experiencing these problems just what it is like to live with depression or bulimia: What is the process for coping with such disorders? So you craft a qualitative study. Maybe, as a means of better understanding what it is like to live with depression, you design a phenomenological study to discover the essence of living with depression or going through treatment and utilize consensual qualitative research (CQR; a new qualitative methodology we touch on in Chapter 11). Maybe you adopt more of a systems perspective and are curious about the process of support seeking among those experiencing bulimia. Here you design a grounded theory study to explore the process that clients with bulimia go through when seeking support. Given your postpositivist stance, you seek a phenomenology, or a grounded theory method that is congruent with a postpositivist stance (e.g., Moustakas, 1994; Strauss & Corbin, 1998) or CQR as a uniquely postpositivist methodology, as I have defined previously. Thus, you want a research design with clear procedures to assist in maintaining objectivity, methods that bracket the influence of your values or beliefs on the understanding of the data (more on this below in the section on what constitutes data in qualitative research), and a means of confirming that your results stem from the participant's data—so the data speak for themselves, so to speak. This may mean an inquiry auditor, as in

Strauss and Corbin's (1998) grounded theory, nor using a team of researchers seeking consensus as an outcome in data analysis as with CQR (Hill et al., 2005; Hill, Thompson, & Williams, 1997).

Critical Theory

Let us now move along the philosophical inquiry spectrum to positions more firmly embedded in critical theory (e.g., feminist, queer, and race theories of knowledge). Accessing the scholar component of your role as practitioner-scholar within a critical theorist stance means that you now see the potential of research not only to inform understanding of your clients, or other counselors and their clients as consumers of research, but also to be used by other counselors to further advocacy efforts on behalf of clients.

Let me mention Lincoln, Lynham, and Guba again and their description of adopting a critical theorist view of research. Within this stance toward knowledge, the research you create sheds light on the larger cultural contexts in which your clients reside, interact, construct meaning and value, and are restrained. Individual client issues are no longer seen primarily as under the control of clients but as strongly influenced by the various systems or contexts within which clients interact, which calls for some form of counselor advocacy on behalf of clients. Poverty, racism, sexism, homophobia, oppression of all forms, and their influence on clients' well-being are highlighted in your research. Pedersen's (1991) view of multiculturalism as the counseling profession's fourth force is congruent, and I might say central, to a critical stance toward counseling practice and research. Your responsibility as a practitioner-scholar is to research ways in which the various contexts of your clients' lives impact their overall mental health and call for counselors to take action in the form of advocating for policy change, community-level programming to lessen the impact of racism and poverty, and so on. However, your role as scholar within this stance is one of "transformative intellectual" (Lincoln et al., 2011, p. 102). The use of the results of your research is in the hands of the consumer. It is up to your fellow counselors to learn from your research, to take back to their work with clients and their clients' communities, and to impact systemic and cultural influences on mental health. Your job is to conduct well-designed research and disseminate results that provide help to clients through increasing emphasis on the contextual influences on the well-being of individuals, couples, families, and communities.

How does this sound to you as a professional counselor? This stance calls for the practitioner-scholar to further engage in advocacy on behalf of clients. If this fits your notion of being a professional counselor, great! In many ways, this is where the profession has developed over the past 20 or more years as multiculturalism, counseling's fourth force, has directly impacted not only the practice of counseling but also research that examines better ways to enhance the overall mental health of individuals and communities.

You might be asking yourself, "Are we done yet with this philosophical babble so we can just get on to learning how to do qualitative research?" No, not quite yet. You see, conducting qualitative research is so much more involved than the mere doing of it. These philosophical conversations are essential for you not only to further refine your counseling theory but also to ensure that you are conducting research that is congruent with your counseling stance.

Constructivism

Next we step into the constructivist stance toward knowledge and its related research forms. Much has been written on constructivism, and I could go on for pages making distinctions between distinctions. I will broadly say that the stances toward knowledge discussed from here forward could be placed on a wide continuum from an individually oriented constructivism (sometimes called *interpretivism* [Denzin, 2001], *cognitive constructivism* [Perry, 1999], or *weak constructivism* [Schwandt, 2000]) to a relationally oriented constructivism (i.e., strong constructivism [Schwandt, 2000] or social constructionist stances [Gergen, 2015]). From these positions, your practitioner role as counselor shifts from seeing reality as existing outside of you and your clients' meaning making to constructing reality through the meaning making of conversation between you and your clients. Your epistemology no longer seeks a closer and closer approximation of some outside reality; instead, you accept that the best you can understand about your client is his or her interpretation of his or her experience of the world, and your related interpretation of your client's interpretation of his or her mental health problem(s).

Hold on. "What is that?" you ask. Yes, please reread that, as it is important. Adopting a constructivist stance means accepting that the best you can know about a client's reality is his or her interpretation of it expressed via language (or through other symbol systems) and understood via your use of language to conceptualize the client's situation. The counseling theory or theories you integrate to assist your clients are clearly understood merely as agreed-upon means of understanding clinical issues and your methods to help clients.

Collaborative is the word most familiar to any counseling theory within this framework. Pragmatism is also aligned with these counseling theories, as your ultimate goal is to assist in bringing about change in your client and his or her world. You still embrace the importance of research-supported use of theory, but you are more open to embracing the reality that counseling theory and technique cannot be uniformly applied or useful across people and settings (i.e., contexts). The phrase "It depends" is further embraced, as you know that your relationship with clients is more negotiated with them (hear the collaborative stance?) rather than imposed onto them through strict adherence to evidence-based treatment protocols. Assessment is still valuable in determining counseling's impact, but you are more aware of the limits of assessment tools as well as generalizations across time and place of any assessment result. Mental health problems are more embedded in one's construction of them through language (and society's construction of mental health or illness), and the focus of change is in new constructions of meaning, which primarily will occur through language. Termination of counseling is truly a shared decision in which clients' perspectives on change are as important as an assessment instrument's conclusion. The more firmly you support a constructivist stance toward the world and your clients' experience, the more you realize the contextual or multicultural contexts that influence your clients. There is a growing sense toward advocacy, social justice, and action for your own counseling community and the communities of your clients that surpasses the stance toward advocacy taken within the critical theorist stance. (I am not saying that interest in advocacy is lacking among those who adopt a postpositivist stance; I am simply saying that interest in action is seen as the duty of an ethical counselor more so with a constructivist stance, particularly a strong or social constructionist one.)

In terms of the scholar component of the practitioner-scholar role within this stance, research is firmly interpretive, moving toward much more relational and action-oriented approaches. As a counselor you are keenly aware of the stories and the narratives your clients share about living with interpersonal violence, anxiety, or eating-disordered behavior. You may be profoundly moved by hearing the larger cultural discourses that impact your clients' struggles with a variety of mental health problems and their processes toward health and wellness. Over time we may call such learnings the *development of clinical wisdom,* which will serve you well to manage the nuances of clinical work. Now imagine capturing the value of such wisdom and sharing it with other professional counselors! Your goal as a scholar within this stance is to utilize research to better understand your clients' experience and process while valuing their participation in the research itself. Your client-participants are viewed as coresearchers in your projects. You understand that your clients' interpretations of their experiences and processes are informed by your own interpretation as a counselor-researcher. You understand that you bring yourself as a person to the research endeavor in the same fashion you do as a counselor. You are authentic, congruent, and aware of the values you bring into the counseling room, cognizant of both positive and negative influences. The same exists in your role as researcher. You see yourself as a person interpreting meaning, which is influenced by your own values, beliefs, and ideas. From this stance bracketing them out of the research project is impossible. Research is clearly a relational task that is negotiated with participants, just as counseling is with clients.

Research in this stance can vary according to your adoption of either a weak to strong or cognitive to social constructionist stance. What I described in the previous paragraph could be said to lean more toward the former: a weak or cognitive constructivist position. However, the more relational you make your research, the more you involve your client-participant in the research endeavor, the more you probably move toward the latter end of the stance: social constructionist.

An aspect of the social constructionist stance that takes the relationship between researcher and participant to another level is new developments within qualitative research framed as participatory action research. Such research is firmly embedded in a social constructionist stance toward the development of knowledge, but it goes further. The role of the scholar here is not simply to disseminate results through professional journals in the hopes that the larger community of counselors use the results in their own practice. Rather, the researcher, along with the client-participant, takes the results of a study back to the community within which the participant resides and implements some form of action—an intervention, a new community-based program—into the relational system of which the participant is a part. Research of this ilk has been framed as *participatory action research,* and it is beginning to find its place in some corners of the world of the professional counselor—particularly those that strongly identify with the action-oriented responsibilities of being social justice advocates. The knowledge generated from such research has more value to the actual communities of clients than the professional journals we read as counselors, though the dissemination of such action-oriented research in professional forums is still vital.

"Okay, stop. Now you have gone too far!" I am sure some of you are saying this as you read this. Never before, or only rarely and secretly, have you heard that research can be so relational, action oriented, and directly impactful to the lives of clients and their communities. I know that allowing space for the relationship between researcher and participant goes against all that we may have learned in our undergraduate research classes or even our master's-level research classes. Here's the deal: We have been taught research in a way that separates it from its philosophical groundings and their consequences for how research is conducted. Once we realize that all research, quantitative and qualitative, is grounded in philosophies of knowledge that have a direct impact on how studies are designed, including the roles and relationships of researcher and participant, we realize we have choices. Within qualitative research, you have many choices, as there are varied philosophical stances to adopt toward knowledge and its production: research. That cannot be said for quantitative research. There are options regarding research methods and statistics, but they all live in the same philosophical home. Remember when I said earlier that Rick once told me "A MANOVA is a MANOVA is a MANOVA"? Well, that is because there is a clear, singular philosophical stance that informs present-day quantitative research: postpositivism.

So with all of these choices of philosophies toward structuring and conducting qualitative research, is there any form to qualitative methods? Is there not anything in common? Well yes, there is. And well, guess what? It depends.

Components of a Qualitative Study

Now we take a breather from philosophy and its role in shaping qualitative research possibilities (sort of). In the remainder of the chapter I speak to the major structural components of a qualitative study, offer important questions to ask yourself as a researcher developing a study, and provide some description of variations within each component. Yes, these variations will link us back to philosophy.

Qualitative research is not the same as quantitative research. You know this by now, I know. It bears repeating when thinking about the structure of a qualitative study. Why? Well, the scientific method, the one my children were taught via a mnemonic device to remember in elementary school, is uniquely foundational to quantitative research, not necessarily qualitative research. The steps, in simple form, are as follows: Ask a question, do background research, construct a hypothesis, test your hypothesis via experimentation, and analyze your data and draw conclusions. Quite simply, the scientific method is a formidable method when deductive reasoning is the overarching framework for making sense of the world around us. Rick spoke of this clearly earlier in the book. However, the hallmark of qualitative reasoning is not deductive but rather inductive reasoning—developing knowledge from the ground up (the local context, a situation, an event, participants' own experience, etc.) versus applying a priori knowledge (theory) to understand the local context, the participants' experience, and so on. Steps 3 (construct a hypothesis) and 4 (test your hypothesis via experimentation) of the scientific method are not present in qualitative research. (Now some qualitative methodologists would say it is possible, though unlikely, to conceive of a hypothesis in qualitative research; see Maxwell, 2013.) What I present in the following paragraphs is truly an amalgam of a number of qualitative research methodologists' views on the structure of qualitative research (see also Creswell, 2013; Patton, 2015).

The Purpose of Qualitative Research

To understand the structure of a qualitative study is to first understand what the purpose of qualitative inquiry is. Qualitative research produces knowledge that allows us to understand the human meaning of events, situations, contexts, experiences, or actions; the particular contexts within which actions and experiences take place; social and psychological processes by which events and actions take place; and the unanticipated phenomena and influences of experiences and processes (Maxwell, 2013). Thus, the first step involves asking yourself, "What do I wish to understand?" Yes, this is similar to the first step in quantitative research. What I like about Maxwell's (2013) model of qualitative research design is his emphasis on the goals of research being personal, practical, and/or intellectual (scholarly). The latter is what I bet most of you think about research and is the prime reason you shy away from it. If you can remember, ask yourself, "Personally, as a counselor, what would I wish to understand about counseling/my clients/coping with loss/etc.?" Or for pragmatic (practical) reasons you can ask, "What do I need to understand to better help my client cope with the loss of his job?" or "What do I need to understand to work with lesbian, gay, bisexual, transgender, questioning, and intersex clients?" To realize that you can conduct research that has direct, pragmatic, and personal implications for your practice of counseling is to see the wide relevance of qualitative research to your role as counselor.

The Conceptual Framework of Qualitative Research

Once you have made your decision on your study's purpose, or focus, you move into *construction of the conceptual framework* (Maxwell, 2013). A number of qualitative research methods books use the more common term *literature review.* However, what I like about Maxwell's (2013) use of the term *conceptual framework* is the emphasis on the researcher's active construction of a framework of literature that is directly relevant to the purpose of the study. *Literature review* has historically meant an exhaustive review of all of the previously developed knowledge that supports the focus of the study. Gaps in the literature are noted, along with limitations of previous research. From such an exhaustive review the specific area of inquiry comes to light, along with the research question. The limitation of this view of knowledge accumulation within the context of the qualitative research paradigm is that knowledge is not developed in sequential building block fashion, as it is in the quantitative research paradigm. In the qualitative research paradigm, knowledge is uniquely tied to context and time. Thus, what worked in one context, in one place in time, with one particular sample cannot be assumed to further solidify the foundational knowledge of a given field, as it may not be relevant in another context, at another time, with a different sample.

What the conceptual framework provides a qualitative study, and the qualitative researcher, is an organized set of concepts. This set of concepts may inform an understanding of the study's purpose and provide the researcher with ideas to consider when collecting and analyzing data. In some ways, the conceptual framework provides a potential description of, or answer to, the research question. No, I am not talking about a hypothesis to be tested. The conceptual framework is a set of ideas and concepts constructed by the researcher that can inform his or her understanding of data collection and analysis. A conceptual framework is an active organization of ideas and concepts, much more than is found in the exhaustive review of the literature found in quantitative research.

A unique aspect of constructing the conceptual framework is including concepts and ideas from you, the researcher, yourself. You (as the researcher) are the main tool used in qualitative research, and so it is vital that you select a topic, or better a phenomenon, to which you are somehow connected. Included in the conceptual framework are ideas and concepts that you conceive from your own experiences with the phenomenon of interest. The conceptual framework is grounded in both ideas and concepts from literature relevant to your phenomenon and your own experience. From the completion of the conceptual framework could come the study's research question, or a revision of the research question, and purpose, which you may already have formulated. The whole notion of the research question is seen as fluid and emergent. Qualitative research is quite nonlinear, and the research question could be altered or even developed during data analysis. Remember, knowledge is constructed inductively in qualitative research, and the research design must be fluid to respond to emergent understanding. You must start somewhere with your actual research design. Let us discuss some options and variations as we speak about data collection and data analysis.

Data Collection

You have identified an intended purpose of your study, an initial focus constructed through the conceptual framework, and a working research question. To research the various potential purposes of qualitative inquiry, you need to first find people who have experienced, or are currently experiencing, the phenomenon that you seek to understand. The common sampling procedure used in qualitative research is called *purposeful sampling* (Lincoln & Guba, 1985). There are slight variations to purposeful sampling, but for now just remember that it means to intentionally seek out those people or participants who have gone through the event, lived in the context, engaged in the process, and so on, that you seek to understand. Each qualitative methodology book you read is going to add its own unique slant to participant selection. I encourage you to be clear and embody fidelity in your use of the procedures described in whichever qualitative methods book you select to guide your study.

The next important decision to make once you have identified a purposeful sample of participants and the means to enlist them in your study is the number of participants from which to collect data. The "How many?" question has caused great consternation among qualitative researchers, journal editors, and even qualitative research methodologists themselves. There truly is no one right answer. A recent research paper that gathered the opinions of 19 experts on qualitative methodology worldwide provided perspectives on just this issue. Answers ranged from 0 (I am not kidding) to 60 (Baker & Edwards, 2012). Now that is not helpful. The experts left the discussion encouraging researchers to consider what is deemed "excellence" for qualitative research within the profession of the researcher. With qualitative research being so new to the counseling profession, we truly have not had this important conversation. Now what?

Here are my suggestions. The oft-quoted phrase you by now have heard in your training to become a counselor is relevant here: It depends. It depends on the purpose of your study, which is influenced by your philosophical stance toward knowledge. (I warned you we would be back to philosophy!) If you adopt a post-positivist stance toward knowledge, which is more interested in commonalities across people and thus more generalizable results, you will lean toward a larger sample size. If you adopt a social constructivist stance, your interest is more in rich description and deep understanding, which would mean a smaller sample size. There is a simple principle that I consider: A larger sample size provides more breadth and less depth; a smaller sample size provides more depth and less breadth. You must decide what is most important for your particular research question and its intended purpose. Again, attend to the research methodology and its informing philosophy, along with the realities of your professional community regarding qualitative research, when considering sample size. The profession of counseling is still developing a fuller understanding of the place of qualitative research and is far from a specific discussion on adequate sample sizes across the various qualitative methods and how they are influenced by the various philosophies mentioned previously. For now, let us assume that we have struggled with these important issues and are ready to design the data collection portion of our study.

Data, first and foremost in qualitative research, are related to how people communicate the meaning of their lived human experience. Qualitative researchers believe that the best way to access meaning is through the use of text as the metaphor for meaning making. Text and its related symbolic expressions is the focus of data collection. The researcher's written descriptions of participant behavior and/or participants' own communications (i.e., words) have historically been the focus of data collection. Put simply, collected written or verbal descriptions of some process, experience, event, and so on represent data in qualitative research. Data can be collected in the form of written journals, in the form of responses to open-ended prompts, or most commonly through researcher-guided interviews with participants. It is fair to say that the majority of qualitative articles published across professions have utilized one to one interviews with participants. These interviews can take place face to face; over the phone; or, with improvements in Internet function and security, through video-based programs on a person's computer.

Meaning can also be communicated via other forms of symbolic representation. "A picture is worth a thousand words." I am sure you have heard this phrase before. But what does it mean? To me, it means that instead of needing to describe my experience in words, I could communicate it through the use of pictures. Sound strange? The use of photos or pictures as a form of data is quite common in the professions of sociology, anthropology, and health education (e.g., photovoice; Wang & Burris, 1997). Within the counseling profession, there has been an increase in the number of qualitative studies that integrate participant-generated pictures as data (e.g., Koltz, Odegard, Provost, Smith, & Kleist, 2010). Pictures have also been used as a catalyst for, or means of eliciting, meanings and stories (e.g., Wathen & Kleist, 2015). For some people, reflecting on a picture provides easier access to memories, associated thoughts, and feelings than being asked to respond to a direct question. Such integration of more art-based forms of data collection or elicitation is slowly on the rise in the counseling profession.

Please do not stop at pictures, as other forms of meaning expression are beginning to take hold in a variety of professions, even counseling. Music is another means of accessing meaning and related thoughts and feelings. Though the use of music, like pictures, may be more familiar in arts-based professions, music has been used as a form of data in a study of cohort development among counselors and counselor educators (Minor, Moody, Tadlock-Marlo, Pender, & Person, 2013). Given that the profession of counseling is a blend of art and science, and given increasing attention to creativity in mental health counseling, I would not be surprised to see further explorations into the use of more creative means of data collection or elicitation.

Data Analysis

As with quantitative data, once qualitative data are collected they must be transformed and analyzed. As said previously, the most common form of qualitative data is the written or spoken word. Interviews with participants, done either one on one or in groups (e.g., focus group research), are recorded. These recorded conversations are transcribed, most commonly by hiring a professional transcriptionist, in preparation for analysis. Once you have the transcripts, data analysis commences, but it is influenced by the type of qualitative analysis being conducted (e.g., phenomenology or grounded theory), as each type of qualitative research seeks to understand a different aspect of some phenomenon (i.e., process, essence of experience, themes). The philosophical stance toward knowledge will also impact the data analysis process. A postpositivist stance toward data analysis will keep a boundary between the researcher and participant during this phase of the research. In CQR (Hill et al., 1997) or phenomenology (Moustakas, 1994), as just two examples, the researcher is responsible for coding the data into themes, categories, and so on. The participant may only be involved for a final member check to verify the accuracy of codes or themes after the completion of the study. For a researcher or research team that adopts a social constructionist stance toward knowledge, the boundary between researcher and participant is more permeable. Various mutations are possible, but it is not uncommon to have participants play a more active role during data analysis, for all intents and purposes acting as coresearchers and actively influencing the coding process as well as ensuring the final accuracy of codes and themes. Sound strange? You will need to remember that the form a qualitative research project can take is thoroughly impacted by the philosophical stance taken toward knowledge and research. All aspects of research design are influenced by the various philosophical stances discussed previously.

Reporting of Results

Reporting the results of qualitative research is very similar to the reporting process for quantitative research, though the actual results look very different. Qualitative studies report the transformed and analyzed data in themes (e.g., phenomenology) or a description of the process of some phenomenon in the form of a theory (e.g., grounded theory), for example. Whereas in quantitative research tables of figures and statistical analysis are given, in qualitative research themes are provided along with excerpts from transcripts to verify the themes or codes or a process description that emerged from the data analysis. In many ways, the results of qualitative research come in story form. Figures may be used to provide a visual representation of the theme structure or process. And you will find qualitative research ending as it began: by focusing on representing understanding through the text metaphor and an emphasis on symbolic meaning represented through words, the same means we use as counselors to promote change.

As with quantitative results, qualitative results are not accepted without having proved their rigor and value. The hallmarks of the rigor of quantitative research results are represented by the terms *reliability, validity,* and *generalizability.* Because of the underlying differences in the nature of knowledge produced through quantitative means and qualitative means, the hallmarks of rigor in quantitative research cannot be applied to assess the rigor of qualitative research results.

Now here is where assessing rigor in qualitative research gets interesting. You might have other words to describe what follows! There are as many different ways to conceptualize rigor in qualitative results as there are philosophical stances toward knowledge that inform the various forms of qualitative methodology. Let me be clear: There are *not* universal criteria for assessing the rigor, or trustworthiness, of qualitative research and its results. Each form of qualitative research, be it phenomenology, grounded theory, narrative inquiry, conversational analysis, or CQR, for example, has its own criteria for assessing rigor. Here is the really interesting part: The research methods just listed could potentially be viewed from different philosophical stances toward knowledge, each with its own different stance toward rigor. A simple example would be phenomenology. Moustakas (1994) adopted a postpositivist stance toward knowledge and developed criteria for rigor that fit this stance. Van Manen (1990) has his own form of phenomenology, specifically *hermeneutic phenomenology,* which adopts a more interpretivist/constructivist stance and calls for yet a different set of criteria to evaluate rigor. So again, we must be open to embracing the phrase "It depends." For now, know that we will look at some examples of these procedures in Chapter 11.

At this point you may have had enough of the uncertainty of qualitative research and the array of methodologies and philosophical stances influencing these methodologies. Or you are excited to learn of a means of conducting research that is congruent with your role as professional counselor, a way of conducting research that directly emanates from, and connects to, your practice as a professional counselor. As a professional counselor you are already trained in the skills essential to being a skilled qualitative researcher. You know how to facilitate reflexive conversations, to find and coconstruct meaning, and to provide an empathic environment that encourages understanding.

Chapter Summary

In this chapter I have attempted to provide an overview of fundamental concepts unique to qualitative research. I began by preparing you for a new way of knowing, a way of knowing that represents a truly different paradigm for developing knowledge that can inform the practice of counseling. Considerable time was spent discussing the importance of philosophical stances toward inquiry, or knowledge, and the various stances' impact on qualitative methodologies. This is imperative. Qualitative research is not simply finding common themes in spoken words, as quantitative research is not simply counting occurrences of some behavior. Qualitative research seeks to understand a wide variety of human experiences and processes. Qualitative methodologies can be as rich and varied as these human experiences and processes. By no means can a couple of chapters in a book fully prepare you for all of the ways qualitative research can inform your role as practitioner-scholar. But it is a start. What follows in Chapter 11 is the examination of a phenomenon from three different qualitative methodological viewpoints. For a couple of these approaches, examples are given of how different philosophical stances toward knowledge impact the design and process of the same qualitative methodology.

Suggested Activities: Thought Experiments

I. Finding Your Philosophical Stance Toward Inquiry

Start with your counseling theory. Ask yourself the following questions:

1. What is my counseling theory's view of the primary pathway of change? Is it affect? Cognitions or meanings? Behaviors?
2. How do I know that change is occurring along any of these pathways?
3. How does my counseling theory view the relationship between myself as counselor and my clients?

4. What role does advocacy have in my counseling theory? The answers to these questions will overlap with the different philosophical stances we spoke of regarding what is viewed as data and the degree of separation or connection you have with research participants.

II. Curiosity Quiz

Walk through the day and be mindful of your thoughts, feelings, and actions.

1. What interests you most about your own thoughts, feelings, and actions?
2. How do you explain what influences your thoughts, feelings, and actions?

   Yes, even in these simple reflective exercises it comes down to your own self-awareness. Finding your fit with a philosophical stance is a personal journey. Safe and enjoyable travels!

References

Baker, S. E., & Edwards, R. (2012). *How many qualitative interviews is enough? Expert voices and early career reflections on sampling and cases in qualitative research.* Retrieved from http://eprints.ncrm.ac.uk/2273/4/how_many_interviews.pdf

Bogdan, R. C., & Biklen, S. K. (2007). *Qualitative research for education: An introduction to theories and methods.* Boston, MA: Pearson.

Creswell, J. W. (2013). *Qualitative inquiry and research design: Choosing among five approaches.* Thousand Oaks, CA: Sage.

Denzin, N. K. (2001). *Interpretive interactionism* (2nd ed.). Thousand Oaks, CA: Sage.

Erford, B., Miller, E., Schein, H., McDonald, A., Ludwig, L., & Leishear, K. (2011). *Journal of Counseling & Development* publication patterns: Author and article characteristics from 1994 to 2009. *Journal of Counseling & Development, 89,* 73–80.

Gergen, K. J. (2015). *An invitation to social construction* (3rd ed.). Thousand Oaks, CA: Sage.

Hill, C. E., Knox, S., Thompson, B. J., Williams, E. N., Hess, S. A., & Ladany, N. (2005). Consensual qualitative research: An update. *Journal of Counseling Psychology, 52,* 196–205.

Hill, C. E., Thompson, B. J., & Williams, E. N. (1997). A guide to conducting consensual qualitative research. *The Counseling Psychologist, 25*(4), 517–572.

Kleist, D. M. (2013). *Socially constructing the role of qualitative research in counselor education, supervision, and counseling.* Unpublished manuscript, Department of Counseling, Idaho State University, Pocatello.

Koltz, R. L., Odegard, M. A., Provost, K. B., Smith, T., & Kleist, D. M. (2010). Picture perfect: Using photo-voice to explore four doctoral students' comprehensive examination experiences. *Journal of Creativity in Mental Health, 5,* 389–411.

Lincoln, Y., & Guba, E. (1985). *Naturalistic inquiry.* London, England: Sage.

Lincoln, Y. S., Lynham, S. A., & Guba, E. (2011). Paradigmatic controversies: Contradictions, and emerging confluences, revisited. In N. K. Denzin & Y. S. Lincoln (Eds.), *The Sage handbook of qualitative research* (pp. 97–128). Thousand Oaks, CA: Sage.

Maxwell, J. (2013). *Qualitative research design: An interactive approach* (3rd ed.). Thousand Oaks, CA: Sage.

Minor, A. J., Moody, S., Tadlock-Marlo, R., Pender, R. L., & Person, M. (2013). Music as a medium for cohort development. *Journal of Creativity in Mental Health, 8,* 381–394.

Moustakas, C. (1994). *Phenomenological research methods.* Thousand Oaks, CA: Sage.

Patton, M. Q. (2015). *Qualitative research and evaluation methods.* Thousand Oaks, CA: Sage.

Pedersen, P. B. (1991). Introduction to the Special issue on multiculturalism as a fourth force in counseling. *Journal of Counseling and Development, 70.*

Perry, W. G. (1999). *Forms of ethical and intellectual development in the college years.* San Francisco, CA: Jossey-Bass.

Schwandt, T. (2000). Three epistemological stances for qualitative inquiry: Interpretivism, hermeneutics, and social constructionism. In N. K. Denzin & Y. S. Lincoln (Eds.), *Handbook of qualitative research* (pp. 189–213). Newbury Park, CA: Sage.

Strauss, A. L., & Corbin, J. M. (1998). *Basics of qualitative research: Techniques and procedures for developing grounded theory.* Thousand Oaks, CA: Sage.

Van Manen, M. (1990). *Researching lived experience: Human science for an action sensitive pedagogy.* Albany, NY: State University of New York Press.

Wang, C., & Burris, M. A. (1997). Photovoice: Concept, methodology, and use for participatory needs assessment. *Health Education Behavior, 24,* 369–387. doi:10.1177/109019819702400309

Wathen, C., & Kleist, D. M. (2015). Internationalization of counselor education: Exploring the lived experiences of counselors-in-training internationally. *The Qualitative Report*, *20*, 59–83.

Multiple Perspectives on a Phenomenon: The Qualitative Lenses

Overview

Congratulations! You decided to turn the page and read on about the potential for qualitative research informing your, and others', counseling practice (or maybe it's your faculty's assigned reading, whatever). However you came to this chapter, your clients thank you. Why? Because if you are willing to read this chapter on the potential of qualitative research to assist your and others' counseling practice as a practitioner-scholar, you somehow agree that allowing clients' more direct voice in producing the knowledge that informs our work might just be a very useful way to expand and enrich our clinical insight, wisdom, and knowledge base. As I (David) said in the previous chapter, I can by no means say all I wish to say about qualitative research in two chapters. My hope is to excite you to the possibilities. In this chapter I discuss a population that may seek the range of counseling services, from preventive to remedial. We look at what we, as professional counselors, may wish to understand about this population and then devise three different qualitative studies to expand our knowledge base. We actually consider five different studies, as I show you two variations on a qualitative theme by highlighting how one's philosophical stance toward knowledge impacts research design.

The Phenomenon of Interest

As discussed in the previous chapter, to start the qualitative research process we must have a question. What do we seek to understand? Our question will relate to understanding some phenomenon or some aspect of a phenomenon. For the purposes of this chapter, I highlight the potential of research to inform our work with those individuals, couples, and families in the lesbian, gay, bisexual, transgender, questioning, and intersex (LGBTQI) population who may seek counseling services. A doctoral student at my institution, Jennifer Gess (2016), found ample research for her dissertation that supports the potential for mental health services for the LGBTQI population. Be it from experiencing heterosexism, transphobia, heteronormativity, and social injustices (e.g., Eubanks-Carter, Burckell, & Goldfried, 2005; Hatzenbuehler, 2011; Hatzenbuehler, McLaughlin, Keyes, & Hasin, 2010; Hein & Scharer, 2013) or discrimination, prejudice, rejection, stigmatization, and violence (e.g., Israel, Gorcheva, Burnes, & Walther, 2008; Meyer, 2003), the LGBTQI population experiences depression, anxiety, eating disorders, substance abuse, and suicidality at a higher rate than heterosexual people (Israel et al., 2008). The potential interest in mental health services for these individuals, couples, and families is broad. Let us put on our creative hats, get curious, and see what we might wish to understand.

Okay, I have one! How about the LGBTQI experience of stigmatization? As a counselor, I need to be able to empathize and build a therapeutic relationship. Research also clearly communicates (Hubble, Duncan, & Miller, 1999) the importance of the therapeutic relationship as a major influence on positive client outcomes. Obviously I need to have some contextual understanding to initiate the relationship-building process. I wonder what it's like for an LGBTQI person to encounter stigmatization? Having some description of this experience will help me to better understand, empathize, and initiate therapeutic conversations. Time to plan a qualitative study!

Phenomenology

Van Manen's (1990) Phenomenology

As our focus of interest is *understanding the experience of stigmatization,* we will conduct a phenomenological study. Broadly speaking, the common focus for any phenomenological approach is understanding how human beings make sense of their lived experience

(Patton, 2015). Okay, great. "Now are we going to be going back to all those philosophical mumblings again?" you might ask. Well, yes, yes, we will. As I communicated in the previous chapter it is vital to steep yourself in your own understanding of the philosophical stance toward knowledge as it impacts which phenomenological methods, or approach, you utilize. For this example, let us say we are somewhere in the middle of the constructivist stance: not too weak, not too strong, but leaning more toward a social constructivist stance. This means that we value an interpretivist stance toward the construction of knowledge and firmly embrace ourselves as interpreting beings who are influenced by our own lived experience, values, beliefs, and so on. As we are not on the weak end of constructivism, we acknowledge the impossibility of interpreting another person's experience without some influence from our own interpretive lens. Given our philosophical location, we also value and accept the relationship between researcher and participant as one that cannot be objectively separated. We see its value in facilitating the generation of rich data, similar to how we see the value of the therapeutic relationship as a means of developing mutual understanding in the clinical context. After reviewing our phenomenological options, we believe Max Van Manen's (1990) hermeneutic phenomenology to be our best philosophical fit. So we have our question and our purpose, and now we have selected a particular type of phenomenological method, or approach, that fits our philosophical stance.

With all phenomenological approaches it is the understanding of the phenomenon by the participants themselves that is the focal point of understanding, not any presuppositions you might have (as a researcher) about what stigmatization might be like for an LGBTQI person. Thus, the conceptual framework (remember, that's the qualitative research version of quantitative research's literature review) is constructed around concepts from the relevant literature, previous research, and personal experience connected to the phenomenon that could sensitize us, as researchers, to the possible meanings that participants could share. An aspect of the conceptual framework that I have mentioned but really need to say more about is the personal experience component. Part of the constructed conceptual framework requires us, as researchers, to lay transparent our thoughts and ideas around the topic of study. Any preconceived notion of the experience of stigmatization, or experience with the phenomenon directly or indirectly, should be shared openly with the reader. Such transparency as to what we as human-beings-as-researchers bring conceptually to the study is a vital component that the reader, or consumer, of our study can use to assess the credibility, or trustworthiness, of our knowledge claims.

The next step is data collection. Obviously for us to collect data on the experience of stigmatization among persons in the LGBTQI population, we will need to find people to collect data from! Purposeful sampling is the intentional selection of persons who have experienced the phenomenon of interest. Relationships are important in all aspects of research, but particularly here for the qualitative researcher. As practitioner-scholars we can use our professional contacts to determine the best place in the community to find suitable participants for our study. There may be certain agencies in town that advocate for or provide services to the LGBTQI population. Maybe the community has social groups for the LGBTQI population. Finding interested stakeholders, or individuals respected by the community you are interested in, is essential to gaining access to potential participants.

Once we have identified possible contexts, we have to strategize the best means of advertising our study and need for participants. Be it old-fashioned flyers available at the entrance of agencies or newer possibilities for advertising on agency websites, Facebook, and so forth, all should be considered. I must digress to ethics for a moment. Unless you are conducting your study as part of your work for an established entity, like a university or large-scale agency, you will probably not have your research protocol reviewed by an institutional review board. Research protocol review processes are seldom established for researchers in small agencies, group practices, or solo private practices. However, as a professional counselor you are still obligated to follow the guidelines for research discussed in the *ACA Code of Ethics* (American Counseling Association [ACA], 2014). In addition to ensuring that your research advertisements meet ethical guidelines, you must specifically describe what criteria you are using to secure participants. Most important for our study, we are seeking members of the LGBTQI population who have experienced stigmatization. Though it is not an absolute requirement, we may provide a definition of what stigmatization means in this research context. We can also attend to diversity in our sample, intending to have participants from various perspectival standpoints: male, female, transgender, various ages, and so on. I need to be clear: We seek maximum variation not for the goal of generalizing results but for the sake of having the potential to identify diverse experiences of stigmatization. For our phenomenological study, we seek the essence of the experience of stigmatization, which would be even more potent if we understood it across a diverse array of perspectives.

On to the dreaded question in qualitative research, phenomenology included: How many people do we want in our sample? For Van Manen's hermeneutic phenomenology it is not an issue of the breadth of participants but the potential for depth of description about the phenomenon. In theory, this could be achieved with a very small sample of one to five. (These numbers are mine, not specifically suggested by Van Manen.) Patton (2015) said quite simply of the sample size issue, "It depends" (p. 311). As I said in the prior chapter, it depends partly on the purpose of the study. Here we seek rich description of stigmatization and thus will seek a small number of participants (let us say five): two rounds of one-on-one interviews followed up by a member check interview to get the job done. Later on I discuss how Van Manen's phenomenology assesses rigor and why I chose two rounds of interviews along with a member check interview. Many other factors influence sample size as well, such as time and the number of researchers. Given our resources—you and I, and let us say 1 year—we should be able to accomplish our goal.

Remember, our place along the philosophical continuum has us as middle-of-the-road constructivists with a slight lean toward the social constructivist end. Thus, we value relationships and are open to the impact of relational dynamics on data collection (Pitts & Miller-Day, 2007); in fact, we see this as essential to the gathering of rich data (Collins & Cooper, 2014). As a consequence, we are going to prize face-to-face interviews or, at worst, video-based interviews in which visual contact can still be made between us as researchers and the participants. We will find a secure and confidential setting in which to conduct our interviews, which will be planned for roughly 60 minutes. We want to be respectful of participants' time while still having enough time to gather rich descriptions of stigmatization.

In his phenomenological approach Van Manen spoke of six methodological themes that will guide the research endeavor rather than of particular methods or techniques that must be present. I chose Van Manen for just this reason. He highlighted the relationship in data gathering and the nuanced dance between researcher and participant that are restrained by more technique-driven phenomenological approaches (e.g., Giorgi, 1992; Moustakas, 1994). (This is another example of how philosophical stance may show its influence. More on this later with a variation of this study from a different research stance toward knowledge.) Let us look at these themes and how they inform our research process.

Methodological Themes

Theme 1: Turning to the nature of lived experience. This may sound trivial, yet in many ways it is profound. To conduct phenomenology, according to Van Manen, we first need to fully commit ourselves to examining the phenomenon of interest with deep, focused, thinking. Think, "Patience!" Mindfulness practice is certainly applicable to the level of focus Van Manen suggested that we as researchers assume in our endeavors. In our case, we need to fully give ourselves as researchers to understanding, as deeply and thoroughly as possible, what it means for an LGBTQI person to experience stigmatization.

Theme 2: Investigating experience as we live it. Again, I can see so much of mindfulness practice relevant here. Van Manen suggested that within our deep focus on a phenomenon we be attentive to the fullness of the experience investigated, as a human being. In other words, we cannot fully understand the experience of our participants if we are not simultaneously attuned to the fullness of our experience as researchers in relationship to the participants we are trying to understand. See any link to what you are learning about your role as counselor and relationship with clients? I told you earlier that you are well grounded in the essential skills of a qualitative researcher!

Theme 3: Reflecting on essential themes. Doing phenomenological research for Van Manen is not merely describing the superficial, apparent, surface understanding of participants' experience of some phenomenon. Instead, as researchers we need to reflect on the not-so-obvious meaning or significance of some experience. We need to see beyond the content description of an experience to the underlying, hidden-yet-present, essential meaning of an experience. Again, I would like to ask, have your faculty ever encouraged you to focus on process, not just the content of a counseling session? Yes, I thought so. That is very much what Van Manen's phenomenology asks of us.

Theme 4: The art of writing and rewriting. This theme, in phenomenological phrasing, highlights an essential distinction between the writing of results in quantitative and qualitative research. In quantitative research the writing of results happens after the analysis. Some would say that the writing of quantitative results is quite straightforward. Not so with qualitative research! The *act* of writing results of qualitative research, particularly for Van Manen's phenomenology, *is* the doing of research. Phenomenological analysis, as Van Manen put it, is "always a *bringing to speech* of something" (p. 32, italics in the original), which commonly presents itself in written form. We must be open to new understandings of the experience we are researching as we write up what we *thought* we understood about the experience.

Theme 5: Maintaining a strong and oriented relation. It's all about relationships. (Sorry, another phrase borrowed from the counselor educator's manual of overused clichés.) However, Van Manen spoke clearly of the loyalty, the fidelity, that must be shown by the researcher to the phenomenon of study and to the participants from which understanding of the phenomenon is to be gleaned. The notion of the disinterested researcher, valued in positivist and postpositivist research, has no place in Van Manen's hermeneutic phenomenology.

Theme 6: Balancing the research context by considering parts and whole. As qualitative research asks, "What is the phenomenon in its whatness?" (p. 33), a potential consequence of following Van Manen's themes is ending up in deep description of the essence of a phenomenon without understanding the bigger picture, the whole, of the experience. We may identify four major themes related to the experience of stigmatization among LGBTQI persons and so deeply explore these major themes that they seem to exist in isolation versus existing in a larger textual, or thematic, context. We must be able to ask, and answer, the question "How are the themes related?" No, we are not asking, "How do the themes influence one another?" That would be a grounded theory question related to the data. We are asking how themes derived from phenomenological analysis are related (e.g., Are themes experienced alongside one another? Are themes found deeper within other themes?)

In reviewing Van Manen's six methodological themes we can clearly see that we are not presented with a qualitative methods cookbook. Rather, we are presented with a stance, a standpoint, from which we engage with the phenomenon and the participant. Engaging in this form of research will not lead to reflectively asking yourself, "Did I do it right?" but lead to asking something more along the lines of "To what degree did I stay loyal, or true, to the stance necessary to conduct a hermeneutic phenomenological study?" Let us get back to our study.

Our data collection will be guided by our overall research question: What is the experience of stigmatization for an LGBTQI person? For Van Manen, and all phenomenologists I would say, the data collection interview must retain the focus and intent of the overarching research question. In this way, while the interview unfolds, focus is maintained and conversation does not stray in ways preferred by the researcher (which would be a potential undue influence of presuppositions of the phenomenon) or by the participant that move away from the phenomenon of interest. Yes, we will need to use the counseling skill of focusing here. In terms of interview questions, Van Manen would suggest a few broad questions to initiate the interview, but a skilled qualitative researcher is very much like a skilled counselor. Both have exceptional listening skills to communicate understanding and facilitate further conversation. So I cannot present some magical list of *the* questions to ask in each and every phenomenological study based on Van Manen's approach. It can be as simple as "What's your understanding of stigmatization as an LGBTQI person?" or "In what ways, or contexts, do you experience stigmatization as an LGBTQI person?" Your skill in conducting a rich data-producing interview is not in the beauty of your interview questions but in how you attend to the verbal and nonverbal communication of potential themes during the interview. Yes, like I said, very much like the skilled practice of counseling. I knew you were a researcher!

After data have been collected via face-to-face interviews captured on digital audio, we will take our recordings to be transcribed by a professional transcriptionist. I do want to suggest that you try transcribing your own interviews at some point in time. Yes, this task may remind you of transcribing your counseling sessions for some course assignment, and you may be shrinking in dread at the thought of the time it will take. Though using a professional transcriptionist is more efficient, there can be great value in transcribing your own interviews. Quite simply, you begin analyzing the data while you are transcribing. It is almost impossible not to! I have had a couple of students transcribe their qualitative interviews, and to a person they strongly believed that they listened differently, more intensely, as they transcribed. This different form of listening allowed them to hear themes, patterns, and other subtleties in ways very different than if they had read transcripts prepared by someone else. But I get it: Transcription is a long process in which to engage. Your choice. But I ask you to at least try it once and see what happens with your process of hearing themes and making sense of the data.

Data Analysis

As hinted at in the previous chapter, data analysis begins even in the midst of interviewing. According to Van Manen, we are making sense, or interpretations, while interviewing participants. Nonetheless, data analysis is a more distinct process for Van Manen. Now that we have transcripts in front of us, let us first adopt the attitude called for by Van Manen. Phenomenological reflection, the process of grasping the meaning or essence of a lived experience, requires us as practitioner-scholars to approach reading transcripts not as practitioner-scholars, professional counselors, but from inside the experience of an LGBTQI person experiencing stigmatization as it is lived via their symbolic interpretation of their experience communicated in the interviews. Such an attitude requires attention to relationship, to our humanness, to our ability for awareness and empathy. There are no simple techniques to bring this about. Van Manen's phenomenology highlights the artistic human quality of such research. Once we challenge ourselves to adopt this attitude, we approach transcripts with various options for analyzing themes.

Van Manen (1990) suggested three approaches for analyzing and developing themes. The first approach is called the *holistic* or *sententious* approach. Here we look at the text as a whole and ask ourselves, "What sentence(s) captures the fundamental meaning communicated in the text?" In many ways, this is akin to a counselor providing an in-session summary to the client as to what has occurred so far in the session. For our research we may read the entire transcript and construct a sentence that captures the overall meaning expressed in the interview. I do not suggest, however, that you see this approach to developing themes as all that there is to thematic analysis. Van Manen spoke of text but not necessarily text-as-whole transcript. I would suggest that we understand the holistic approach as related to smaller pieces of the transcript—a page or paragraph—and then ask ourselves, "What sentence can I use to summarize this page of the transcript or this paragraph of the transcript?"

The second approach is called the *selective* or *highlighting* approach. Here we ask ourselves, "Is there a sentence(s), partial sentence(s), or phrase(s) in the text that captures a theme I am interpreting in the text?" We then paraphrase what we interpret as the meaning of these selective phrases or sentences. To reiterate, the process is bigger than this in terms of emergent themes. Qualitative research analysis across methodologies is an iterative process of tacking back and forth between data (here, text) and our sense making or interpretation of themes, connecting back to the data to ground our interpretation of emerging themes, and so on, moving the process onward. As with the first approach, what we as researchers select as the segment of text that best captures a developing theme may be different from what a different researcher would conceive and select. I know. That post-positivist part of your prior training cannot take this fact. You want *the* theme or set of themes to be found! Sorry! As we are residing in the world of hermeneutic phenomenology, we accept and embrace the interpretive nature of meaning making in research.

The third approach for analyzing and developing themes put forth by Van Manen is the *line-by-line* or *detailed* approach. Here sentences or sentence groupings are pulled from the text and listed. Each sentence is wondered about for its meaning and its significance to the larger whole of the paragraph, the text, and ultimately the interview. In these three approaches you see different levels of analysis to which our attention as researchers is directed differently. Though not specified by Van Manen, their use seems interactional. One would not simply conduct a thematic analysis of a text using the holistic or line-by-line approach; rather, thematic analysis is also an iterative process of tacking back and forth from the whole to a particular phrase and back again.

After we have thematically analyzed our interview transcripts, it's time for us to form some cohesive understanding of what we currently understand of stigmatization among LGBTQI persons. For this to occur, Van Manen uses the task of writing and rewriting, of linguistically transforming our analysis into a more coherent description of our current understanding of the phenomenon. At this point we may feel confident in some aspects of our understanding of stigmatization and unsure in other areas. For both, a return to data collection, a second interview, is common practice. During our second interview we can inform participants of our emergent understanding of stigmatization. We focus our second interview on two areas: confirmation of what we think we have come to understand and richer description of areas not yet fully understood. This second interview is thus more focused than the first. Our questions are much more pointed. We seek verification of understanding simultaneously with the hope for even richer description of the phenomenon. Van Manen indicated, and I strongly concur, that participants take on a different level and form of involvement at this stage of inquiry. Participants tend to be drawn into the unfolding description of their experience and experience an increased ownership of the developing knowledge product, one they value as shown by increased involvement in the interviews.

These second-round interviews are transcribed as in the first round. And again, we engage in the process of thematic analysis utilizing the same approaches we used previously. At this point we are both confirming and enriching our understanding through the art and task of writing our evolving understanding of what Van Manen called *essential* versus *incidental* themes. The goal is to identify those themes that if removed, would lead to the dissolution of the experience of the phenomenon itself. These are the essential themes. Incidental themes are those whose removal does not impact the essence of the experience. Incidental themes might be unique to a person but are not experienced by all in our phenomenon of stigmatization.

Writing, rewriting, reflection, and reflection on what one has written are central to the research process for Van Manen. The act of writing as central to phenomenological research sets Van Manen's approach off as quite distinct from other phenomenological approaches. I cannot emphasis this point enough. Whereas other, more postpositivist approaches view writing as a necessary component of communicating results, Van Manen's stance would be that our linguistic transformation of our interpretation of the interviews is so vital, so key to attempting to grasp participants' meaning that writing must be prized as central to all aspects of the research process. Writing facilitates the act of thinking. Writing and reading what we have written is our way of understanding our own thinking. So be ready at this point of the research process to be patient. We cannot rush good interpretive reflection and writing.

Once we get to the point of trusting our writing of the essential themes as best capturing and communicating our understanding of the phenomenon (for us stigmatization among LGBTQI persons), we take our results back to the participants for a final member check. Member checks are a way to ensure the trustworthiness of the results (more will be said in the next paragraph—patience, remember?). During member checks we are primarily seeking verification of our final results. However, we do not want participants to simply agree with us. We must be open to further refinement of our understandings, even at this point of the process. Though we as researchers and the participants themselves may be tired of the project at this point, we must be attentive to the possibility of being wrong or partially wrong. I know. We have spent countless hours in interviews, thematic analysis, and writing. Such is the world of the practitioner-scholar conducting qualitative research.

Quality

We all were taught as far back as some undergraduate research class, maybe even further back than that, the hallmarks of quality research: validity, reliability, and generalizability. Qualitative research is research, so these hallmarks must be the criteria to use when evaluating qualitative research. Right? Wrong—oh, so wrong. Yes, you may have heard or seen these terms applied to qualitative research, and in some situations they may fit, particularly if the research is conducted within a postpositivist stance. However, there are almost as many different sets of criteria for assessing quality in qualitative research as there are different methodologies and philosophical stances, which all can vary by degree and be integrated in numerous creative ways. Patton (2015) described seven sets of such criteria in his latest book on qualitative methods. The answer again, my friends, is not blowing in the wind, but "It depends." Again, I encourage fidelity to the particular methodology that you have selected for the given study. For us, that means turning to Van Manen's criteria for assessing quality.

Van Manen conceptualized four criteria that can be used to assess the quality of a given hermeneutic phenomenological study. The first is *orientation.* The research results, or the text of the results, must be oriented toward the phenomenon of interest within the relevant field of study. Sounds odd or overly simple. But we must look at the results of our study and ask, "Are the results oriented toward helping counselors understand the stigmatization of persons who identify as LGBTQI?" This becomes a judgment call—the judgment call of the consumer of the research. We do our best to be transparent in our research process and our stance as persons-in-the-role-of-researcher (remember the personal connection to the phenomenon discussed in the conceptual framework). Our work's potential now becomes the focus of the professional counselor who wishes to inform his or her practice of counseling with the LGBTQI population.

The second criterion is *strength.* For our text of the results to be strong, it must communicate explicit interpretation to the context of counseling. Qualitative research is about local, contextual knowledge, and our results must stay exclusively directed toward the context of counseling.

The third criterion is *richness.* Our description of the phenomenon of interest in a given study must be concrete and deeply descriptive of all aspects of the essential themes, leaving the reader with a truly experiential understanding of the essential themes and thus the phenomenon. Whether we adequately meet this criterion is again up to the reader. For our part, we attempt through our linguistic transformations in writing to fully capture the experience of the phenomenon (for our study, the experience of stigmatization among LGBTQI persons).

The fourth criterion put forth to assess quality in Van Manen's hermeneutic phenomenology is *depth*. *Depth* refers again to our ability to write about the essence of a phenomenon in a way that captures the subtle contours of experiencing the phenomenon. I know what you are thinking: "Where the heck are the statistics to support *depth* or *richness*?" You are in a different world—yes, a qualitatively different world of research (I could not help but use the pun). In many ways, what Van Manen's hermeneutic phenomenology asks of the results is "Have I been moved, emotionally, cognitively, and experientially, by reading the text describing the essence of the phenomenon?" Humanism is alive and well in such a qualitative methodology.

Moustakas's (1994) Phenomenology

We have just moved through one way of conceiving phenomenological research. There are many others. Although it is not the purpose of this chapter to walk through examples of all possible phenomenological approaches, I do want to show a variation on the phenomenological theme. So let us look briefly at how a phenomenological study based in a postpositivist stance toward knowledge would structure the same phenomenon. I wish to focus on the differences here, not the similarities with Van Manen (1990), of which there are many.

Let us start with your attitude as a practitioner-scholar, which resonates more with a postpositivist view toward knowledge and thus research. You believe that a world, a reality, exists beyond yourself, beyond a person's experiencing of it. The use of rigorous methods and procedures, in and of themselves, lends credibility to the results of research. As reality exists beyond a person's experiencing of it, methods and procedures must be used to keep human experiencing from tainting, or biasing, the collection, analysis, and presentation of results. A separation between the researcher and participants must be sought. Yes, a relationship of some sort must exist to gather rich data, but like some approaches to counseling, the therapeutic alliance is merely the groundwork on which the real counseling work is to be done. It is a necessary component for change to occur, but not *the* component for change. Do you hear the different attitude toward the relationship between the researcher and participant? It is still there, but it's of a different quality, value, and purpose. Let us start here and mention a key concept in Moustakas's phenomenological approach that sets it apart from Van Manen's.

Moustakas, and those who utilize his approach, spends much time talking about *epoche*. This should come as no surprise, but there is not one agreed-on description of epoche. Go ahead, sigh. Let me give one conceptualization. Epoche represents the researcher's own experiences that may connect to the phenomenon of interest. For us, in our example, it would be our direct and/or indirect understanding of stigmatization among LGBTQI persons. As researchers within this stance, we must reflect on our past experiences and be transparent with them to ourselves and ultimately to the audience of our research results. We can communicate that we used memoing as a technique to identify our epoche. Once our epoche has been identified, and this is a continuous process throughout the study, we must *bracket* these experiences when we are in relationship with participants, from interview through analysis. To bracket one's epoche means to suspend these experiences and their meaning, to pause their potential influence on one's ability as a researcher to hear, to truly hear and understand, participants' stories, meanings, and understandings of the phenomenon. According to Moustakas our epoche must be bracketed until it is time to interpret the results of the study. At this time, our previous experiences may prove useful in empathically communicating the essence of the participants' experiences in rich fashion.

Data Analysis

Distinctions in the data analysis stage of Moustakas's approach set it apart from Van Manen's (1990). Remember, Van Manen did not speak of specific data analysis methods or techniques; rather, he spoke of methodological themes to integrate into data analysis. Moustakas discussed the techniques of *horizontalization* (listing every quote relevant to the experience of the phenomenon) and *reduction and elimination* (finding the invariant constituents by eliminating overlapping, repetitive, or vague language; or developing more abstract labels). Once invariant constituents are found, you move on to *clustering* or *thematizing* the invariant constituents. Then, in similar iterative fashion as described by Van Manen, you go back to the transcript and find explicit and compatible examples of the invariant constituents of the experience. This is done for each participant, concluding with the development of an *individual textural description* of each participant's experience. Next, an *individual structural description* is developed that describes the connection between main themes for each participant. After this is done for each participant, a *composite description* is provided that highlights the common experiences across participants, resulting in the essence of the experience.

Rounds of data collection are not rigidly specified. I have reviewed a number of phenomenological studies that ultimately seek the emergence of no new understandings of the phenomenon under study. Some have only one round of interviews with four to 15 participants, whereas others have multiple rounds of interviews with eight participants. When multiple rounds of interviews take place, there is greater potential to achieve added depth, which can limit the number of participants needed.

Quality

Quality in Moustakas's phenomenological approach, let alone any phenomenological approach that comes from a postpositivist stance (i.e., Giorgi, 1992), places considerable emphasis on the rigor and thoroughness of procedures conducted by the researchers. I am reminded of *Field of Dreams,* the movie from which came the phrase "If you build it, he will come." I see this phrase echoed in the quality efforts of Moustakas and other postpositivist researchers. Build a detailed and thorough methods procedure or technique, and quality will come (and so too the faithful readers trusting the message of the results).

As I stated previously, my intention is not to walk step by step through all phenomenological approaches. I have chosen one to highlight (i.e., Van Manen, 1990) and then have sought to mention the most significant differences with another phenomenological approach that is based in a different philosophy of research (i.e., Moustakas). For the confused and interested reader I would encourage further reading of Moustakas (1994) and Giorgi (1992) directly. And guess what? A relatively new phenomenological method is finding its way into the research world from across the pond (that means England, by the way). The interpretive phenomenological analysis approach by Smith, Flowers, and Larkin (2009) is a fine addition to your options to consider as a practitioner-scholar finding an affinity toward phenomenology. I will not go into this model here, but I find it resides between Moustakas's and Van Manen's on the philosophical continuum. "Oh gosh! Please, please, please! Just *tell me* how to *do* phenomenological research!" you shout. I must remind you, I cannot. I can only hope that you are excited, maybe even a bit liberated by the fact that you have research options to choose from—ones that you get to decide how well they fit your theoretical and philosophical stance toward counseling and research.

Summary

I hope you walk away from this phenomenological section realizing the clinical benefits of conducting research for your counseling practice and how you can impact other professional counselors' practice. If relationship is foundational to the practice of counseling, then let us conduct research that is directly applicable to enhancing how we as professional counselors develop and maintain a positive therapeutic alliance through empathy. Likewise, more fully empathizing with clients' lived experience fuels advocacy for those in the LGBTQI community. Now to explore what other learnings can come from another form of qualitative research, it is time to turn to grounded theory.

Grounded Theory

We need to remember what our phenomenon of interest will be for the grounded theory section. Stigmatization within the LGBTQI population fueled our phenomenological interest in understanding the experience of stigmatization among this population. With grounded theory our attention turns to process. Specifically, grounded theory seeks to understand the social and/or psychological process of some phenomenon. Embracing the core counseling value of wellness and strengths-based practice, let us structure the focus of our grounded theory study around the following research question: "How do persons who identify as LGBTQI overcome stigmatization?" For our practice as professional counselors such a question has relevance for remedial counseling work as well as structuring prevention programs or mental health promotion programs. Our role as advocates can definitely be informed by an answer to this question.

Here again there are many grounded theory approaches to consider (e.g., Charmaz, 2014; Clarke, 2005; Corbin & Strauss, 2015; Glaser & Strauss, 1967; Corbin & Strauss, 2008). "Here we go again" I hear echoing in the background. Yes, here we go again. The examples I give vary across positivist, postpositivist, constructivist, and social constructivist stances toward knowledge. Oh, the options! For our study, we will morph into a new research group, one that is coming from a postpositivist-weak-constructivist stance toward knowledge. For this stance we choose to use Strauss and Corbin's (1998) grounded theory approach. Grounded theory methodology has gone through various iterations of conceptual development since Glaser and Strauss's (1967) text *The Discovery of Grounded Theory.* Strauss went off on his own later to develop a reconceptualized grounded theory approach with his wife, Juliet Corbin (e.g., Corbin & Strauss, 2008; Strauss & Corbin, 1998). They were in the process of developing another revision when Strauss died; Corbin finished their work, which advanced a more postmodern version of their grounded theory methodology (see Corbin & Strauss, 2008, 2015).

Let us again start with our attitude toward the current research endeavor. We believe that people construct meaning of reality, but we believe that there is a reality beyond our experience of it. We understand our interpretive nature as humans but believe that through rigorous use of detailed research techniques and procedures we can minimize our interpretive influence. We accept that participants are giving us their interpretation of their process, and their descriptions through language are the data from which we will derive an understanding of the process of overcoming stigmatization for LGBTQI persons. We acknowledge that our relationship with participants is very important to facilitating their descriptions, but we need to be persistent in monitoring our potential for interpreting the data through our own personal experience and framework and not letting the data speak for themselves. So we have our phenomenon, and we have our research question. I guess we had better find a sample.

Participant Selection

In grounded theory, as with phenomenology, we will utilize *purposeful sampling* procedures. We need to find participants within the LGBTQI community who have experienced the process of overcoming stigmatization. Just what is overcoming stigmatization? Well, we could review previous research on overcoming any phenomenon, or we could let potential participants self-identify as overcoming stigmatization. I like the second option better. Why? Allowing participants to define and articulate the process of overcoming values local knowledge over the theorized description of overcoming or using another study's definition of overcoming. We are coming from a postpositivist-weak-constructivist stance, but we as qualitative researchers still prize the local, contextualized meaning of experience. Our purpose is to develop a local, contextualized theory of the process of overcoming stigmatization among LGBTQI persons. Toward this end we will use *maximum variation sampling,* what I frame as a subsampling strategy within purposeful sampling.

Our goal is to develop a rich and powerful theory of a process. The rigor of our findings is enhanced if we develop a theory that has been informed by diverse perspectives. So we reflect back on our conceptual framework, which encompasses any concepts from the world of ideas related to overcoming stigmatization, as well as our direct or indirect personal experience with overcoming stigmatization among LGBTQI persons. From our conceptual framework we may find that persons of different ages might overcome stigmatization in different ways, or we may find that gender or region of the country might impact the process. Therefore, we are going to attempt to maximize the presence of these participant characteristics in our purposeful sample. Our strategy must be to find persons in the LGBTQI community who identify as having overcome stigmatization.

Creativity must be present in all aspects of research, I believe, but certainly here. How are we going to reach out across the country to find participants? Here is one option, and one we will use for the sake of this example. Fortunately, ACA has ACA Connect (https://community.counseling.org/home), which is an electronic means for ACA members to interact with one another. We can craft our call for participants via this venue. Like in the phenomenological example, we also must be certain to follow the *ACA Code of Ethics* (ACA, 2014) regarding conducting research.

How Many to Sample?

Here we go again with just what adequate sample size is with qualitative research (and specifically, grounded theory). I refer you back to what I said about sample size in the phenomenology example. In a grounded theory methodology, there is no singular view of a required or minimum sample size. In fact, given its inductive nature, in theory you may start with some small number of participants and achieve saturation of codes, and your overall understanding of the process, or you may need to continue to sample more participants as nuanced understanding unfolds that requires further elucidation. However, there is a slight difference. We are seeking to understand process and hearing the description of process from only one person. So we do need to think of the purpose of our study. Are we looking to generalize to the larger population of persons in the LGBTQI community, or do we want to provide a detailed and rich description of the process for our particular sample? I suggest we stay truer to the overarching purpose of qualitative inquiry, which is to value the local, contextual meanings as informed by the participants themselves. I am going to suggest that we seek between six and 12 participants to engage in a minimum of two rounds of interviews, concluding with a member check. This means that we will plan on between 12 and 24 interviews, along with 12 to 24 member check interviews.

At the outset, this appears to be adequate to provide a rich description of the process we wish to understand. It is possible that we may not need this many participants if we hear redundancy in the data with only, say, eight participants. We are not obligated to interview 12 just because we indicated that number at the outset. Our process of data collection is emergent and truly driven by the data. We must be open to the possibility of needing more than 12 participants if after data analysis there are still conceptually thin areas in our understanding of the process. Or we may begin to hear new data, which requires seeking additional rounds of interviews or quite possibly new participants. Remember and embrace the concept of emergence—the process of coming into view or becoming exposed after being concealed—as it is an essential aspect of qualitative research. As with phenomenology, sample size is affected by human resources (how many researchers) and time (the time frame within which we would like to complete the study). So our plan is to get between six and 12 participants, and we will give ourselves a window of a month for people to respond to our post on ACA Connect. We will look to get participants who vary in terms of gender and region of the country.

Our data collection plan is definitely impacted by proximity to participants. Given that we are seeking regional differences, odds are some participants will live too far away to consider in-person, face-to-face interviews. We can think of using a secure digital means of interviewing, possibly Skype or Adobe Connect. These technologies are being utilized in studies at present, but there are issues, such as trusting the security of connections, participants' willingness to trust such technology, and the inconsistent connection speeds of the present-day Internet. Given this, we will go with phone interviews, and digital recording software will be used to capture the interviews. We will be missing out on nonverbal data, but phone interviews have a long history in qualitative research, and we will go with this time-honored standard. We will structure our interviews with very broad questions like "How would you describe your experience of overcoming stigmatization?" and "What started your process of overcoming stigmatization?" and "What allowed overcoming to take place?" As with phenomenology, our skill is not simply in the beauty of these initial questions but in our ability to listen keenly for meaning, descriptions of process, and facilitation of more finely focused conversations around these areas. Once we have completed our interviews, they will need to be transcribed in the same fashion as our transcripts in our phenomenological study to ready the data for analysis.

Data Analysis

Strauss and Corbin (1998) were instrumental in detailing techniques and procedures for data analysis in grounded theory research. Remember, I am seeking to give a broad overview of their analysis procedures. What follows is not a how-to grounded theory discussion. Go seek out the books listed in the reference list for more details! For each and every transcript that now lies before us will seek to conduct an initial *microanalysis* of the data. For Strauss and Corbin, this means *line-by-line* and even *word-by-word* analysis. Such a micro focus is vital during the initial stages of coding in grounded theory. These initial stages of data analysis seek to develop an initial list of codes related to concepts found in the data. Such concepts are compared with other examples of codes, utilizing the oft-mentioned *constant comparison method* of Glaser and Strauss (1967). This initial stage of analysis is referred to as *open coding*. The emphasis is on attending to all plausible meanings that can be packed into a single word, line, or sentence. The goal is to develop an initial understanding of the emergent *categories* along with their *properties* and *dimensions.*

I had better say something about each, as regardless of whose grounded theory you use, some aspect of categories and their properties and dimensions are included. Imagine if "running" were a *category* of some set of data. Part of the open coding process is to identify in the data properties of a category. So for running one *property,* or characteristic, could be "pace" and another might be "posture." Once properties are identified in the data, further constant comparison of words and phrases that relate to the property of posture is performed to look for ways in which a property *dimensionalizes*. In our example, we may find that the data suggest that the property posture of the category running dimensionalizes from upright to slumped. Categories can clearly have multiple properties, and most do, and properties can dimensionalize in a number of ways.

In the process of open coding it is possible to find relationships between categories. In Strauss and Corbin's (1998) grounded theory analysis, looking for relationships between categories is referred to as *axial coding.* In axial coding, relationships between categories tend to show at the property and dimensional levels. In the running example, we might find data to suggest that the properties pace and posture are related at the dimensional level. This means that as running pace increases, posture becomes more upright. Now this example is extremely simplistic, but I hope you begin to understand what the early stages of analysis may look like in grounded theory.

For our study, let us say we found eight participants and are now engaged in open coding, maybe even some axial coding, with the eight transcripts we have as our data. If your mind wandered with the running example, how many properties of running did you come up with? How about ways each property could dimensionalize? See how thorough and complex just these two features of grounded theory analysis can be? And we are just talking about one category: running. Now imagine we have analyzed our eight first-round transcripts of the process of overcoming stigmatization among persons who identify as LGBTQI. How many categories might emerge in the open coding process? Three, seven, 12, 20, more? Let us add in properties for each of these potential three to 12 categories. "Stop! Do not even ask me to think about dimensionalization of these categories!" I hear you. That is a lot of data to sift through and code. For myself, a good rule of thumb is to focus on developing a grasp of all of the potential categories as a goal for first-round data analysis. Typically I can find properties also, but the dimensionalization process might not be very clear yet. Our analysis of first-round interview data is complete when we can account for all transcript data as fitting into one of the categories or more deeply as a property of a category and maybe even an example of a property dimensionalizing.

We now want to look back at our developing understanding of the data and ask, "What do I still not understand?" "Which categories need further description and development?" So on goes the process with the properties, along with the dimensions, of each category. As some axial coding was possible, we will also be asking ourselves, "In what ways are the categories related?" "What allows the categories to be connected?" "What conditions bring about the connection?" and so on. To conduct good qualitative analysis is to be good at asking questions. From these questions we ask ourselves about the data come the second-round interview questions. Second-round interview questions have more focus than first-round questions. Now that we have a developing sense of the process, we need to gather more information about the categories we initially conceptualized, along with their properties and related dimensions. Likewise, we are tending to process how the categories are related to one another, how they influence one another, what conditions bring them about, how aspects of the context and time have an impact, and so on.

Second-round data analysis proceeds in similar fashion as the first. Great attention to open coding is important, as we wish to leave second-round data analysis with a clearer picture of the main categories, ideally understanding which category is the core category of the process around and through which all other categories interact. We very much want to verify what the main categories are, sifting through our original 20 categories, for example, and winnowing these down to four to seven. This range is not a hard and fast rule. But collapsing categories into smaller yet more abstract categories with richly described properties and dimensions allows relationships between categories to be more clearly known.

Through the analytic process of the second round, a theory of our process of interest begins to take shape. In rare cases, a full understanding of the process is the outcome of second-round analysis, with all categories and properties fully saturated. By *saturation* Strauss and Corbin (1998) meant that no new data about any aspects of our theory are coming out of data analysis. I find it very rare indeed for saturation to be achieved after just two rounds of interviews and analysis. However, many published studies stop after two rounds of interviews. For the sake of an example, let us say we still do not fully understand the process, and some of our properties are without information on how they dimensionalize. Therefore, we must conduct a third round of interviews to fill out our emerging theory of the process of overcoming stigmatization among persons who identify as LGBTQI.

We enter the third round of interviews with very specific questions that must be asked of participants who may have insight into specific aspects of the process we still do not fully understand. These interviews are transcribed, and now *selective* and *theoretical* coding is used. We now look at the data not for the sake of opening up all plausible options but to intentionally look for data that may fill in our conceptual gaps in our effort to develop a more complete theory of our particular process. This level of analysis only takes place after open and axial coding have yielded a fairly rich and detailed description of the process. The outcome of such coding leads to our ability to construct a story of the process in explicit detail. All data existing in our transcripts can be captured by our developed theory. At this point we should be able to tell an audience, the participants themselves, the story of overcoming stigmatization. This last part of the process, of sharing our final story of the process, is the member check interview in which participants give feedback on the accuracy of our grounded theory. In hearing or reading the story they should be able to connect with and see themselves in the described process.

Quality

For the postpositivist-oriented grounded theory of Strauss and Corbin (1998), no singular hard and fast evaluative rules are suggested. However, procedural evidence is vital. The final presentation of the study, from design through theory presentation, should provide a detailed picture of the procedures used to develop concepts; to describe their linkages, or relationships; and ultimately to develop the final theory. Obviously any lack of rich description speaks to potential flaws in the analytic process and overall procedures. Consistency in the logic of the design and findings speaks to the postpositivist groundings of this version of grounded theory methodology.

I have taken a very detailed process and oversimplified it terribly, but my intent is to provide an overview of grounded theory analysis as conceived by Strauss and Corbin (1998). Do you like group work? How about working with couples and families? If you do, you probably enjoy the process-level work in these counseling contexts. If so, you might also find your interest piqued by grounded theory. Or at least this one form of grounded theory piques your interest. "Aw, come on, do not say it, and do not tell me there are other options and forms of grounded theory." Yes, you are catching on. Grounded theory is not grounded theory is not grounded theory. Here is an example of another form of grounded theory, this one firmly grounded in social constructivism and postmodern ideas.

The most recent iterations of grounded theory by Corbin and Strauss (2015) and Charmaz (2014) are two examples of grounded theory that are embedded in a social constructivist stance toward knowledge and research. Let me again, as I did with the example of Moustakas's phenomenology, summarize only the distinctions between Strauss and Corbin's (1998) postpositivist-oriented grounded theory and more social constructivist (or postmodern) grounded theory approaches (i.e., Charmaz, 2014; Corbin & Strauss, 2015).

We must again start with the attitude of the researcher. A social constructivist stance toward grounded theory is going to value more highly in data collection and analysis than postpositivist grounded theory the interpretive relationship between researcher and participant in data collection and analysis. Whereas Glaser and Strauss (1967) and Strauss and Corbin (1998) spoke of *discovering* grounded theory, social constructivist grounded theorists intentionally speak of *constructing* grounded theory. There is the philosophical commitment to constructing meaning, and thus the realities we know, through relationships between people as evidenced by the language used to capture their shared understandings. Social constructivist grounded theory is coconstructed by researcher and participant. Data, according to this philosophical stance, do not and cannot speak for themselves. Data related to understanding the process of stigmatization are given life by the use of words to capture both the participants' and researcher's interpretation of the process.

An example of such coconstruction is Jane Coe Smith's (2007) dissertation research on the process of relationship in supervision. Unlike in the postpositivist example above, in which the researchers were responsible for data analysis and development of the grounded theory, Coe Smith engaged participants in what she called *interpreting dialogues.* Between each formal round of data collection she would share her evolving understanding and tentative categories, properties, and so on with participants. In this fashion, participants were provided the opportunity to contribute to the evolving theory throughout each round of the data analysis process rather than being brought in for the final theory presentation during the member check interviews. Such valuing of the participant as coresearcher empowers him or her to have more say in the use of language to best portray his or her understanding of the process under study. In essence, what Coe Smith did was embody the relational focus of meaning making that is the cornerstone of the social constructivist stance toward knowledge and research.

The social constructivist stance toward the construction of theory rather than its discovery also points to greater flexibility in the analytic process. Charmaz (2014) most aptly stayed away from restricted use of linear analytic procedure and technique merely for the sake of following procedure to show quality in grounded theory studies. She encouraged methodological flexibility to meet the needs of a particular study and highlighted the nonlinear process of coding, analysis, and theory building. Flexibility also shows in the final product of a grounded theory study. Whereas postpositivist grounded theory seeks a grand theory that captures, in rich detail, a singular process (yes, still variation at the dimensional level, but a singular primary process), social constructivist grounded theory allows varied processes to be included in the final research product. To put it succinctly, postpositivist grounded theory may communicate the process of stigmatization among persons who identify as LGBTQI, whereas social constructivist grounded theory communicates the processes of stigmatization among persons who identify as LGBTQI. The social constructivist stance removes the search for a core category or grand theory and instead views multiple categories as having influence, with none seen as *the* singular, most impactful category within one grand theory.

In terms of the quality of research, social constructivist grounded theory places primacy in its resonance and usefulness in the lives of participants and the audience of research consumers. Though there is overlap with postpositivist criteria for evaluating quality in terms of rich description of categories and their logical relations, the aspect of utility in the lives and worlds of participants sheds light on an increased focus on social justice implications for research. In short, a study is evaluated in terms of how the results make the world a better place. I again must remind you that I only seek to highlight one variation to postpositivist grounded theory that I detailed in much greater depth earlier. Reflect on your philosophical stance and find the grounded theory that best fits you.

As we transition out of grounded theory, I hope you see the potential impact of focusing on process. In our current clinical world, with increasing requirements for evidence-based practice, we need more than to know an intervention works. We need to understand how it works. Process research, like that using grounded theory methodology, can serve this purpose. Toward the other end of potential counseling services, we can choose to focus on strengths-based, wellness-oriented processes. Our focus on overcoming stigmatization is one example that can lead to the development of prevention programming that speaks to a core component of the foundation of counseling that can easily be forgotten in our daily practice of counseling.

Consensual Qualitative Research (CQR)

We end our foray into highlighting how three different qualitative methodologies examine the same phenomenon of stigmatization among persons who identify as LGBTQI with an overview of a relative newcomer to the qualitative research scene. CQR (Hill, Thompson, & Williams, 1997) has its origins in psychology, unlike phenomenology and grounded theory, whose home disciplines are education and sociology, respectively. Hill et al. (1997) developed CQR as an integration of phenomenology, grounded theory, and comprehensive process analysis. In this regard, I view it as leaning toward what Patton (2015) described as a general qualitative research approach. Hill and associates developed CQR with clear, stepwise procedures out of frustration with other qualitative approaches they saw as vague and confusing to understand conceptually and implement. They have definitely come up with a much clearer qualitative approach.

Though Hill et al. (2005) place CQR as constructivist in its philosophical stance with a "post-positivist flair" (p. 198), I would flip this emphasis. In terms of the framework of Lincoln, Lynham, and Guba (2011) introduced in Chapter 10, I view CQR as firmly postpositivist with a constructivist flair (i.e., postpositivist weak constructivism). They have developed an integrative qualitative approach that values the following (this is not an exhaustive list, just some prime examples): minimizing the relational impact on data, enhancing objectivity while minimizing bias through the use of multiple perspectives of the research team and external auditor to minimize bias, seeking replication across settings to increase generalizability, using a realist view of language (i.e., words represent reality vs. an interpretation of reality), and prizing consistent procedures (Hill et al., 2005). The attitude of the researcher and research team is one of investigative reporter. Very few of you are old enough to remember the line "Just the facts" spoken by Joe Friday in the 1960s show *Dragnet*, but this is the way I would describe the researcher attitude necessary for CQR. So let us morph again as researchers and adopt the CQR researcher attitude to see how the CQR approach would explore the phenomenon of stigmatization among persons who identify as LGBTQI. We will move on under the guise of having asked the following research question: "What is the experience of stigmatization among persons who identify as LGBTQI?"

The Research Team

Before we go further, we need to ensure that we have an adequate research team with appropriate training in CQR. As an aside, training or education in the given method is implied in other qualitative methodologies, but in CQR it is an explicit component of the research protocol. CQR guidelines recommend at least three research team members, so we may have to enlist colleagues from our office or find interested professionals nearby to make up our team. If they have not heard of CQR or been trained, we will first have to spend time preparing them for the tasks at hand. Team members will play various roles. Let us move forward with a team of three members, two of whom will be data analyzers and one of whom will serve as an external auditor. Now this is not ideal: Because CQR uses a team perspective to minimize bias and enhance objectivity, having more team members (e.g., four to 12) would be preferred, but finding that number proved difficult for us in our present study.

Participant Selection

As researchers conducting qualitative inquiry we must find potential participants who actually are experiencing the phenomenon. We will use snowball sampling, in which we make contact with someone who might know a person who identifies as LGBTQI, and then ask the identified LGBTQI person for more names, and so on. This will get us going with participants in our local context. However, we also seek to generalize to some degree to the larger population, so we will also utilize ACA Connect to gain access to potential applicants from across the country. Once we have heard from initial respondents we will select a random sample of 12 participants (our preferred range is eight to 15) to participate in one round of interviews along with, hopefully, a member check meeting. Hill et al. (2005) suggested two interviews, and at times more, but their overview of all CQR studies to date indicated that most researchers do one round of interviews with a follow-up interview that seems to mirror more of a member check interview rather than an attempt to gather more detailed descriptions of the phenomenon.

Interview Protocol Development

Our goal is to develop a scripted interview protocol with eight to 12 questions. Our questions will be developed from our review of the literature and past research, so we can ask questions to extend the knowledge base and build on what is already known. We will talk with people from our target population (persons in the LGBTQI population who have experienced stigmatization) to assist in the development of the interview questions. Once we have developed our list, we will pilot the questions with people from our target population to better refine the questions to best elicit the information we seek in the interviews.

Data collection will utilize the refined interview protocol with participants via phone interviews. Though technology provides us with other interview options, phone interviews will allow for a greater degree of objectivity and lessen the potential for relational influence. Phone interviews are also more affordable and feasible than face-to-face interviews. All interviews will be transcribed and readied for analysis.

Data Analysis

Within the CQR framework, data analysis is a team process that concludes with consensus on all coding processes and results. Three steps are involved in the data analysis. First, we come up with *domains,* which are topics used to initially organize the data. Domains ideally should come from the explicit meaning of the participants, but we could also start with topics informed by our interview questions and/or literature review. Second, we take the meaning segments that have been organized within the domains and develop *core ideas.* Core ideas should again remain close to the data, or the explicit words and meanings communicated by participants, but are refined similarly to how we as counselors might use the basic skill of paraphrasing. Our goal is to edit down core ideas and free them from what CQR refers to as *nonrelevant* aspects of the interview, such as "ums," pauses, and repetitive phrasing. Third, we *cross-analyze* the data. Cross-analysis involves looking at the core ideas of each the participant and finding commonalities across all participants. Here we will institute frequency counts and label core ideas as *general* if they apply to all participants, *typical* if they apply to at least half of participants, *variant* if they are found in at least two cases up to the cutoff for typical, and *rare* if they are applicable to only two or three participants. At this point the results are written up in as clear a fashion as possible, and our *auditor* will review our process and results.

Quality

In CQR, adherence to the defined structure of the research process as outlined by Hill et al. (1997), or procedure fidelity, is the prime theme for ensuring valid and trustworthy data. Though a hallmark of qualitative inquiry is the use of participants during member check interviews, with Lincoln and Guba (1985) even describing this as the hallmark of credibility for qualitative research, very few of the CQR studies conducted between 1997 and 2005 (only 25%) engaged in a process resembling a member check interview. A good number of these merely mailed the results to participants for feedback and comments.

A Discussion of Qualitative Methodology

We now have had an overview of three different qualitative methodologies (and within two of these an added philosophical variation) and their respective views of the same phenomenon. What do you think? At this point I do not want you to draw any firm conclusions given what I have provided (truly a sketch of these three methodologies). I merely suggest that you wonder and you ponder how such an approach to research and knowledge may be beneficial to not only your practice but also the counseling practice of others. How might hearing directly, in rich detail, how counseling is experienced, what life is like living with a particular mental health problem, or what life is like living with stigmatization impact your ability to provide therapeutic counseling services? How might hearing such stories change the way you advocate or design preventive programming? Whatever answers you just thought about, be aware that we walked through only three qualitative methodologies! There are so many other possibilities. Let me tempt you further with the potential of qualitative research in your role as practitioner-scholar with a list of other methodologies, their focus, and their relevance to this chapter's phenomenon of interest:

- *Action research/participatory action research:* Utilizes qualitative research to focus on pragmatic strategies of action and social justice and their implementation in the lives and communities of the people most connected to a phenomenon. Relevance to our phenomenon: assisting persons who identify as LGBTQI in breaking down the walls of stigmatization (e.g., Stringer, 2014).
- *Autoethnography:* Examines a person's own experience of his or her culture, a situation, an event, or way of life. Relevance to our phenomenon: understanding an LGBTQI-affirming counselor's work with stigmatization in the LGBTQI community (e.g., Muncey, 2010).
- *Conversational analysis:* Examines talk-in-interaction and how participants organize their interactions in conversation. Relevance to our phenomenon: understanding how the therapeutic alliance built between LGBTQI clients and non-LGBTQI counselors is enacted in therapeutic conversations (e.g., ten Have, 2007).
- *Discourse analysis:* Examines the structure of language usage and how it informs the creation and maintenance of patterns and rules for relating to ourselves and others. Relevance to our phenomenon: understanding the societal discourses that maintain LGBTQI stigmatization.

- *Ethnography:* Examines culture, seeking to understand the forms of relationships, behaviors, and beliefs within a given culture and the rules and perspectives that guide actions toward others in and out of the culture. Relevance to our phenomenon: understanding LGBTQI cultural responses to stigmatization (e.g., Fetterman, 2010).
- *Narrative analysis:* Focuses on examining human lives and lived experience for the sake of understanding personal patterns across time. Relevance to our phenomenon: understanding stories of stigmatization: the life of an LGBTQI person (Schiffrin, Tannen, & Hamilton, 2001).

"Oh my gosh!" you are hopefully saying. "All these topics are relevant to the counseling profession!" They sure are, particularly if we wish to fully embody the values of the counseling profession (Kleist & White, 1997). As a practitioner-scholar you face choices. In what ways does not only your counseling practice but what and how you choose to research further the profession of counseling? The profession of counseling is embedded in a philosophy of prevention and advocacy in addition to the more common remedial interventions of one-on-one counseling. How do your research choices promote prevention and advocacy efforts? How are your areas of research interest working toward the embodiment of the full character of the counseling profession? "Oh great," you mumble under your breath. "Even research is steeped in ethical quandaries and imperatives." Yes, well said.

I am a staunch advocate for qualitative research as a means of producing and disseminating knowledge that directly impacts clients and the communities in which they reside. I see the place for quantitative research, but I write Chapters 10 and 11 to tease you, the reader, into realizing the significant place for qualitative research in the profession of counseling. Your actions as a counselor and as a practitioner-scholar will help shape not only your professional identity but simultaneously the identity of the profession of counseling.

Qualitative research, quite simply, is new to the counseling profession. First being encouraged to utilize phenomenological methods in 1989 (Brown, 1989) and finding the first qualitative study in *Counselor Education and Supervision* in 1995 (Bruce, 1995) means that counselor educators like myself are still trying to figure out qualitative research. Just what is it? How can it inform the training of counselors? We are integrating research methods that were born in other professions: grounded theory in sociology, phenomenology in education, and CQR in psychology. This newness might explain why we find chapters on qualitative research in the back of research texts. We counselor educators and supervisors who are teaching counselors as practitioner-scholars clearly need to open dialogue about knowledge, research, and the place of qualitative research *methodologies* in the counseling profession. But please, do not wait for us. As a counselor educator for more than 20 years I have found that we are slow movers, sometimes followers. So go read more about qualitative research! Get moved to tears, and action, by understanding people through their own words, meanings and stories of living, and stories of striving toward mental health and wellness. "Counseling is a professional relationship that empowers diverse individuals, families, and groups to accomplish mental health, wellness, education, and career goals" (Kaplan, Tarvydas, & Gladding, 2014, p. 366). Toward this end, qualitative research methodologies provide an avenue for researching *with,* versus *on,* the people we wish to help in our roles as practitioner-scholars (Gergen, 2009).

Chapter Summary

Whew! You made it! You took the risk to expose yourself to looking at research through three different qualitative methodologies (i.e., lenses) along with two different lens prescriptions (i.e., phenomenology and grounded theory from two different philosophical stances). My intent for this chapter was to expose you to the different understandings of human experience that can come from three different qualitative methodologies and how these methodologies are influenced by the philosophical stance you take toward research. By no means did I introduce you to all of the possible qualitative methodologies that are available to you as a practitioner-scholar. However, the six additional methodologies I listed previously give you a great place to engage in further study if interested. In the end, that is my hope for you—that you leave interested in the possibilities of qualitative research to inform your practice and others' practice of counseling. On a related note, I hope you leave these chapters on qualitative research finding not just a place for qualitative research in the counseling profession but a place for yourself, as a practitioner-scholar, in the counseling profession as a researcher who adds to the knowledge base of our profession.

Suggested Activities: Mindful Curiosity

In Chapter 10, I laid out some brief reflective questions to assist you in becoming aware of your philosophical stance toward knowledge. The suggested activities here are also thought experiments focused on your own self-awareness. You could in fact ask yourself the same questions to get started, if you would like. However, the attention to your self-awareness in each moment is even more acute here.

I. Observation and reflection: What is your lens?

This exercise seems simple yet requires acute attunement, or mindfulness, to your experiences with thoughts and feelings. Find a public place in which to people-watch. Spend 20 to 30 minutes watching a person or persons (your choice) move through the moment or situation they are in. Allow your mind to be open to attend to whatever and to shift attention to whatever your mind wishes to shift attention toward.

1. To what degree did you attend to individuals or groups?
2. To what degree were you curious about what was going on for one person internally or what was going on for a person in relation to other people or the context?

Be very aware of what you find most curious about your interest in understanding people and their situation. Your answers will guide you toward preferences for the internal experiences of individuals in relationships or the influences of the situation in which people find themselves.

II. Let your counseling theory guide you toward a research methodology.

I ask my students to reflect on this notion all the time. Over the years I have found great parallels between a student's preferred counseling theory and role of counselor and the qualitative methodologies that interest that student. Jot down lists of what you like most about your counseling theory. Now, as you learn about different qualitative methodologies (in all of their aspects, from relationships with participants, to data collection, to analysis), jot down not only what you like the most but also what you like the least about each methodology. I guarantee you will find some degree of overlap. Though this is not the sole means of determining which qualitative methodology to use in a given study, it does shed light on your own personal leanings toward and fit with various methodologies. Good luck on your journey as a developing practitioner-scholar!

References

American Counseling Association. (2014). *ACA code of ethics.* Alexandria, VA: Author.

Brown, D. (1989). Logical positivism and/or phenomenology. *Counselor Education and Supervision, 29,* 5–6.

Bruce, M. A. (1995). Mentoring women doctoral students: What counselor educators and supervisors can do. *Counselor Education and Supervision, 35,* 139–149.

Charmaz, K. (2014). *Constructing grounded theory: A practical guide through qualitative analysis.* London, England: Sage.

Clarke, A. E. (2005). *Situational analysis: Grounded theory after the postmodern turn.* Thousand Oaks, CA: Sage.

Coe Smith, J. (2007). *Being in relationship: Dialogic constructions with master's level counseling supervisees* (Unpublished doctoral dissertation). Idaho State University, Pocatello.

Collins, C. S., & Cooper, J. E. (2014). Emotional intelligence and the qualitative researcher. *International Journal of Qualitative Methods, 13,* 88–103.

Corbin, J., & Strauss, A. (2008). *Basics of qualitative research: Techniques and procedures for developing grounded theory* (3rd ed.). Thousand Oaks, CA: Sage.

Corbin, J. M., & Strauss, A. (2015). *Basics of qualitative research: Techniques and procedures for developing grounded theory* (4th ed.). Thousand Oaks, CA: Sage.

Eubanks-Carter, C., Burckell, L. A., & Goldfried, M. R. (2005). Enhancing therapeutic effectiveness with lesbian, gay, and bisexual clients. *Clinical Psychology Science and Practice, 12,* 1–18.

Fetterman, D. M. (2010). *Ethnography: Step-by-step.* Thousand Oaks, CA: Sage.

Gergen, K. J. (2009). *Relational being.* Philadelphia, PA: Taylor & Francis.

Gess, J. (2016). *Queering counselor education: Situational analysis of LGBTQI competent faculty* (Unpublished doctoral dissertation). Idaho State University, Pocatello.

Giorgi, A. (1992). Description versus interpretation: Competing alternative strategies for qualitative research. *Journal of Phenomenological Psychology, 23,* 119–135.

Glaser, B. G., & Strauss, A. L. (1967). *The discovery of grounded theory: Strategies for qualitative research.* Chicago, IL: Aldine.

Hatzenbuehler, M. (2011). The social environment and suicide attempts in lesbian, gay, and bisexual youth. *Pediatrics, 127,* 896–903.

Hatzenbuehler, M. L., McLaughlin, K. A., Keyes, K. M., & Hasin, D. S. (2010). The impact of institutional discrimination on psychiatric disorders in lesbian, gay, and bisexual populations: A prospective study. *American Journal of Public Health, 100*(3), 452–459. http://doi.org/10.2105/AJPH.2009.168815

Hein, L. C., & Scharer, K. M. (2013). Who cares if it is a hate crime? Lesbian, gay, bisexual, and transgender hate crimes: Mental health implications and interventions. *Perspectives in Psychiatric Care, 49*, 84–93.

Hill, C. E., Knox, S., Thompson, B. J., Williams, E. N., Hess, S. A., & Ladany, N. (2005). Consensual qualitative research: An update. *Journal of Counseling Psychology, 52*, 196–205.

Hill, C. E., Thompson, B. J., & Williams, E. N. (1997). A guide to conducting consensual qualitative research. *The Counseling Psychologist, 25*, 517–572.

Hubble, M. A., Duncan, B. L., & Miller, S. D. (1999). *The heart and soul of change: What works in therapy.* Washington, DC: American Psychological Association.

Israel, T., Gorcheva, R., Burnes, T. R., & Walther, W. A. (2008). Helpful and unhelpful therapy experiences of LGBT clients. *Psychotherapy Research, 18*, 294–305.

Kaplan, D. M., Tarvydas, V. M., & Gladding, S. T. (2014). 20/20: A vision for the future of counseling: The new consensus definition of counseling. *Journal of Counseling & Development, 92*, 366–372. doi:10.1002/j.1556-6676.2014.00164.x

Kleist, D. M., & White, L. J. (1997). The values of counseling: A disparity between a philosophy of prevention in counseling and counselor practice and training. *Counseling and Values, 41*, 128–140.

Lincoln, Y. S., & Guba, E. G. (1985). *Naturalistic inquiry.* Beverly Hills, CA: Sage.

Lincoln, Y. S., Lynham, S. A., & Guba, E. (2011). Paradigmatic controversies: Contradictions, and emerging confluences, revisited. In N. K. Denzin & Y. S. Lincoln (Eds.), *The Sage handbook of qualitative research* (pp. 97–128). Thousand Oaks, CA: Sage.

Meyer, I. H. (2003). Prejudice, social stress, and mental health in lesbian, gay, and bisexual populations: Conceptual issues and research evidence. *Psychological Bulletin, 129*, 674–697.

Moustakas, C. (1994). *Phenomenological research methods.* Thousand Oaks, CA: Sage.

Muncey, T. (2010). *Creating autoethnographies.* Thousand Oaks, CA: Sage.

Patton, M. Q. (2015). *Qualitative research and evaluation methods.* Thousand Oaks, CA: Sage.

Pitts, M. J., & Miller-Day, M. (2007). Upward turning points and positive rapport-development across time in researcher–participant relationships *Qualitative Research, 7,* 177–201.

Schiffrin, D., Tannen, D., & Hamilton, H. E. (2001). *The handbook of discourse analysis.* Malden, MA: Blackwell.

Smith, J. A., Flowers, P., & Larkin, M. (2009). *Interpretative phenomenological analysis: Theory, method, and research.* Thousand Oaks, CA: Sage.

Strauss, A. L., & Corbin, J. M. (1998). *Basics of qualitative research: Techniques and procedures for developing grounded theory.* Thousand Oaks, CA: Sage.

Stringer, E. T. (2014). *Action research.* Thousand Oaks, CA: Sage.

ten Have, P. (2007). *Doing conversation analysis: A practical guide* (2nd ed.). London, England: Sage.

Van Manen, M. (1990). *Researching lived experience: Human science for an action sensitive pedagogy.* Albany: State University of New York Press.

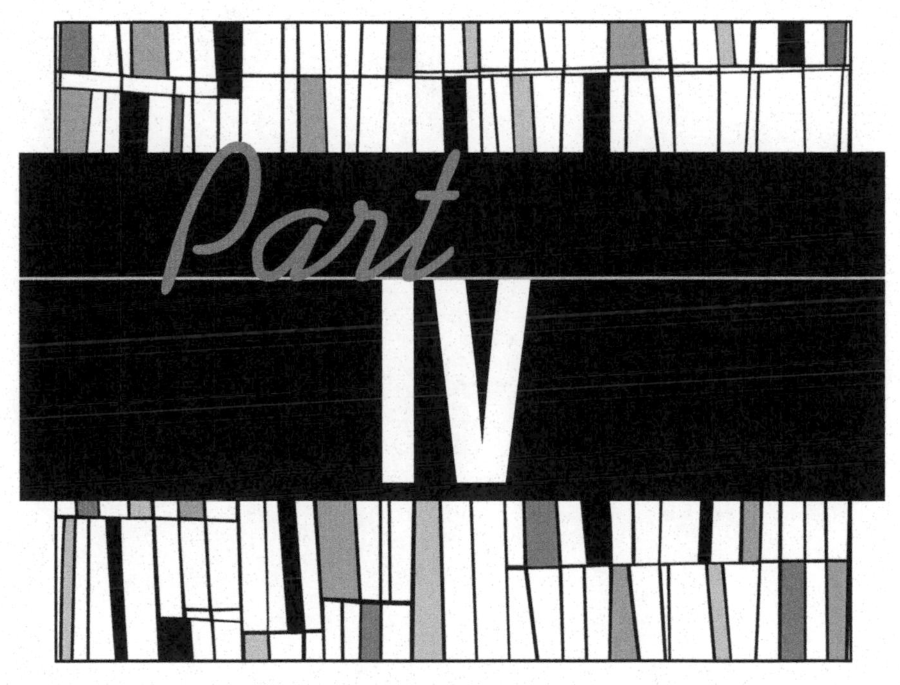

Part IV

Practice-Based Research

In this section we look at the more practical bases of conducting research, including facets of assessment, program evaluation, and the evaluation of counseling outcomes. Researching just for the sake of doing research is a fruitless endeavor. A major emphasis of the practitioner-scholar model is that research is beneficial to informing practice. Measuring client progress and evaluating programs in agency, school, and organizational settings in order to identify useful, beneficial procedures to help the population that receives counseling services is the ultimate goal of counseling research.

Many counselors are trained that counselors at the master's level should be informed consumers of research, and counselors at the doctoral level should be producers of research. But as shown throughout this textbook, and particularly in the upcoming chapters, research that informs practice at a personal or more generalizable level can be done ethically and can produce results that improve client care. The following chapters present an overview of processes used to measure important constructs relevant to counseling and to evaluate programs and interventions.

Measurement in Counseling Research

Overview

Measurement is a foundational element of research and assessment. Measurement is multifaceted and can refer to many aspects of counseling, including client symptoms, improvement, academic progress, and even client processes. Measurement can be used in counseling to evaluate the working alliance between the client and counselor or the client's satisfaction with services. Many of the ideas about measurement in counseling stem from Sir Francis Galton (1822–1911), a cousin of Charles Darwin who believed that *anything* could be measured. This included constructs such as emotional states and intelligence, phenomena that could not be directly observed (Balkin & Juhnke, 2014).

Why Focus on Measurement in Counseling Research?

A rather safe bet is that most professional counselors (but certainly not all) do not aspire to be psychometricians and develop measures in counseling and education. That being said, counselors and stakeholders want to know whether services being provided are making an impact, and measuring this impact can be integral to the practice of counseling. Clearly there is a lot more to assessing constructs than simply asking a single question. For example, the Beck Depression Inventory–II (Beck, Steer, & Brown, 1996) evaluates the presence and severity of depressive symptoms in order to help a counselor ascertain the presence and severity of depression in a client. The Beck Depression Inventory–II has 21 items. Hence, the assessment goes far beyond asking the simple question "Are you depressed?" Rather, it is used to evaluate the presence of specific symptoms that contribute to depression. The result is a highly utilized and consistent measure for evaluating clients who can identify having depressive symptoms.

Using appropriate and consistent measures requires counselors to have some awareness of how measures are designed. Furthermore, counselors who are more on the *scholar* end of the practitioner-scholar model may have a desire to know how to develop instruments to be used in counseling research. If, as Sir Francis Galton indicated, anything can be measured, it is easy to conceive that counselors may wish to develop measures that do not yet exist or improve on or add to the existing set of tools that already exist.

What Constitutes a Well-Designed Measure in Counseling Research?

If accurate and consistent measurement is a foundational element of counseling research, then comprehensively addressing constructs of interest must be a cornerstone of measurement in counseling. This brings us to two important components of any measure used in counseling: construct underrepresentation and construct irrelevance.

Construct Underrepresentation

When a measure is being developed, it is likely that elements will be left out that may be considered important to other professionals or users. A serious problem in instrument development is *construct underrepresentation,* which occurs when a measure lacks comprehensiveness, particularly because it lacks items that accurately and completely assess the construct of interest (American Educational Research Association [AERA], American Psychological Association [APA], & National Council on Measurement in Education [NCME], 2014). The theoretical framework from which the items on a measure were derived and the operational definition used to conceptualize the construct are extremely important to developing a comprehensive instrument. However, when researchers do not thoroughly review the literature, develop the theoretical framework of the measure, or adequately define the construct of interest, measures and the research resulting from such measures will be inadequate and lack utility. For example, a measure that evaluates trauma symptoms but focuses only on physiological responses to trauma and not on emotional or affective symptoms could be considered inadequate for measuring trauma.

Construct Irrelevance

Sometimes the intent to measure a construct is affected by other phenomena or processes. "Construct irrelevance refers to the degree to which test scores are affected by processes that are extraneous to the test's intended purpose" (AERA, APA, & NCME, 2014, p. 12). This can be a common problem in both educational and counseling assessment. In educational settings, for example, difficulty with word problems in math for some students could be due to issues with reading comprehension rather than applications of math concepts. These sections of a test may be designed to evaluate math concepts, but problems in reading comprehension could lead to inaccurate assessment of these students. Although reading comprehension is not the intended construct of interest, it could have an effect on evaluation of the intended construct—math applications.

As another example, the Crisis Stabilization Scale (Balkin, 2014) was developed as a clinician-response instrument to measure progress among adolescent clients identified as in crisis. The items on the Crisis Stabilization Scale evaluate the extent to which counselors believe that an adolescent client has met specific goals related to crisis stabilization. However, each of the items pertains to therapeutic goals as evaluated by the counselor, not the client. Hence, as with any measure there could be response bias on the counselor's part in overreporting or underreporting therapeutic progress. In this respect, response bias could be considered irrelevant to the construct of interest.

Whether counseling researchers are using a survey or a more formal measure, the multitude of issues that could result from inadequate measurement exemplify the need to provide evidence of the content, use, application, and interpretation of the measure. AERA, APA, and NCME (2014) identified five essential types of evidence for validating a measure: evidence based on test content, evidence of response processes, evidence of internal structure, evidence of relationships to other variables, and evidence of consequences of testing. An overview of these five types of evidence follows, as does a heuristic example using the Forgiveness Reconciliation Inventory (FRI; Balkin, Harris, Freeman, & Huntington, 2014) to demonstrate the process of developing a measure for counseling research.

Evidence Based on Test Content

Counselors who develop measures need to demonstrate the relationship between the content of the measure and the construct of interest. The *content* of a measure is defined as the "themes, wording, and format of the items, tasks or questions" (AERA, APA, & NCME, 2014, p. 14). Counseling researchers demonstrate alignment between the items and the theory from which the items were derived by demonstrating a review of the literature and having experts review the items to ascertain that they adequately measure the intended construct. Researchers typically provide the items or examples of the items to demonstrate the format of the items and their relevance to the construct of interest.

To demonstrate evidence of test content with the FRI, researchers aligned the FRI with a theoretical model of working with clients through forgiveness and conflict identified as the forgiveness reconciliation model (Balkin, Freeman, & Lyman, 2009). Hence, the development of the measure included a review of the forgiveness reconciliation model. In addition, a draft of the items was presented to expert reviewers; their feedback was solicited; and minor changes were made to the items to improve clarity, conciseness, and alignment with the forgiveness reconciliation model (Balkin et al., 2014). Counselors should be able to review a clear explanation of evidence of test content when reading a review of an instrument or an article on the development of the measure.

Evidence of Response Processes

Evidence of response processes is demonstrated through an indication of theoretical and empirical evidence related to the cognitive processes used to respond to items. Because many instruments rely on subjective interpretations of items based on self-report and ratings by others, empirical evidence is often difficult to demonstrate and not included in many test reviews or articles on the development of the measure. Theoretical evidence can be provided by demonstrating the process involved in completing the measure. For example, Balkin et al. (2014) described the theory and process for completing the FRI:

> The FRI utilized semantic differentials (Osgood, 1957), establishing dichotomous choices of opposing adjectives that represent each stage and are aligned with the [forgiveness reconciliation model].

Between each of the dichotomous adjectives are five points that represent the respondent's agreement with one or the other differentials. Thus, two points lie close to one adjective, two points lie close to the opposing adjective, and the midpoint is neutral. Under each of the four stages respondents select a point of agreement for each pair of dichotomous adjectives presented. Each stage consists of a preliminary statement followed by six adjective pairs. A sample item not included in the instrument was provided to explain how to complete the FRI. Instructions for the instrument are as follows:

> *Below you will find a statement written in bold and a list of word pairs. Between each word pair are several boxes (☐). For the following word pairs, place a check (✔) in the appropriate "☐" that indicates the extent to which you feel more closely to one of the words. You will have only one "✔" for each word pair.*
>
> *Example:* **Most people are**
>
> **Trustworthy** ☐ ☐ ☐ ☐ ☐ **Untrustworthy**
>
> *So, you would check the box above if you felt strongly that most people are trustworthy. The extent to which you feel different could be represented by checking one of the boxes to the right of the present mark.* (p. 6)

Other types of evidence to consider could include the reading level of the instrument. Measures that use a higher reading level (e.g., above eighth grade) might not be appropriate for the general public.

Evidence of Internal Structure

Evidence of internal structure refers to the outcome of statistical analyses used to identify the relationship between the items and scales that support the organization and scoring of the measure. Three common analyses may be used to provide evidence of internal structure: exploratory factor analysis (EFA), confirmatory factor analysis (CFA), and reliability analyses. The computations for these analyses tend to be complex and performing them generally requires the use of statistical software (e.g., SPSS, SAS, Mplus, AMOS).

EFA

EFA is used as a preliminary process to evaluate the factor structure of a measure. A *factor*, also known as a *latent variable*, is a variable that is not directly observed but rather is hypothesized based on the items that correlate or *load* on the factor. *Factor loading* refers to the relationship of the item to the identified factor. Researchers collect data on a population, which serves as a normative sample for the measure. Generally speaking, 10 to 20 participants per item are needed to conduct an EFA; hence, EFA is a large data procedure. In an ideal situation, a factor loading for an item will be .40 or greater for the identified factor and lower for other factors on the measure. EFA is an appropriate tool to use when researchers believe that items measure the intended construct but are uncertain as to whether the measure is *unidimensional* (i.e., all items can be combined to produce a single score) or *multidimensional* (i.e., two or more factors emerge from the EFA).

CFA

When counseling researchers use a strong theoretical framework to design a measure, they may hypothesize the structure of the measure and test the model based on scores from a normative sample. Similar to EFA, CFA is a large data procedure. Often both an EFA and a CFA are conducted, and when this occurs, separate samples—each of 10 to 20 participants per item—should be used. Hence, when both EFA and CFA are conducted for a study, the sample size will need to be doubled. In CFA, the model based on the scores from the normative sample is tested against the hypothesized model. A chi-square test is used to determine whether the distribution of the normative sample is significantly different from that of the hypothesized model. It is very common for the chi-square test to be significant, which indicates that the model from the researcher's data does not fit the hypothesized model. There are two common reasons for this problem: (a) The researcher may have misspecified the model; or (b) the large sample size is contributing to a stronger likelihood of statistical significance, despite minor deviations from the hypothesized model. There is really no way to ascertain when a statistically significant chi-square is the result of either of these scenarios. However, researchers typically use alternative indices in order to make minor adjustments and provide evidence of model fit.

The FRI was based on a published theoretical framework (Balkin et al., 2009), and therefore Balkin et al. (2014) developed a reasonable hypothesis based on a four-factor structure of the measure with specific items loading on each factor. With this hypothesis identified *a priori*—before data analysis—Balkin et al. (2014) chose to conduct a CFA rather than an EFA. When a theory is driving the development of a measure and the theory includes an identified factor structure, CFA is preferred over EFA. Balkin et al. (2014) reported the following CFA results: $\chi^2(244) = 598.49$, $p < .001$.

The fit indices indicated an acceptable model fit for the data: comparative fit index = .91, Tucker–Lewis index = .90, standardized root-mean-square residual = .069 (Balkin et al., 2014, p. 7). The chi-square test was significant, which, as explained previously, indicated differences between the tested model and hypothesized model. Alternative indices (comparative fit index, Tucker–Lewis index, standardized root-mean-square residual) were used to evaluate the fit because of the large sample size used. To reemphasize, there is no way of knowing whether the statistically significant result of the chi-square test is due to model misspecification or a large sample size, but common practice is to use alternative indices to suggest model fit or lack thereof.

Reliability

Reliability refers to the accuracy and consistency of the scores on a measure. Although reliability is not identified as a type of evidence of internal structure by AERA, APA, and NCME (2014), reliability analyses are used to identify items that should be included or discarded from a measure, particularly if scores on specific items lower the accuracy or consistency of the measure. The reason reliability is only loosely associated with internal structure is because reliability is a function of scores, not the scale. In other words, scores on a scale may be accurate or consistent, but the measure itself can never be described as accurate or consistent. The reason is that scores come from varied populations, and a measure that is accurate or consistent for one population or sample may not be for another. Reliability analyses are inherently tied to correlation coefficients, and there are a variety of ways to demonstrate the reliability of scores on a scale.

Test–retest reliability is used to demonstrate the relationship between scores when a measure is administered more than once. For example, a reasonable assumption is that individuals who complete a measure and receive no intervention will score similarly on the measure if it is taken a second time within a reasonable time period (e.g., within 2 weeks). Scores should be quite consistent and correlate rather strongly (e.g., .70 or greater). *Parallel-forms reliability* is similar to test–retest reliability except that the researcher compares two or more alternative versions of a measure rather than evaluating the same measure more than once. Another form of evaluation is *split-half reliability,* in which one half of a measure is compared to the other half of the measure. This can be done in numerous ways (e.g., comparing odd vs. even numbered items, comparing the top half vs. the bottom half). The most common type of reliability estimate is *Cronbach's alpha* or *coefficient alpha.* This type of analysis creates a coefficient from all of the possible split-half analyses; coefficient alpha is the most common estimate of reliability for scores on a measure. Balkin et al. (2014) reported strong reliability estimates for scores on each of the FRI subscales.

Evidence of Relationships to Other Variables

Correlational analyses (see Chapter 6) are at the heart of demonstrating evidence of relationships to other variables. This type of evidence demonstrates how a measure is similar to or different from other measures that evaluate the intended construct. For example, Rye et al. (2001) developed the Forgiveness Scale to evaluate forgiveness toward a particular offender. Because of the similarity to the intended construct of the FRI—evaluating the process of forgiveness—moderate to strong correlations and a statistically significant relationship between scores on the FRI and the Forgiveness Scale were expected. Balkin et al. (2014) demonstrated *convergent evidence*—evidence of similarities between constructs of interest. Sometimes researchers may also wish to demonstrate that the construct being measured is different from other constructs; such relationships, also demonstrated through correlational analyses, are referred to as *discriminant evidence.*

Another aspect of evidence of relationships to other variables refers to *test criterion relationships* (AERA, APA, & NCME, 2014)—evidence that scores on a measure might predict scores on another measure of a different construct. For example, aptitude tests (e.g., SAT, ACT) may serve as an indicator of freshman grade point average in college. In the current heuristic example, Balkin et al. (2014) demonstrated a relationship between FRI scores and likelihood of forgiving based on scores on the Forgiveness Likelihood Scale (Rye et al., 2001).

Evidence of Consequences of Testing

As most measures are constructed without longitudinal research designs, evidence indicating the consequences of testing tends to be theoretical and derived from how scores should be interpreted and used with clients. Interpretation and use of scores should be clearly delineated and tied to the purpose and theory related to the measure. Balkin et al. (2014) provided scoring and sample interpretations from three types of common profiles to demonstrate how scores may be used with clients addressing issues of forgiveness and conflict and summarized how scores should be used:

> An important facet for establishing validity evidence of an instrument is the manner in which the scores on the instrument are interpreted and used . . . Perhaps this area is where the FRI is more distinct. The FRI is not a diagnostic instrument or problem inventory. Rather, the FRI may be used as part of the process in counseling. The FRI is very brief (approximately 5 minutes) and easy to score. Counselors are encouraged to process the score profile with the client in order to illustrate if the client is moving toward interpersonal forgiveness, intrapersonal forgiveness, or is conflicted. (p. 11)

Should You Develop a Measure?

Probably not. However, many beginning researchers in counseling (e.g., doctoral students) will not heed this advice. Creating a measure involves large sample sizes, is time consuming, and requires an understanding of sophisticated statistical procedures. Often creating a measure to use for research in a dissertation can feel like doing two dissertations—one to validate the measure and the other to conduct the research.

A plethora of well-designed measures in the counseling profession evaluate relevant constructs. Before taking on the task of developing a measure, be certain that an appropriate measure does not already exist. Library databases such as the *Mental Measurements Yearbook* provide reviews of published, commercial measures. The *Mental Measurements Yearbook* can be searched using Boolean search strategies, similar to other library databases. Noncommercial measures can be found in library databases such as EBSCOhost, PsycTests, PsycINFO, ProQuest, and Academic Search Complete. Simply because a measure has not been sold for commercial use does not mean it is not reputable or useful. Specific to counseling research, the Association for Assessment and Research in Counseling publishes test reviews on its website. Many measures are developed specifically for research purposes, and researchers can simply review the permissions to determine whether they can be used.

The decision to develop a measure should be based on need. If, after thoroughly reviewing the measures available, a researcher determines that he or she has a unique perspective on measuring a construct, or a specific measure does not exist or can be improved on, then the development of a new measure makes sense. A researcher should undertake the following when considering developing a measure for counseling research:

1. A thorough review of existing measures to ascertain whether an adequate measure currently exists
2. A thorough review of the extant literature to align the measure with the theoretical underpinnings of the intended construct
3. Solicitation of expert reviewers related to the construct of interest
4. Pilot testing and modifications to the measure to address item development, clarity, and content
5. Consideration of item format and response tasks to best measure the intended construct
6. Identification of methods to obtain an appropriate normative sample (generally 10–20 participants per item; if conducting both EFA and CFA, separate samples should be used)
7. Selection of methods to evaluate internal structure (e.g., EFA, CFA, reliability estimates)
8. Selection of other measures with relevant constructs to evaluate relationships to other variables
9. Uses and limitations of the measure clearly conveyed to potential users

Chapter Summary

Measurement is a foundational element in research design. Measures that are poorly designed or inaccurately scored can render a study useless. In this chapter we described the process of validating a measure, with particular attention to evidence of validity (AERA, APA, & NCME, 2014). Keep in mind that tests are never valid; rather, evidence is presented to evaluate the validity of a measure for a particular use. The reliability of scores is also an important consideration, as evidence that the scores represent an accurate and consistent measure is pertinent to the usefulness of the measure with a given sample. In a research study, reliability estimates for scores from the norm group and from the study participants should be provided so that the accuracy and consistency of the scores can be assessed. Resources, such as the *Mental Measurements Yearbook* library database or test reviews from the Association for Assessment and Research in Counseling, are available to inform counselors of the design, validity, and utility of published measures.

Suggested Activities

I. Read the following articles:

Balkin, R. S., Freeman, S. J., & Lyman, S. R. (2009). Forgiveness, reconciliation, and mechila: Integrating the Jewish concept of forgiveness into clinical practice. *Counseling and Values, 53,* 153–160. doi:10.1002/j.2161-007X.2009.tb00121.x

Balkin, R. S., Harris, N., Freeman, S. J., & Huntington, S. (2014). The Forgiveness Reconciliation Inventory: An instrument to process through issues of forgiveness and conflict. *Measurement and Evaluation in Counseling and Development, 47,* 3–13. doi:10.1177/0748175613497037

1. How did the first conceptual article inform the creation of the FRI, as described in the latter article?
2. In the development of the FRI, participants were administered three measures related to forgiveness so that the scores on the scales could be correlated. Why is this process important?

II. Review the following article:

Davis, R. J., Balkin, R. S., & Juhnke, G. A. (2014). Validation of the Juhnke-Balkin Life Balance Inventory. *Measurement and Evaluation in Counseling and Development, 47,* 181–198. doi:10.1177/0748175614531796

In what ways was the validation of the Juhnke-Balkin Life Balance Inventory similar to or different from the validation of the FRI as described in this chapter or in Balkin et al. (2014)?

References

American Educational Research Association, American Psychological Association, and National Council on Measurement in Education. (2014). *Standards for educational and psychological testing.* Washington, DC: Author.

Balkin, R. S. (2014). *The Crisis Stabilization Scale manual and sampler set.* Menlo Park, CA: Mind Garden.

Balkin, R. S., Freeman, S. J., & Lyman, S. R. (2009). Forgiveness, reconciliation, and mechila: Integrating the Jewish concept of forgiveness into clinical practice. *Counseling and Values, 53,* 153–160. doi:10.1002/j.2161-007X.2009.tb00121.x

Balkin, R. S., Harris, N., Freeman, S. J., & Huntington, S. (2014). The Forgiveness Reconciliation Inventory: An instrument to process through issues of forgiveness and conflict. *Measurement and Evaluation in Counseling and Development, 47,* 3–13. doi:10.1177/0748175613497037

Balkin, R. S., & Juhnke, G. A. (2014). *Theory and practice of assessment in counseling.* Columbus, OH: Pearson.

Beck, A. T., Steer, R. A., & Brown, G. K. (1996). *BDI-II manual.* San Antonio, TX: Psychological Corporation.

Rye, M. S., Loiacono, D. M., Folck, C. D., Olszewski, B. T., Heim, T. A., & Madia, B. P. (2001). Evaluation of the psychometric properties of two forgiveness scales. *Current Psychology, 20,* 260–277.

Chapter 13 Program Evaluation

Michael J. Walsh and Richard S. Balkin

Overview

Program evaluation is a distinctive form of counseling research, and there could be debate as to whether program evaluation is indeed research. In Chapter 3 we introduced the definition of research as offered by the Office for Human Research Protections (OHRP; 2009): "*Research* means a systematic investigation, including research development, testing and evaluation, designed to develop or contribute to generalizable knowledge" (p. 4, italics added). Program evaluation does not meet the OHRP definition of research because it is not a generalizable endeavor. Program evaluation only pertains to a specific program, often through a single agency or organization. The controls needed for generalizable research often do not appear in program evaluation. As a result, program evaluations are generally exempt from institutional review board review (OHRP, 2009).

Nonetheless, program evaluation can be worthwhile in addressing the needs of client systems and providing important information to stakeholders who fund various projects and endeavors to enrich specific populations and communities. Whether or not program evaluation fits the OHRP definition of research is not important; rather, the role of program evaluation in informing decisions and practice in counseling settings cannot be overstated, and counselors can generally take advantage of both narrative and empirical forms of data to address program accountability.

To address the role of program evaluation, it can be important to understand how the counseling profession entered into an era of accountability. Hence, a history of program evaluation is provided, along with pertinent definitions, theories, and design strategies.

Defining Program Evaluation

There are a number of definitions of program evaluation, mostly from the related fields of education or health care policy research. As counselors, we may look to the best of three definitions below, each a bit more specific than the last:

1. Scriven (1991) defined *evaluation* as "the process of determining the merit, worth and value of things" (p. 77).
2. Rossi, Lipsey, and Freeman (2004) defined *program evaluation* as "the use of social research procedures to systematically investigate the effectiveness of social intervention programs" (p. 16).
3. Boulmetis and Dutwin (2000) defined *program evaluation* as "the systematic process of collecting and analyzing information about the efficiency, the effectiveness, and the impact of programs and services" (p. 7).

We might say that, for our purposes, *program evaluation* is the systematic collection of information about a program or aspects of a program in order to make decisions about that program. The key question to ask yourself in terms of program evaluation is "What do I need to know in order to make the decisions that I need to make?"

When we look to extrapolate program evaluation into the counseling field, we can begin by looking at some of the specific ways in which program evaluation is typically used. The important concept here is that the design and type of the evaluation is driven by the fundamental question to be answered.

Powell, Steele, and Douglah (1996) noted that program evaluation can help to answer questions in areas such as program outcome and impacts (Does my program work, and how does it make a difference?), program needs (What might my program need to improve?), program context (Where does my program fit into the service delivery system and/or my client's life?), and program operations (How does my program work?). A key part of understanding the definition of program evaluation is understanding the circumstances in which program evaluation is often helpful. Program evaluation helps counselors to better understand the impact that the *process* or *product* of counseling is having on their clients. In short, program evaluation can help us to answer the following question: How do we know if and/or how a given program is working?

For example, let's say a counselor is working with a group of adults in a psychiatric rehabilitation setting, and a group intervention is targeted at helping clients to stay out of the hospital. The counselor may want to know how effective this intervention is for this group of people. Program evaluation can help to determine the answer to that question.

This is a great example of an *outcome* or *product-based (summative) program evaluation.* This type of evaluation looks at the sum or the bottom line. In this sort of program evaluation, the desired information has to do with the outcome or product of the program. In short, the question being asked in this example is this: Does this program work in helping people stay out of the hospital?

In a *process-based (formative) program evaluation,* the fundamental question is different. It has to do with evaluation of a process. This process looks at the *form* of the process. For example, let's say a counselor is running that same group (people with psychiatric disabilities who are trying to stay out of the hospital), but the question that the counselor wants to answer is not the bottom line question about hospital stays. Rather, the counselor wants to know what role peer feedback is playing in the overall group process. This is an example of a process-based program evaluation. The fundamental question being asked is this: How does peer feedback fit into the process of this intervention? How does this intervention work?

Of course, there are some instances in which counselors may want information on both process and product. In that case, it is natural to ask questions about both process and outcome, and so a mixed program evaluation design is called for. Later in this chapter we will look at some of the essential steps in designing effective program evaluation and the ways in which counselors can make some of those key decisions. Because program evaluation is rooted in this era of accountability, it may be helpful to look at how program evaluation has developed and grown.

A History of Program Evaluation

In the present climate of ever-increasing attention to accountability, it is easy to assume that program evaluation is a new idea. However, program evaluation linked to payment for services rendered has been around for some time. Hogan (2007) provided an excellent overview.

As far back as 1444, schoolmasters in Treviso, Italy, were paid based on students' performance on tests related to areas of the curriculum (Ariès, 1962). This practice was also common in the United Kingdom and the United States in the 1800s (Kellaghan & Madaus, 1982). Known as *payment by results strategies,* these programs were designed to ensure accountability for educational services. These strategies ultimately were found to be less efficient than hoped, as they usually led to a preoccupation with preparing students for the tests as opposed to helping students to learn new things (Kellaghan & Madaus, 1982). As a result, these systems disappeared in the United Kingdom and United States by the 1920s, only to be reenergized in the United States by the No Child Left Behind legislation, which once again tied public funding (in this case, federal funding) to students' performance on standardized tests. It is not surprising that the same problems reasserted themselves, leading to the overhaul of the program in December 2015.

The use and concept of program evaluation has gone through a number of changes over time. Although many of these changes are seen most clearly in the world of education, many of the concepts are also filtering into the areas of government, health care, and psychology/counseling.

The Age of Reform (1792–1900)

Prior to 1792, the predominant form of program evaluation in education was subjective. In other words, teachers would write subjective notes on students' performance, and these were what was used to determine whether a student, or by extension an educational program, was successful. In 1792 William Farish developed the first quantitative methods for scoring students' work, ushering in an era in which educational performance was evaluated using quantitative tests (Madaus & Kellaghan, 1992). In the United States, the first evaluation of a school system using quantitative measures occurred in Boston in 1845. This idea was further championed by Joseph Rice, who from 1887 to 1898 led a comparative study of several school districts related to students learning to spell. Rice was able to provide evidence that there was no link between time spent learning to spell and actual student performance. This was to become known as the first formal program evaluation in the United States (Stufflebeam, Madaus, & Kellaghan, 2000). This trend led to governments taking active roles in the evaluation of educational programs using empirical data.

The Age of Efficiency (1900–1930)

This period was dominated by a dawning focus on efficiency and the use of formative feedback to enhance performance. In the early 1900s, Frederick Taylor developed the idea of *scientific management.* Based on the concepts of observation, measurement, analysis, and efficiency, this idea became influential in the field of education by about 1910 (Biddle & Ellena, 1964). More emphasis began to be placed on the development of objective tests to inform practice and enhance efficiency.

The Tylerian Age (1930–1945)

The Tylerian age marked the birth of behavior-based evaluation and the dawn of the criterion reference age. It was also a critical theoretical link between the educational program evaluation world and the world in which counselors most often find themselves. Specifically, program objectives were for the first time linked with human behaviors. Ralph Tyler (1975) developed the idea that objectives can effectively be linked to a set of desired behaviors and that those behaviors can then be measured as the basis for evaluation. This idea formed the foundation of the criterion-referenced testing movement (Worthen, Sanders, & Fitzpatrick, 1997) and formed the first critical link between program outcomes and client behaviors.

The Age of Innocence (1946–1957)

The end of the Great Depression and the Second World War ushered in a renewed sense of hope and excitement. This era of relative prosperity coincided with a decreased focus on accountability for dollars spent on education. Tyler's ideas continued to gain acceptance, forging a more solid theoretical and practical link between human behavior and program evaluation data. Bloom, Engelhart, Furst, Hill, and Krathwohl (1956) gave that link a boost with the publication of *Taxonomy of Educational Objectives.* This seminal text argued that students' cognitions were complex and could be divided into a number of learning outcomes, some more or less important than others. In this new theoretical world, objectives could be classified in terms of these outcomes, and tests could then be developed to measure these different types of outcomes (Reiser, 2001).

This focus on a hierarchy of objectives was new and represented an advance in the complexity of program evaluation. It also represented another critical link between the theory of program evaluation and counseling. Specifically, for the first time, client behaviors and cognitions were viewed as multidimensional. Gone were the days of considering people based on a single program-related variable. Rather, the human being became a driver of outcomes, and the multidimensional nature of human experience made its way into the science of evaluation. The complexity of how a person experienced a program or intervention was considered for the first time.

The Age of Development (1959–1972)

Two seminal events helped to spur action in program evaluation. First, in 1957 the Soviets successfully launch Sputnik. This fueled early Cold War fears of Soviet dominance in science and technology and spurred the National Defense Education Act, which appropriated millions of dollars for curriculum development and corresponding program evaluation in the areas of science, mathematics, and technology (Stufflebeam et al., 2000).

Second, the Elementary and Secondary Education Act was passed in 1965. This act, which aimed to make sure academic resources and practices supported the needs of lower income children, focused program evaluation on the use of criterion-referenced measures. This shift from norm-referenced measures (those that compare the performance of some students to that of other students) to criterion-referenced measures (those that measure to a set standard) was an attempt to even the playing field and ensure that all students were trained in an equal manner (Weiss, 1998). Today the idea that criterion-based standards can be used effectively is now more widely accepted, which has led to advances in criterion-based instrument research.

The Age of Professionalization (1973–1983)

In the 1970s and 1980s, program evaluation began to be recognized as a profession, spawning several professional journals and sparking preliminary interest in the use of program evaluations in areas outside of education. In 1974 the American Psychological Association revised *Standards for Educational and Psychological Tests* (American Psychological Association, American Educational Research Association, & National Council on Measurement in Education, 1974) while also recognizing a need for a separate set of standards dealing with program evaluation (Stufflebeam et al., 2000). In the early 1980s the development of quality assurance concepts in program evaluation became popular.

According to Stufflebeam (2000) the proposed standards on program evaluation laid out by the American Psychological Association in 1974 indicated that program evaluation should accomplish the following:

- Serve the needs of the clients of the evaluation
- Address central value issues
- Deal with situational realities
- Meet probity requirements
- Satisfy veracity needs

The Age of Expansion and Integration (1983–Present)

The increasing focus on accountability led to greater emphasis on program evaluation. Professional associations such as the American Counseling Association and the American Psychological Association formally incorporated program evaluation into professional standards (e.g., Council for Accreditation of Counseling and Related Educational Programs, 2009, 2016). Within the counseling profession, program evaluation continues to be emphasized within the context of assessment and research. Furthermore, makers of public policy have embraced the accountability aspects of program evaluation and begun to call for its use in fields as diverse as mental health services, education, and health care. For example, decreasing funding streams has led to an explosion in interest in program evaluation in mental health care and counseling. Agencies and organization want to know which services contribute to improvement for clients and stakeholders and which programs are unnecessary. Third-party funders (insurance companies, government health care programs) may require a program evaluation as evidence of the need, and justification, for continued services.

Basics of Program Evaluation

As you likely noted while reading the previous section, the program evaluation process was developed largely outside of the counseling world. As Astramovich and Coker (2007) identified, many program evaluation models either have been developed for use with large-scale projects and populations or focus on the use of evaluation procedures that are impractical in counseling settings. Consequently, counselors are often faced with the task of customizing principles and approaches to fit within the counseling process.

Given the increasing call for program evaluation in this era of enhanced accountability, an understanding of the basic concepts of program evaluation and how to apply them is essential. This section will help to demystify some of these basics and will also help you to begin to develop your own skills in designing and applying these principles in your own settings.

As we noted previously, there are different kinds of program evaluations, and these evaluations are based on what the evaluator wants to know. In addition, each type can be broken down into subtypes, again depending on what information is needed. Here we discuss the two basic types of program evaluation: summative and formative evaluation.

Summative Evaluation

Summative evaluation is concerned with products and/or outcomes—does the program do what it is intended to do? Examples of summative program evaluation include the following:

- *Outcomes:* Is the program doing what it is supposed to do?
- *Impact evaluation:* What is the overall effect or impact of the program?
- *Cost evaluation:* What is the overall cost of the program? What is the cost–benefit analysis of the program?

Formative Evaluation

Formative evaluation, also known as *process evaluation,* examines program delivery. Sometimes this means looking at how things work or the actual process of delivering the program and gathering information. Examples of formative program evaluation include the following:

- *Process:* How does the program work? How does some aspect of the program work in conjunction with or apart from other programs or the overarching mission of the agency or organization?
- *Needs assessment:* What are the needs of the program? What are the needs of the clients, and how does the program meet them (or not)?
- *Conceptualization:* How do clients view the program? How do the clients envision success as a result of the program?
- *Implementation evaluation:* Is the program faithful to the model envisioned and executed according to established protocol (fidelity monitoring)? How is the program delivered?

With these types of summative and formative evaluations in mind, we can begin to address the process of executing a program evaluation pertinent to counseling settings. What follows is a set of practical guidelines for conducting a program evaluation and an explanation of relevant models consistent with the counseling literature.

Conducting Program Evaluation

Many models have been developed over the years for program evaluation. Most of these either are specific to large-scale projects (Kellaghan & Madaus, 2000) or are so discipline specific that they have questionable validity within the counseling world (Astramovich & Coker, 2007). That said, the Centers for Disease Control and Prevention (2011), in an effort to help public health agencies have the flexibility to design program evaluation models in a variety of environments and situations, developed six basic steps that are universal within effective program evaluation programs.

Step 1: Identify and Involve the Stakeholders

Program evaluation works best when it is focused, collaborative, and intentional. This means the counselor must figure out who the stakeholders are (i.e., the people with an interest in the outcome of the evaluation) and get their input into the evaluation process. In counseling, stakeholders can include clients, other staff or professionals in the program, third-party funders, and so forth. Stakeholders can give valuable information on what they find to be of value or most important in a program. This gives clues on where to look for information. Each stakeholder can provide feedback that can help to make sure that the evaluation process is a successful one.

Step 2: Define the Program

A key step in program evaluation is to define the phenomenon that is going to be measured. In short, counselors are looking to answer the following question: What is this program supposed to do?

For example, if a counselor is wondering whether a counseling group is effective, the first step is to figure out what the group is supposed to be doing. If the counselor is running a group intervention designed to help people avoid inpatient hospitalizations, then the counselor has a program that is well defined. The counselor can build an effective evaluation based around the question "Is this group effective in helping people stay out of the hospital?" The counselor starts with the clearly defined purpose of the group (helping individuals stay out of the hospital) and develops an evaluation plan to evaluate the overarching goal of the program.

Step 3: Focus the Design of the Evaluation

In this step the counselor decides what kind of evaluation is needed. What questions need to be answered? Do the program needs call for a formative process evaluation, in which the counselor examines ways in which the program is executed? Or do the program needs call for a summative product or outcomes evaluation, in which the counselor examines the bottom line of whether the program is efficacious? In addition, the counselor needs to ascertain what information is needed and who will provide that information. In this respect, knowledge of quantitative, single-case, and qualitative research designs is helpful. Program evaluation can include any of these methodologies or a combination. The type of methodology is driven by the overarching question or goal of the program evaluation and influences the counselor's choices in terms of what kind of data will be collected, how the data will be collected, from whom the data will be collected, and how data will be analyzed.

Step 4: Gather the Evidence

This step involves executing the plan for data collection and may include such processes as interviewing clients, collecting data from third parties on outcomes, or using some other method appropriate to the question(s) of interest.

Step 5: Analyze the Data and Draw Conclusions

Data analysis requires an understanding of the procedures and processes discussed in previous chapters related to quantitative, single-case, and qualitative research designs. However, keep in mind that counselors engaging in program evaluation do not have to be concerned about experimental validity and the generalizability of the results because of the limited sample size and lack of experimental controls. A combination of quantitative and qualitative analyses provides rich data that measure accountability to address both objective and practical considerations.

Step 6: Present Your Findings and Use Them

Believe it or not, this is the area of program evaluation that most often falls short. Organizations and programs can sometimes get so caught up in the mechanics of collecting data that they forget to use them! A critical step in program evaluation is sharing data with stakeholders and using those data to improve the effectiveness and efficiency of the program. Strong program evaluations use a combination of procedures. Although program evaluation may not fit the traditional definition of research established by OHRP (2009), program evaluation can produce rich data that can inform the profession as well as the client system, counseling professionals, and stakeholders.

For example, based on program evaluation results presented to stakeholders, counselors in an agency or organizational setting have an opportunity to make very intentional and specific changes in specific areas that are likely to do the most good. Program evaluation provides an opportunity to show potential funding sources that there is a constant continuous improvement in both quality and effectiveness and that program changes are made based on empirical evidence. Keeping this framework in mind, let's now look at some program evaluation models that elucidate how these six steps of program evaluation are put into practice.

Logic Modeling

Joseph Wholey (1979) introduced the concept of a *logic model,* which is simply a graphic representation of a program that shows the intended relationships between investments and results. Modern logic models include the program's assumptions and potentiating external factors in order to represent the full logical picture of how a program is supposed to work. Using logic models can be an excellent way of introducing programs to funders and to the general public by providing clear and easily understood graphical representations of the program. Many third-party funding sources, including most grant sources, require the presentation of a logic model prior to considering a funding request. Counselors can benefit from knowing how to conceptualize and construct a good logic model. Taylor-Powell and Henert (2008) defined some key terms in logic modeling:

- *Baseline:* information about a situation or condition prior to intervention
- *Impact indicator:* evidence that an impact is being achieved
- *Inputs:* resources that go into programming, such as staff time, materials, money, equipment, and so forth
- *Outputs:* the activities, products, and participation resulting from program activities
- *Outcomes:* results or changes from a program; outcomes can range from immediate (short term) to intermediate (medium term) to final (long term)

An example of a basic logic model framework follows (Taylor-Powell & Henert, 2008):

Inputs ⟶ Outputs *(Activities, participation)* ⟶ Outcomes *(Short term, medium term, long term)*

With an understanding of the concepts related to logic modeling, we can transition to a heuristic example that demonstrates the implementation of a logic model for program evaluation in counseling.

A Heuristic Example of Logic Model

A counselor is running a group for clients who struggle with anxiety. The group is designed to help people reduce the anxiety that they feel each day and to help them reduce anxiety-related behaviors such as crisis calls and hospital trips. A program evaluation logic model for this program may look something like the following:

- *Inputs:* Two counselors for 1 hour per week, office space at $15 per square foot, utilities at $8 per day, case preparation and documentation for 2 hours at $25 per hour, one binder per client per group at $3.50 per binder
- *Outputs:* Client participation for 1 hour per week; engagement in client homework for 2 hours per week per client; production of a coping skills binder for each client; orientation of clients to other clients; a sharing of contact information, multiplying the support network for each client
- *Outcomes:* 82% reduction in hospital visits from group members in first 2 months (short term), 64% reduction in crisis line calls from active group members over a 6-month period compared to a baseline of 12 calls per month from members prior to group intervention (medium term), 75% reduction in hospital visits among active group members over the course of one full year (long term)

The logic model template (see Figure 13.1) can be used to map the program evaluation process. The idea behind a logic model is to give a graphic representation of the effectiveness (or lack of effectiveness) of an intervention along with a clear chain connecting investments with outcomes.

The Accountability Bridge Model

There are a number of barriers to using program evaluation in counseling. These range from a lack of training (Whiston, 1996), to a general lack of confidence in skills to apply the results of program evaluation back to the program being evaluated (Isaacs, 2003), to a basic fear of finding that the service delivered may not have been effective (Lusky & Hayes, 2001). That said, there are increasing demands for accountability among third-party funders (Houser, 1998) as well as demands to prove the effectiveness of services (Isaacs, 2003). Program evaluation can also be used as a tool to enhance the quality of services provided (Loesch, 2001). In order to do this, the program planning process has to be fluid and informed by the program evaluation process.

Astramovich and Coker (2007) proposed a model called the *accountability bridge*, which argues that measured accountability can achieve the sort of program improvement that is both needed and valued within the counseling field. The accountability bridge takes into account the unique context of a program while acknowledging the need for the program planning process to be both ongoing and dynamic (Astramovich & Coker, 2007). Key to the success of any program evaluation model is taking into account the unique context within which the program operates (Stufflebeam, 1971). A number of models have emerged over the years designed to do just that. The context, input, process, and product model (Stufflebeam & Shinkfield, 2007, p. 351) gained widespread appeal because it considers the unique and dynamic conditions in which services are provided. This sensitivity to context, unique environments, and adaptability makes the context, input, process, and product model singularly adaptable to the types of situations in which counselors find themselves. This focus on context was a vital first part of the development of the accountability bridge.

A second vital link was the inclusion of the program planning, strategic vision, and business sides of programs into the program evaluation process (Ernst & Hiebert, 2002). Adding business considerations allows programs to include cost–benefit analyses into the program evaluation process. The real advance here was the inclusion of business evaluation processes in the program evaluation process, which typically focused exclusively on clinical and help-related questions (e.g., Is this program effective?). The inclusion of business ideas added the question "Is this program efficient?" In a world in which funding is increasingly tied to both effectiveness and efficiency, this is a critical link. Counselors now have a tool that combines an assessment of effectiveness with an assessment of

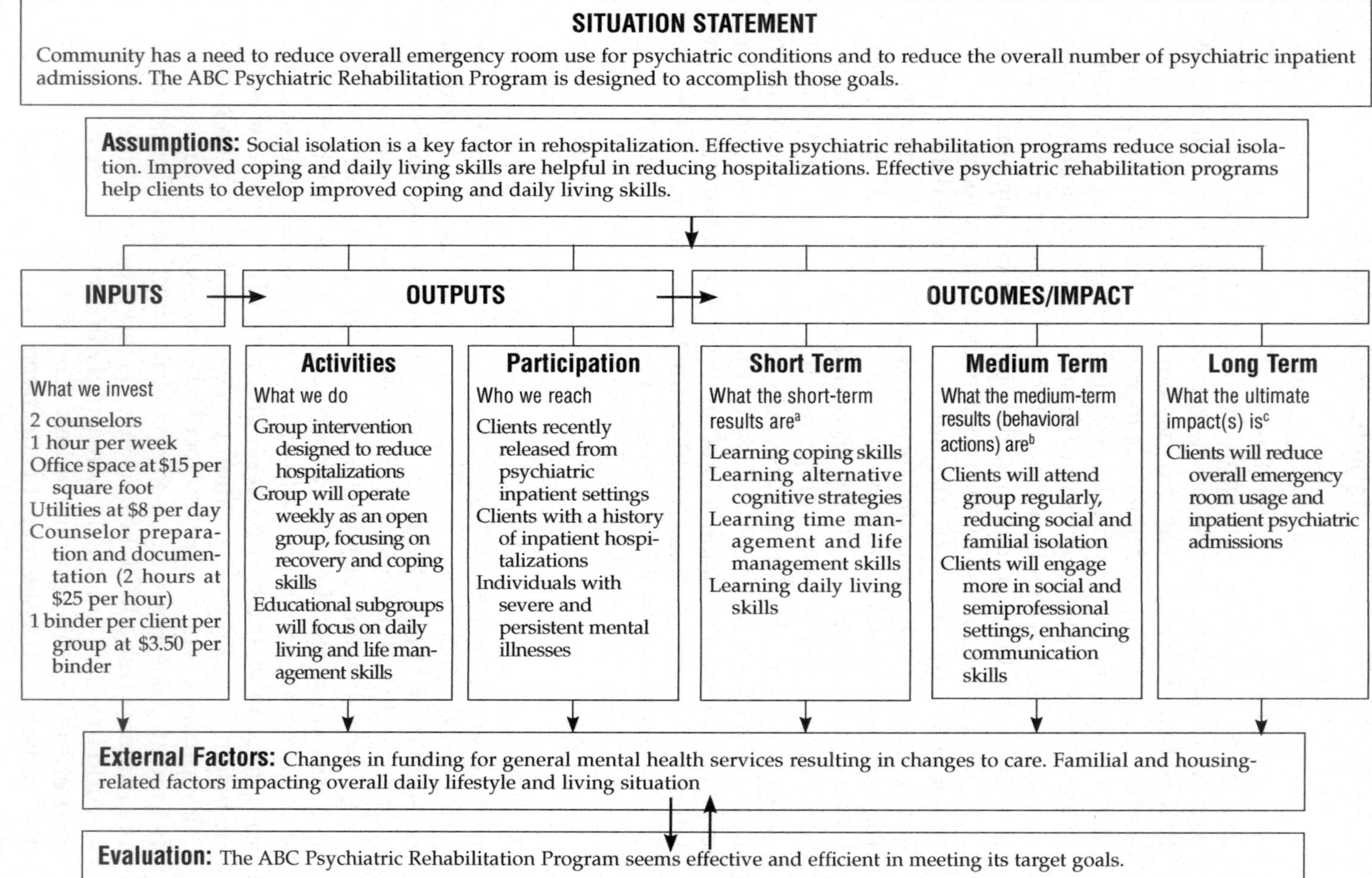
SITUATION STATEMENT
Community has a need to reduce overall emergency room use for psychiatric conditions and to reduce the overall number of psychiatric inpatient admissions. The ABC Psychiatric Rehabilitation Program is designed to accomplish those goals.
Assumptions: Social isolation is a key factor in rehospitalization. Effective psychiatric rehabilitation programs reduce social isolation. Improved coping and daily living skills are helpful in reducing hospitalizations. Effective psychiatric rehabilitation programs help clients to develop improved coping and daily living skills.
INPUTS
OUTPUTS
OUTCOMES/IMPACT
What we invest
2 counselors
1 hour per week
Office space at $15 per square foot
Utilities at $8 per day
Counselor preparation and documentation (2 hours at $25 per hour)
1 binder per client per group at $3.50 per binder
Activities
What we do
Group intervention designed to reduce hospitalizations
Group will operate weekly as an open group, focusing on recovery and coping skills
Educational subgroups will focus on daily living and life management skills
Participation
Who we reach
Clients recently released from psychiatric inpatient settings
Clients with a history of inpatient hospitalizations
Individuals with severe and persistent mental illnesses
Short Term
What the short-term results are[a]
Learning coping skills
Learning alternative cognitive strategies
Learning time management and life management skills
Learning daily living skills
Medium Term
What the medium-term results (behavioral actions) are[b]
Clients will attend group regularly, reducing social and familial isolation
Clients will engage more in social and semiprofessional settings, enhancing communication skills
Long Term
What the ultimate impact(s) is[c]
Clients will reduce overall emergency room usage and inpatient psychiatric admissions
External Factors: Changes in funding for general mental health services resulting in changes to care. Familial and housing-related factors impacting overall daily lifestyle and living situation
Evaluation: The ABC Psychiatric Rehabilitation Program seems effective and efficient in meeting its target goals.

FIGURE 13.1

Logic Model: ABC Psychiatric Rehabilitation Program

Note. Adapted from Taylor-Powell, E., & Henert, E. (2008). *Developing a logic model: Teaching and training guide*. Retrieved from http://www.fs.usda.gov/Internet/FSE_DOCUMENTS/stelprdb5104513.pdf

[a]82% reduction in hospital visits from group members in first 2 months. [b]64% reduction in crisis line calls from active group members over a 6-month period compared to a baseline of 12 calls per month from members prior to group intervention (medium term). [c]75% reduction in hospital visits among active group members over the course of one full year.

efficiency and also suggests that the two concepts are inextricably linked to effective planning of services (Astramovich & Coker, 2007).

As demonstrated in Figure 13.2, the accountability bridge uses both the program and the unique context of the program as central hubs in the evaluation and planning cycle. Each is informed by the other, and both are linked. The advantage of this type of model is that the ways in which services are delivered are naturally informed by the evaluation, which then helps both consumers and staff to evaluate and plan future services. In an era in which third-party funders as well as advocates are calling for increased consumer and client involvement in service planning (Loesch, 2001), an evaluation model that includes clients is a valuable tool.

The ABC Psychiatric Rehabilitation Program from the previous example uses the accountability bridge. In traditional program evaluation, the program would be evaluated, the results shared with program developers and staff, and changes either made or not made. This would likely result in services staying largely the same. After all, the program seemed very effective!

However, often clients are the best experts on what works in mental health services, and often clients develop far more effective ideas than professionals because of the unique context of those ideas within their own lives (Miller & Rollnick, 2013). In fact, consumer-driven service design is acknowledged as a best practice (Fenton, 2003; Fischer, 2006; Hamann, Cohen, Leucht, Busch, & Kissling, 2005; Hamann, Leucht, & Kissling, 2003). When the accountability bridge is used, this expertise is not only acknowledged but utilized to its full potential while continuously being tested and refined. The clients are a vital part of a seamless and continuous feedback loop. This allows

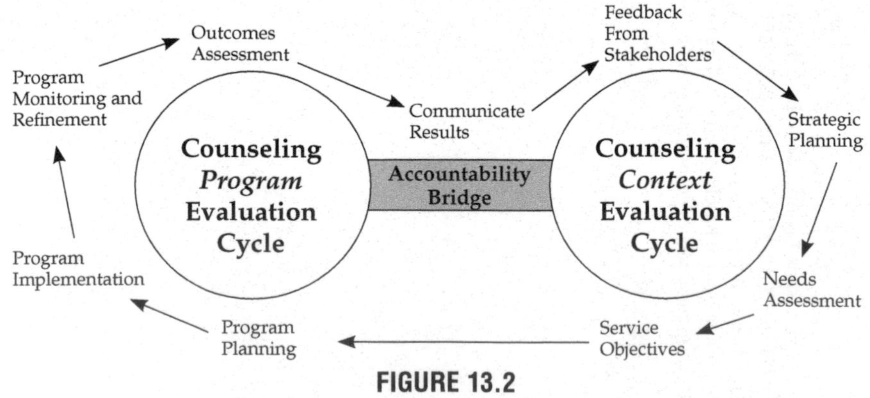

FIGURE 13.2
Accountability Bridge Model (Astramovich & Coker, 2007)

a program to flex and grow within its own unique context and with the active involvement and direction of its consumers.

In today's world of winding budgets and questions over the efficient use of resources, counselors are more than ever faced with the task of justifying the need for ongoing service provision. Indeed, many counselors are often faced with the task of justifying the continuation of their employment to superiors or third-party payers. Effective program evaluation skills are a vital tool that can be used to accomplish these critical objectives.

Putting It All Together

When you consider the nature of program evaluation and the pressure to evaluate accountability for the services offered by counselors in a variety of settings, both quantitative and qualitative research and their various designs may be incorporated. Program evaluation can involve the collection of a variety of data sources, creating an opportunity for analyses at both macro and micro levels! How were individuals affected by the services provided? Were the services effective across all groups? Both qualitative and quantitative methods, respectively, could be used to address these questions. For counseling programs in particular, in which the unit of service is individuals, families, and small groups, qualitative methods and single-case research designs can provide sources of formative and summative evaluation. The sources of measurement or evaluation through formal instruments, surveys, or interviews are commonly incorporated into program evaluation.

Hence, program evaluation is a comprehensive endeavor that cuts across the various methods of research discussed throughout this text. Not only is program evaluation essential to evaluating the efficacy of services for a specific program, but such evaluations can serve as initial steps in identifying best practices and empirically supported treatments. In this regard, program evaluation serves as another mechanism to influence positive change and contribute to knowledge of the counseling profession.

Chapter Summary

We started this chapter by looking at the definition of program evaluation: the systematic collection of information about a program or aspects of the program in order to make decisions about that program.

We then looked at some fundamental questions to be considered in program evaluation: What sort of information do we need to make the decisions that we need to make, and what type of program evaluation do we want to do? One type of design focuses on outcomes (Does my program work, and how does it make a difference?). The goals for this design flow from the basic question being asked. If, however, our program evaluation is focused on other areas, such as program needs (What does my program need in order to grow?), the goals and the design of the program evaluation must change to meet those needs. Likewise, if the program evaluation is focused on program context (Where does this program fit into the service delivery system and/or my client's life?) or program operations (How does my program work?), the questions to be asked and the persons to whom those questions will be directed must change to suit the specific need. The answers to these questions tell us the type of program evaluation we need. A summative program evaluation looks at outcomes. A formative program evaluation looks at process. Counselors may want to use one or both types of program evaluation depending on the circumstances.

We took a good look at the history of program evaluation from the context of counseling, examining the ways in which program evaluation developed over time and the milestones at which counseling-specific ideas and constructs made their debuts. From the use of accountability-based payment structures in 15th-century Italy, to the development of quantitative program evaluation measures in the 18th century, through present-day trends among third-party funders such as insurers and government funding agencies to require program evaluation data for continued funding, the need for effective program evaluation strategies is growing. Fortunately, the technology to develop and deploy program evaluation also continues to grow. This growth became evident as we examined ways in which counselors can design and develop effective program evaluation models.

We then looked at the basics of designing and developing a program evaluation. Key steps in program evaluation design and implementation were identified, and counseling-specific considerations were noted at each step.

We also examined a graphically based method for representing both programs and outcome data. The logic model is a graphic representation of the intended relationships between investments and results. Several counseling-specific examples of logic modeling were presented to help show the power of this approach.

Finally, we examined the accountability bridge model, a program evaluation model that builds on the unique context and business considerations of a program to form a program improvement strategy.

This chapter provides counselors with the tools and strategies for designing, developing, and presenting program evaluation in ways that enhance their ability to determine effectiveness, evaluate processes, and improve the overall efficiency and effectiveness of programs. We hope that you are able to utilize these tools to enhance your own programs and services.

Tools You Can Use: A Cheat Sheet for Designing and Developing a Model for Program Evaluation

1. *Identify the stakeholders.* Who benefits from your program? Clients? Referral sources? Funders?
2. *Define the program.* What does your program do? How does it work?
3. *Design the evaluation.* What question needs to be answered? What type of evaluation do you need? What type of evidence do you need to gather?
4. *Gather the evidence.* Use a method that is most appropriate to the question that you are exploring. For example, in a summative case, in which you want to explore the numbers around an issue or the bottom line outcomes, a quantitative method makes sense. In a formative case, in which you want to explore how something works or the role it may play in people's lives, a qualitative approach that gathers people's thoughts and feeling may be more appropriate.
5. *Analyze the data and draw conclusions.* Use the type of analysis that will be of most help to you. Quantitative analysis will help make sense of numbers, whereas qualitative analysis will help to spot patterns and themes in the way people are experiencing your program. A combination of the two can be especially powerful.
6. *Present the findings and use them.* The best program evaluation in the world is useless unless you use what you find to enhance the quality of your program.

Suggested Activities

Each of the following articles describes an aspect of evaluating the effectiveness of a counseling program:

Cox, R. M., Lenz, A. S., & James, R. K. (2015). A pilot evaluation of the ARRAY program with offenders who have mental illness. *Journal of Counseling & Development, 93,* 471–480. doi:10.1002/jcad.12045

Del Conte, G., Lenz, A. S., & Hollenbaugh, M. H. (2016). A pilot evaluation of dialectical behavior therapy for adolescents within a partial hospitalization treatment milieu. *Journal of Child and Adolescent Counseling, 2,* 16–32. doi:10.1080/23727810.2015.1134008

After reviewing one or both of the articles, consider the following:

1. What type of strategy was used to demonstrate program effectiveness?
2. How could these studies be expanded to provide a comprehensive program evaluation as described in this chapter?
3. How do these studies contribute to accountability in counseling services?

References

American Psychological Association, American Educational Research Association, & National Council on Measurement in Education. (1974). *Standards for educational and psychological tests.* Washington, DC: Author.

Ariès, P. (1962). *Centuries of childhood: A social history of family life* (R. Baldick, Trans.). New York, NY: Vintage.

Astramovich, R. L., & Coker, K. J. (2007). Program evaluation: The accountability bridge model for counselors. *Journal of Counseling & Development, 85,* 162–172.

Biddle, B., & Ellena, W. J. (1964). *Continued research on teacher effectiveness.* New York, NY: Holt, Rinehart, & Winston.

Bloom, B. S., Engelhart, M. D., Furst, E. J., Hill, W. H., & Krathwohl, D. R. (1956). *Taxonomy of educational objectives: The classification of educational goals. Handbook 1: Cognitive domain.* New York, NY: David McKay.

Boulmetis, J., & Dutwin, P. (2000). *The ABCs of evaluation: Timeless techniques for program and project managers.* San Francisco, CA: Jossey-Bass.

Centers for Disease Control and Prevention. (2011). *Evaluation steps.* Retrieved from http://www.cdc.gov/eval/steps/index.htm

Council for Accreditation of Counseling and Related Educational Programs. (2009). *2009 standards for accreditation.* Alexandria, VA: Author.

Council for Accreditation of Counseling and Related Educational Programs. (2016). *2016 standards for accreditation.* Alexandria, VA: Author.

Ernst, K., & Hiebert, B. (2002). Toward the development of a program evaluation business model: Promoting the longevity of counselling in schools. *Canadian Journal of Counselling, 36,* 73–84.

Fenton, W. S. (2003). Shared decision making: A model for the physician-patient relationship in the 21st century? *Acta Psychiatrica Scandinavica, 107,* 401–402.

Fischer, E. P. (2006). Shared decision-making and evidence-based practice: A commentary. *Community Mental Health Journal, 42*(1), 107–111.

Hamann, J., Cohen, R., Leucht, S., Busch, R., & Kissling, W. (2005). Do patients with schizophrenia wish to be involved in decisions about their medical treatment? *American Journal of Psychiatry, 162,* 2382–2384.

Hamann, J., Leucht, S., & Kissling, W. (2003). Shared decision-making in psychiatry. *Acta Psychiatrica Scandanavica, 107,* 403–409.

Hogan, R. L. (2007). The historical development of program evaluation: Exploring the past and present. *Online Journal of Workforce Development,* 2(4), 1–14.

Houser, R. (1998). *Counseling and educational research: Evaluation and application.* Thousand Oaks, CA: Sage.

Isaacs, M. L. (2003). Data-driven decision making: The engine of accountability. *Professional School Counseling, 6,* 288–295.

Kellaghan, T., & Madaus, G. F. (1982). Trends in educational standards in Great Britain and Ireland. In G. R. Austin & H. Garber (Eds.), *The rise and fall of national test scores* (pp. 195–214). London, England: Academic Press.

Kellaghan, T., & Madaus, G. F. (2000). Outcome evaluation. In D. L. Stufflebeam, G. F. Madaus, & T. Kellaghan (Eds.), *Evaluation models: Viewpoints on educational and human services evaluation* (2nd ed., pp. 97–112). Boston, MA: Kluwer Academic.

Loesch, L. C. (2001). Counseling program evaluation: Inside and outside the box. In D. C. Locke, J. E. Myers, & E. L. Herr (Eds.), *The handbook of counseling* (pp. 513–525). Thousand Oaks, CA: Sage.

Lusky, M. B., & Hayes, R. L. (2001). Collaborative consultation and program evaluation. *Journal of Counseling & Development, 79,* 26–38.

Madaus, G. F., & Kellaghan, T. (1992). Curriculum evaluation and assessment. In P. W. Jackson (Ed.), *Handbook of research on curriculum* (pp. 199–154). New York, NY: Macmillan.

Miller, W. R., & Rollnick, S. (2013). *Motivational interviewing: Helping people change* (3rd ed.). New York, NY: Guilford Press.

Office for Human Research Protections. (2009). *U.S. Department of Health and Human Services, Code of Federal Regulations, Title 45 Public Welfare, Part 46, Protection of Human Subjects.* Washington, DC: Author.

Powell, E. T., Steele, S., & Douglah, M. (1996). *Planning a program evaluation.* Madison: University of Wisconsin–Extension, Division of Cooperative Extension.

Reiser, R. A. (2001). A history of instructional design and technology: Part II. A history of instructional design. *Educational Technology, Research and Development, 49*(2), 57–68.

Rossi, P. H., Lipsey, M. W., & Freeman, H. E. (2004). *Evaluation: A systematic approach.* Thousand Oaks, CA: Sage.

Scriven, M. (1991). *Evaluation thesaurus* (4th ed.). Thousand Oaks, CA: Sage.

Stufflebeam, D. L. (1971). The use of experimental design in educational evaluation. *Journal of Educational Measurement, 8*(4), 267–274.

Stufflebeam, D. L. (2000). *Evaluation models: Viewpoints on educational and human services evaluation.* Hingham, MA: Kluwer Academic.

Stufflebeam, D. L., Madaus, G. F., & Kellaghan, T. (2000). *Evaluation models: Viewpoints on educational and human services evaluation* (2nd ed.). Boston, MA: Kluwer Academic.

Stufflebeam, D. L., & Shinkfield, A. J. (2007). *Evaluation theory, models, and applications.* San Francisco, CA: Jossey-Bass.

Taylor-Powell, E., & Henert, E. (2008). *Developing a logic model: Teaching and training guide.* Retrieved from http://www.fs.usda.gov/Internet/FSE_DOCUMENTS/stelprdb5104513.pdf

Tyler, R. W. (1975). Educational benchmarks in retrospect: Educational change since 1915. *Viewpoints, 510*(1), 11–31.

Weiss, C. H. (1998). *Evaluation: Methods for studying programs and policies* (2nd ed.). Upper Saddle River, NJ: Prentice Hall.

Whiston, S. C. (1996). Accountability through action research: Research methods for practitioners. *Journal of Counseling & Development, 74,* 616–623.

Wholey, J. (1979). *Evaluation: Promise and performance.* Washington, DC: Urban Institute Press.

Worthen, B. R., Sanders, J. R., & Fitzpatrick, J. L. (1997). *Educational evaluation: Alternative approaches and practical guidelines* (2nd ed.). White Plains, NY: Longman.

Index

Figures and tables are indicated by "f" and "t" following page numbers.

A

B

C

D

(Continued)

F

G

H

(Continued)

N

Q

R

T

U

V

W

Y

Z